WHY
GRIZZLY BEARS
SHOULD WEAR
UNDERPANTS

Other books by

The **Oatmeal**

→ 5 Very Good Reasons to Punch a Dolphin in the Mouth
(And Other Useful Guides)

→ How to Tell If Your Cat Is Plotting to Kill You

→ My Dog: The Paradox

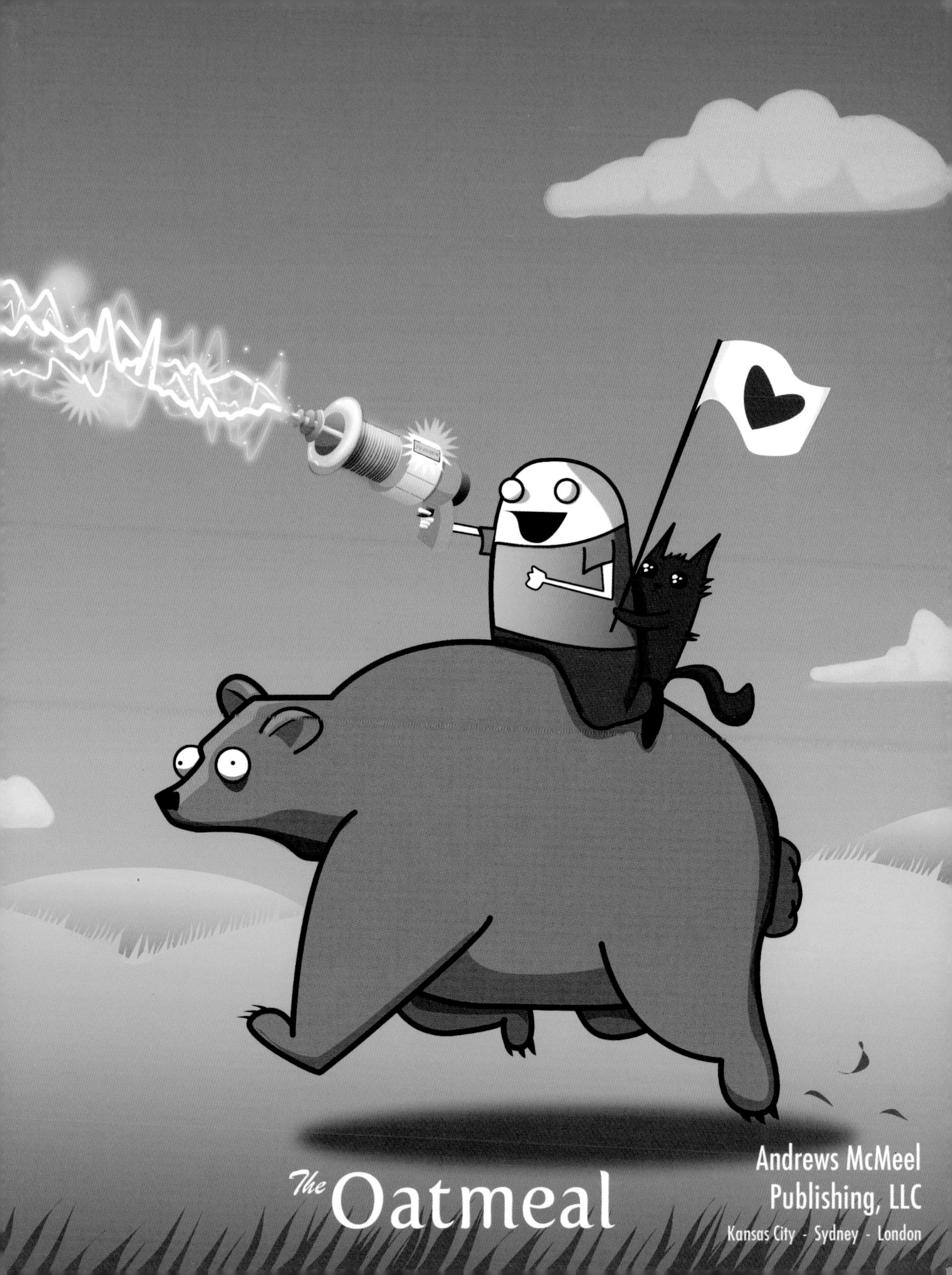

The Oatmeal

Andrews McMeel
Publishing, LLC
Kansas City · Sydney · London

Andrews McMeel Publishing, LLC
an Andrews McMeel Universal company
1130 Walnut Street, Kansas City, Missouri 64106

www.andrewsmcmeel.com

13 14 15 16 17 SDB 10 9 8 7 6 5 4 3 2

ISBN: 978-1-4494-2770-2

Library of Congress Control Number: 2013937114

ATTENTION: SCHOOLS AND BUSINESSES
Andrews McMeel books are available at quantity discounts with bulk purchase for educational, business, or sales promotional use. For information, please e-mail the Andrews McMeel Publishing Special Sales Department: specialsales@amuniversal.com

Contents

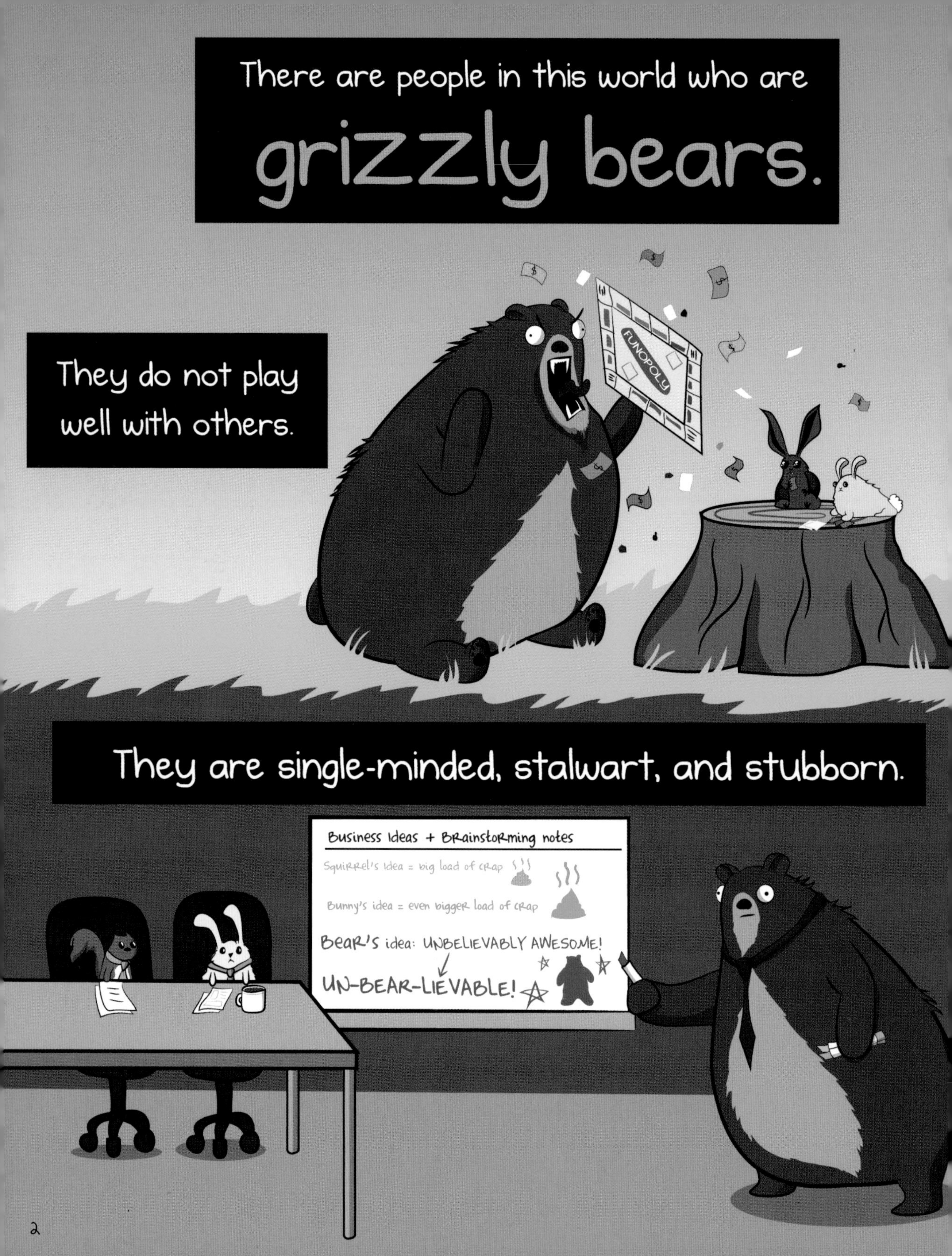
There are people in this world who are
grizzly bears.
They do not play well with others.
FUNOPOLY
They are single-minded, stalwart, and stubborn.
Business Ideas + Brainstorming notes
Squirrel's idea = big load of crap
Bunny's idea = even bigger load of crap
Bear's idea: UNBELIEVABLY AWESOME!
UN-BEAR-LIEVABLE!

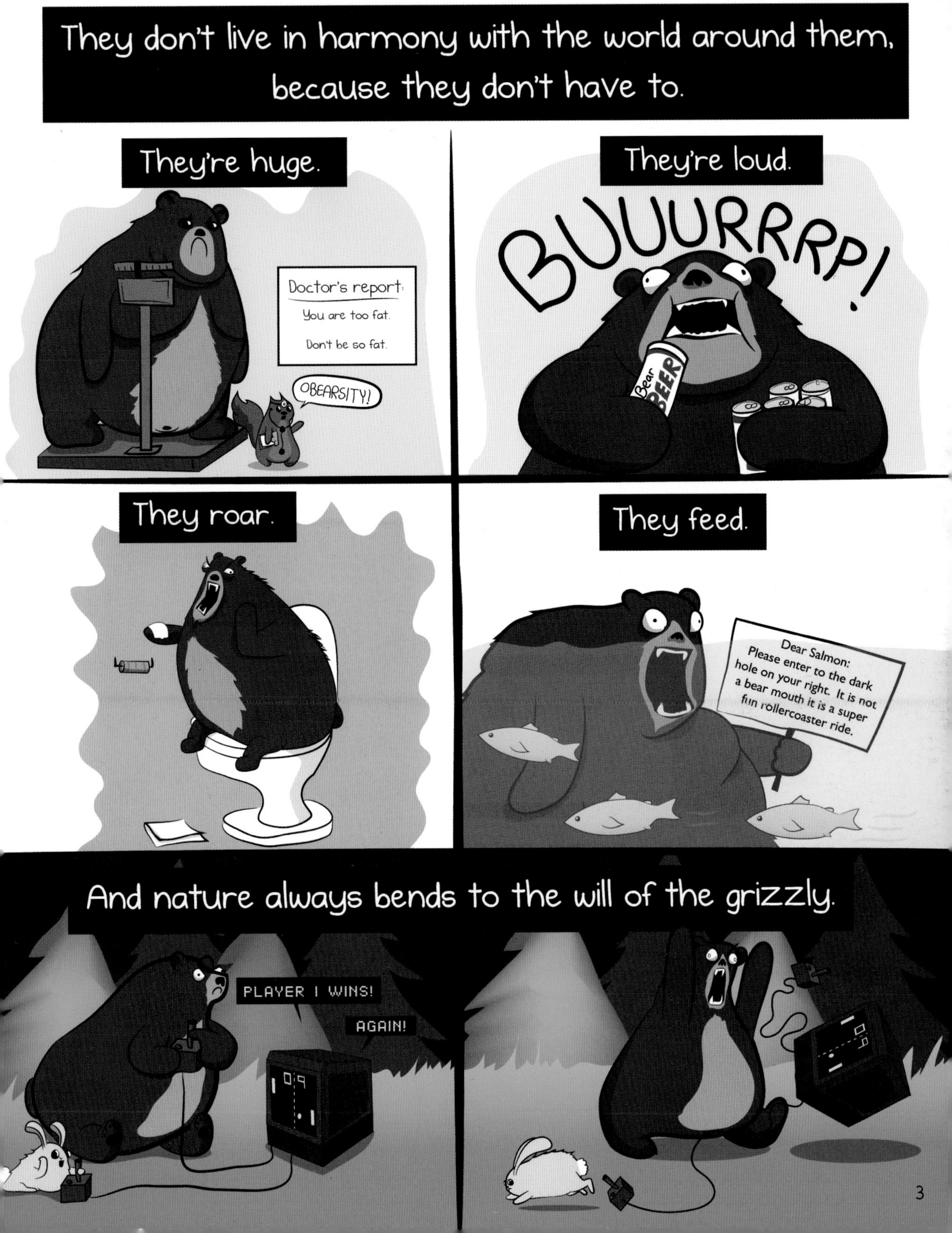
They don't live in harmony with the world around them, because they don't have to.
They're huge.
Doctor's report:
You are too fat.
Don't be so fat.
OBEARSITY!
They're loud.
BUUURRRP!
Bear BEER
They roar.
They feed.
Dear Salmon: Please enter to the dark hole on your right. It is not a bear mouth it is a super fun rollercoaster ride.
And nature always bends to the will of the grizzly.
PLAYER 1 WINS!
AGAIN!
0:9

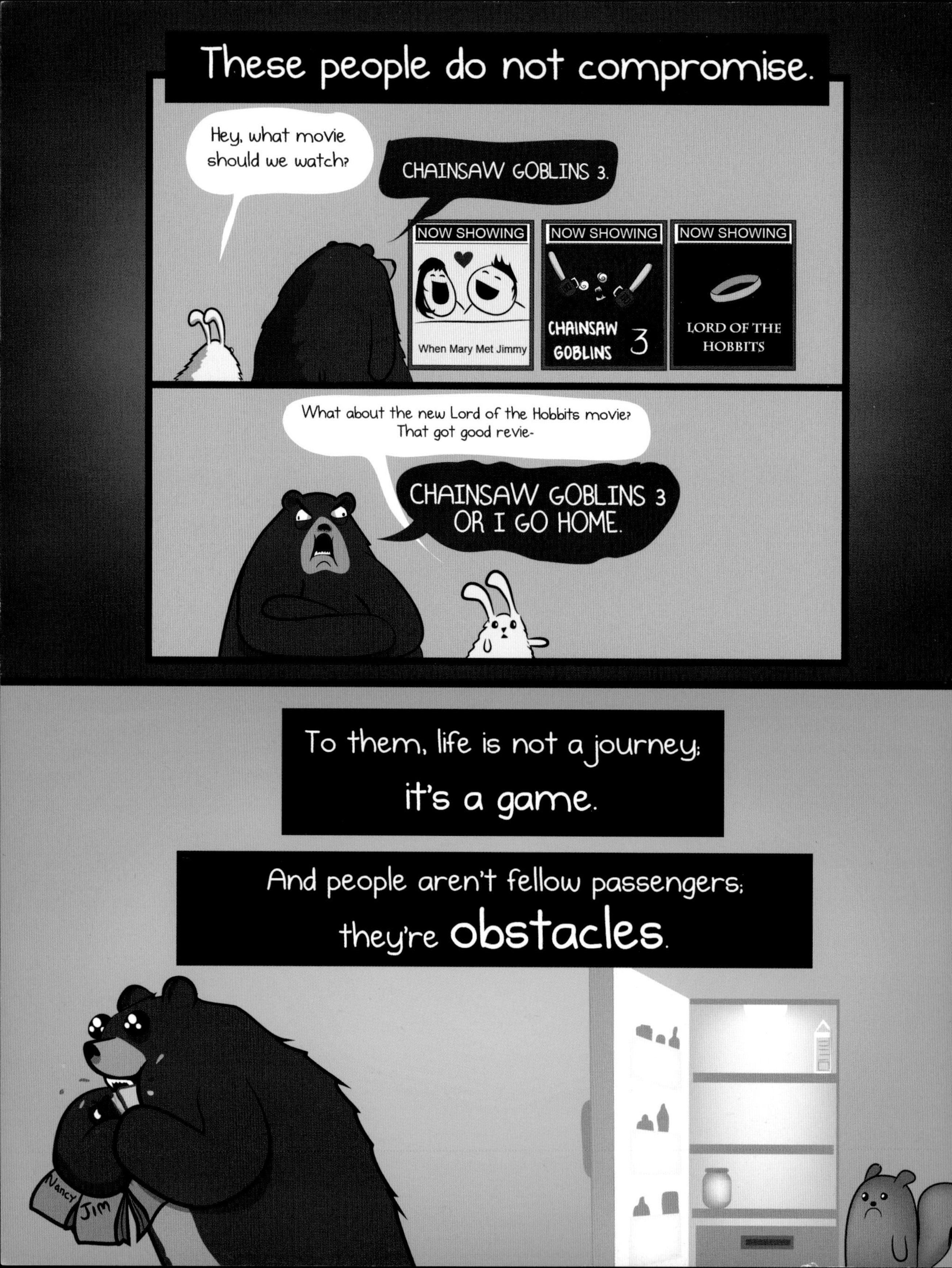
These people do not compromise.
Hey, what movie should we watch?
CHAINSAW GOBLINS 3.
NOW SHOWING
When Mary Met Jimmy
NOW SHOWING
CHAINSAW GOBLINS 3
NOW SHOWING
LORD OF THE HOBBITS
What about the new Lord of the Hobbits movie? That got good revie-
CHAINSAW GOBLINS 3 OR I GO HOME.
To them, life is not a journey;
it's a game.
And people aren't fellow passengers;
they're obstacles.
Nancy
Jim

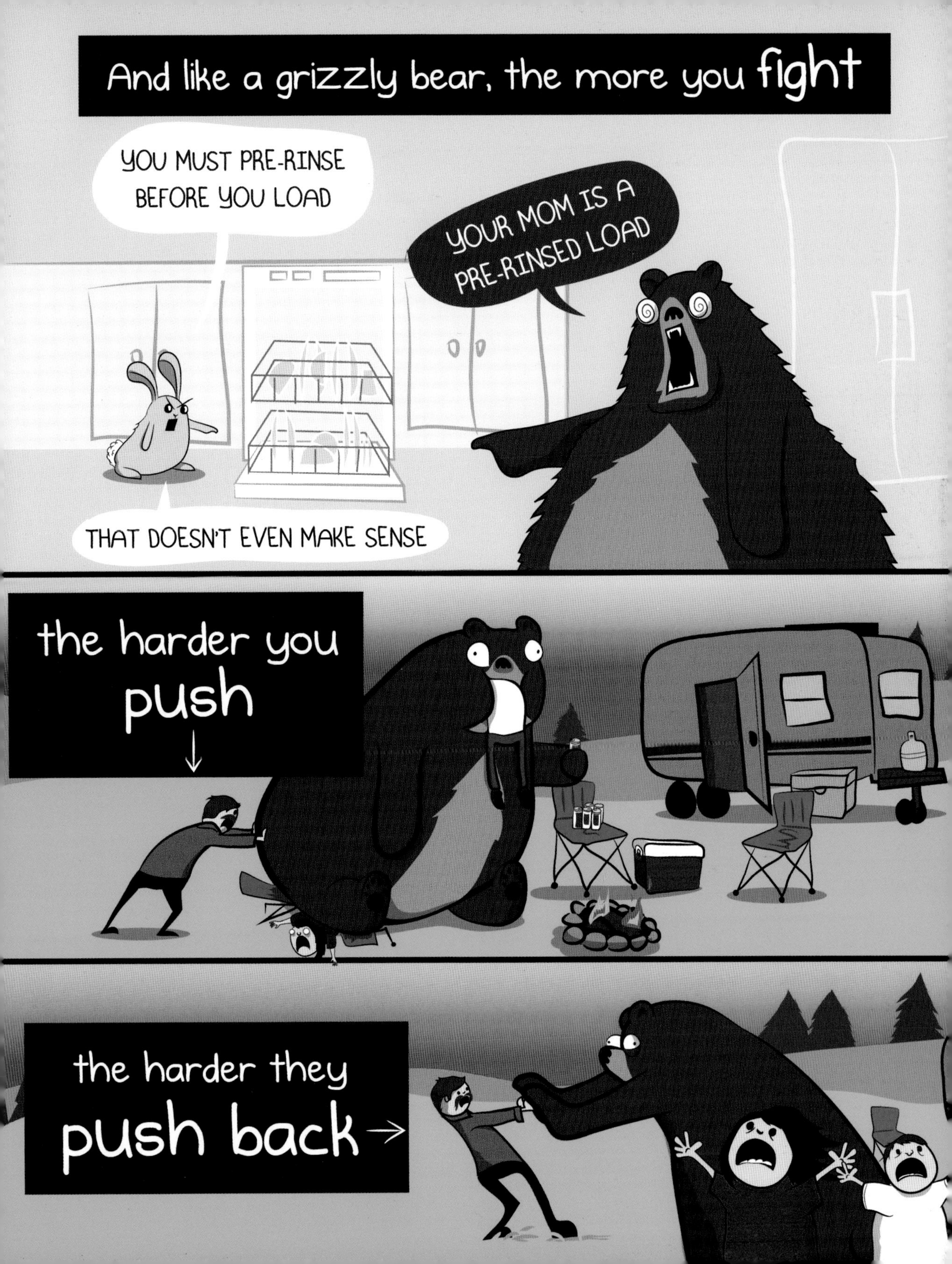

And like a grizzly bear, the more you fight
YOU MUST PRE-RINSE BEFORE YOU LOAD
YOUR MOM IS A PRE-RINSED LOAD
THAT DOESN'T EVEN MAKE SENSE
the harder you push
the harder they push back

BUT, there is a solution to this problem. There is a way to defeat the bear without fighting the bear.

It's been said that the core of the human spirit comes from the

heart.

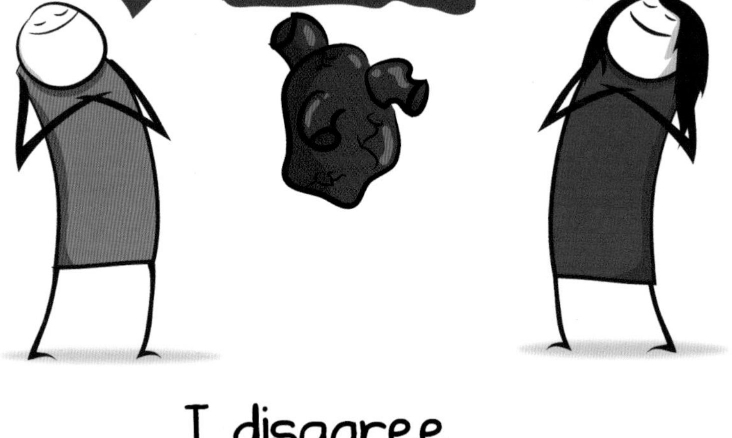

I disagree.

I believe it comes from the

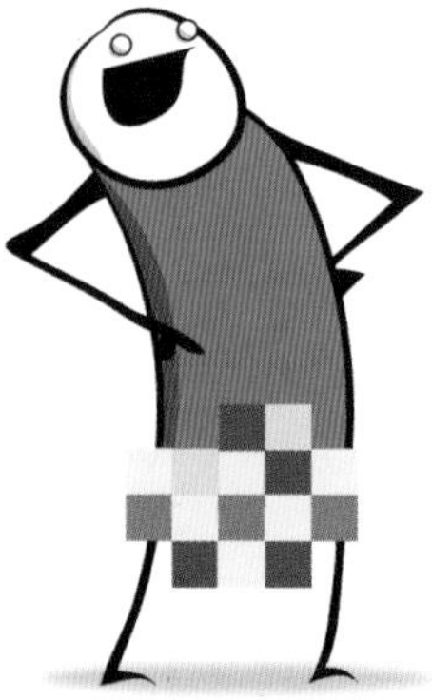

← **PRIVATES.** →

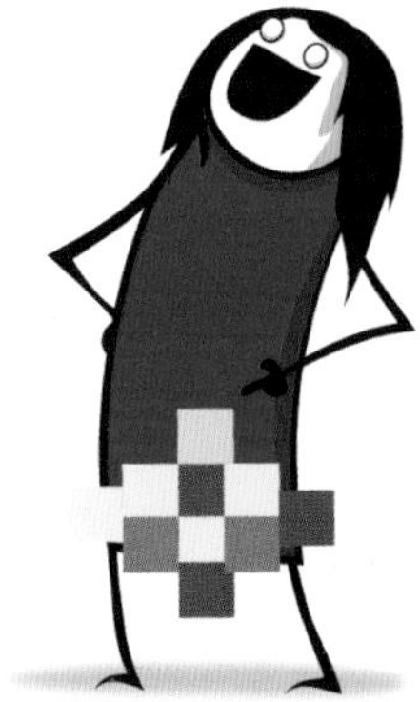

A heart is just a pump:

it moves blood from one place to another.

↓

They can even make an artificial one if yours stops working.

After I install your robot heart, you may develop erections when in the presence of computers and forklifts.

We call these "Skynet boners." Try to ignore them.

Our **privates**, however, are vastly complex organs.

They can grow bigger when it's time for a hot sexy adventure

WOOOOooo I HAVE A BONER!

MY PEEPEE IS REACHING FOR THE STARS!

and get smaller when it's time for a cold not-so-sexy adventure.

Well Nancy, my ding-dong is 45% its normal size. I'd say that puts us right around 28° F.

Roger that, good buddy. My nipples are three times as rigid as they were before, so I concur with your assessment.

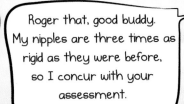

squeeze squeeze

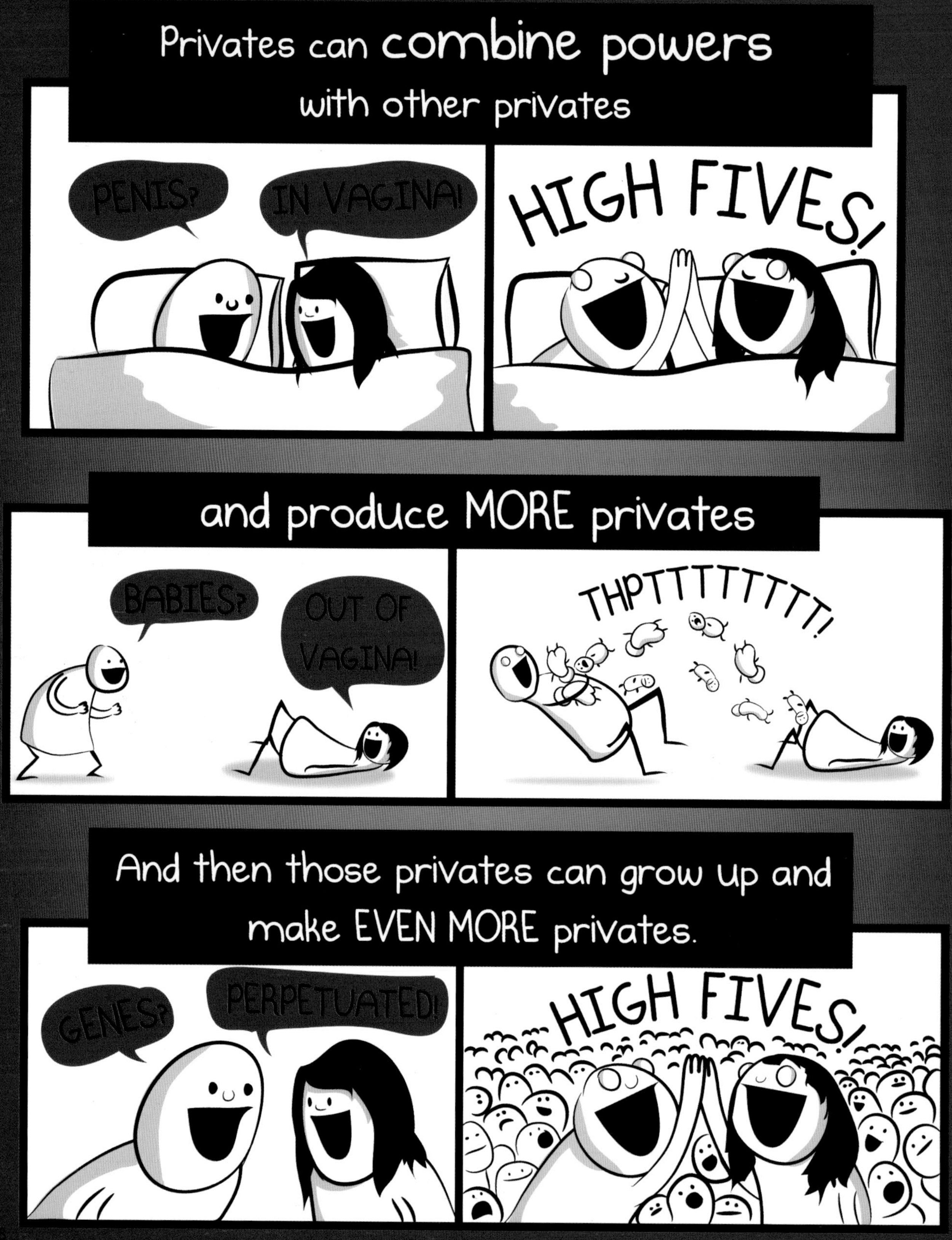

Privates can combine powers with other privates
PENIS?
IN VAGINA!
HIGH FIVES!
and produce MORE privates
BABIES?
OUT OF VAGINA!
THPTTTTTTTT!
And then those privates can grow up and make EVEN MORE privates.
GENES?
PERPETUATED!
HIGH FIVES!

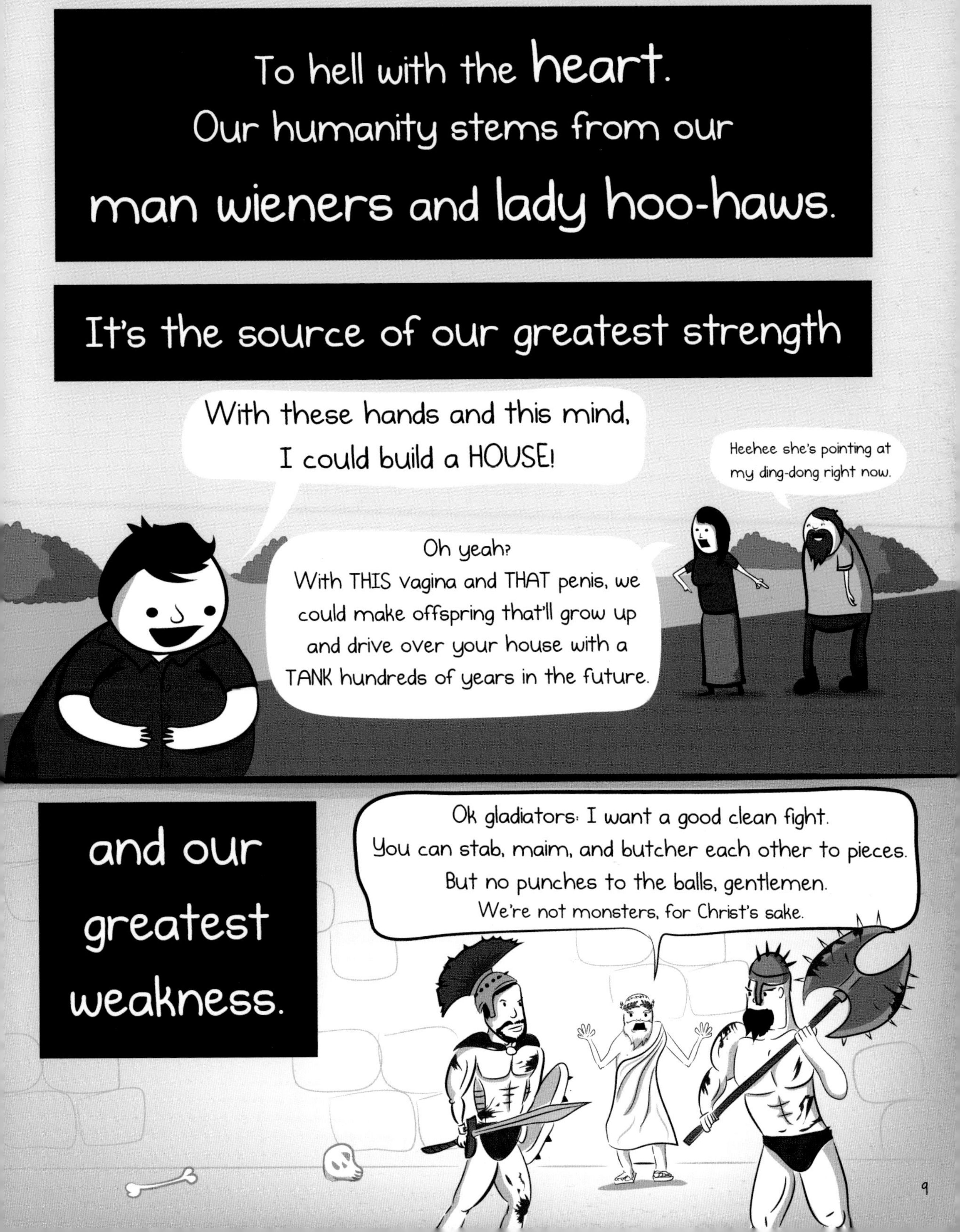

To hell with the heart.
Our humanity stems from our
man wieners and lady hoo-haws.
It's the source of our greatest strength
With these hands and this mind, I could build a HOUSE!
Oh yeah? With THIS vagina and THAT penis, we could make offspring that'll grow up and drive over your house with a TANK hundreds of years in the future.
Heehee she's pointing at my ding-dong right now.
and our greatest weakness.
Ok gladiators: I want a good clean fight. You can stab, maim, and butcher each other to pieces. But no punches to the balls, gentlemen. We're not monsters, for Christ's sake.

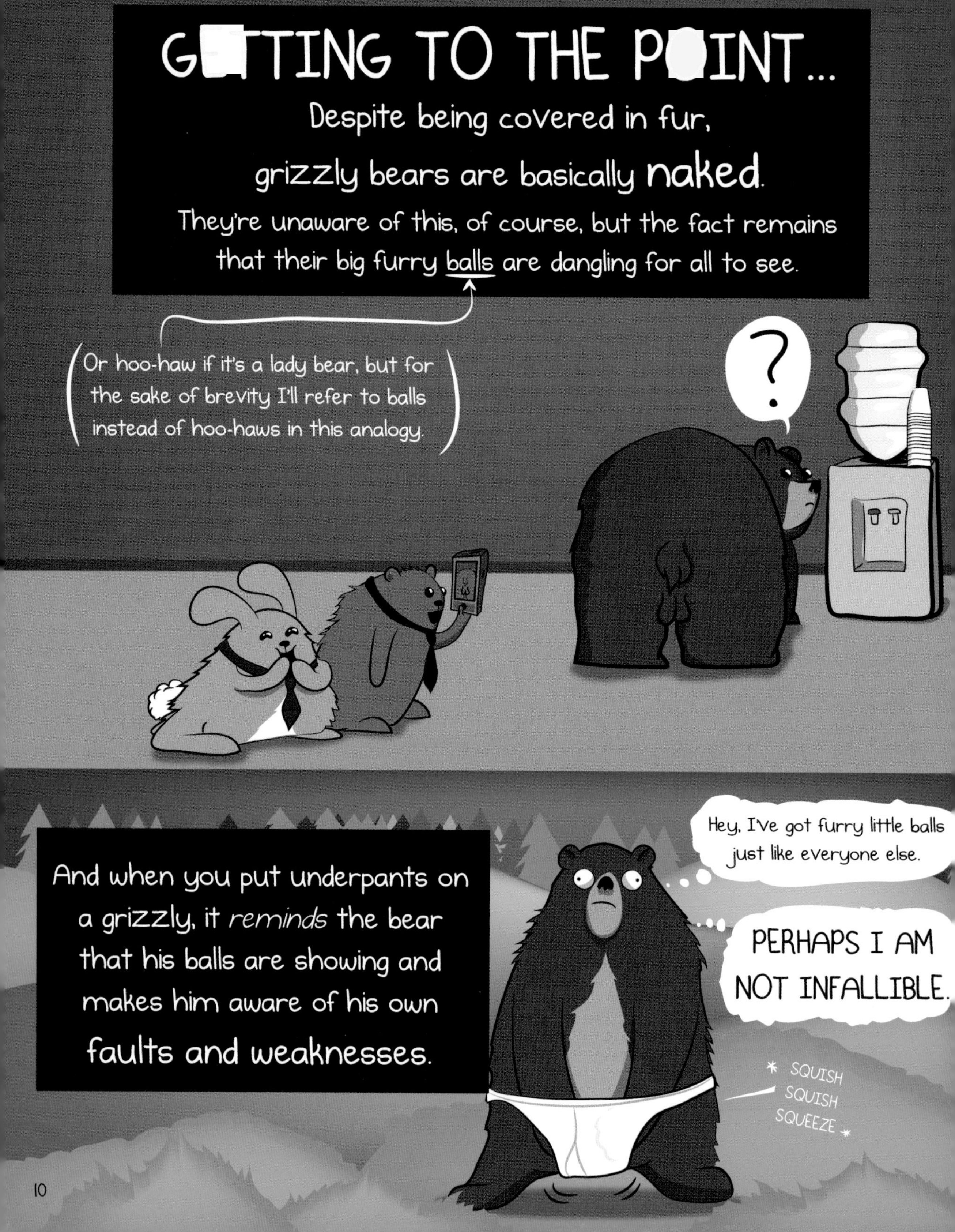

GETTING TO THE POINT...
Despite being covered in fur, grizzly bears are basically naked.
They're unaware of this, of course, but the fact remains that their big furry balls are dangling for all to see.
(Or hoo-haw if it's a lady bear, but for the sake of brevity I'll refer to balls instead of hoo-haws in this analogy.)
?
And when you put underpants on a grizzly, it *reminds* the bear that his balls are showing and makes him aware of his own faults and weaknesses.
Hey, I've got furry little balls just like everyone else.
PERHAPS I AM NOT INFALLIBLE.
SQUISH SQUISH SQUEEZE

Furthermore, wearing underpants might eventually teach the bear that

compromise

can be the best way to endure this bumpy-yet-awesome journey we call **life**.

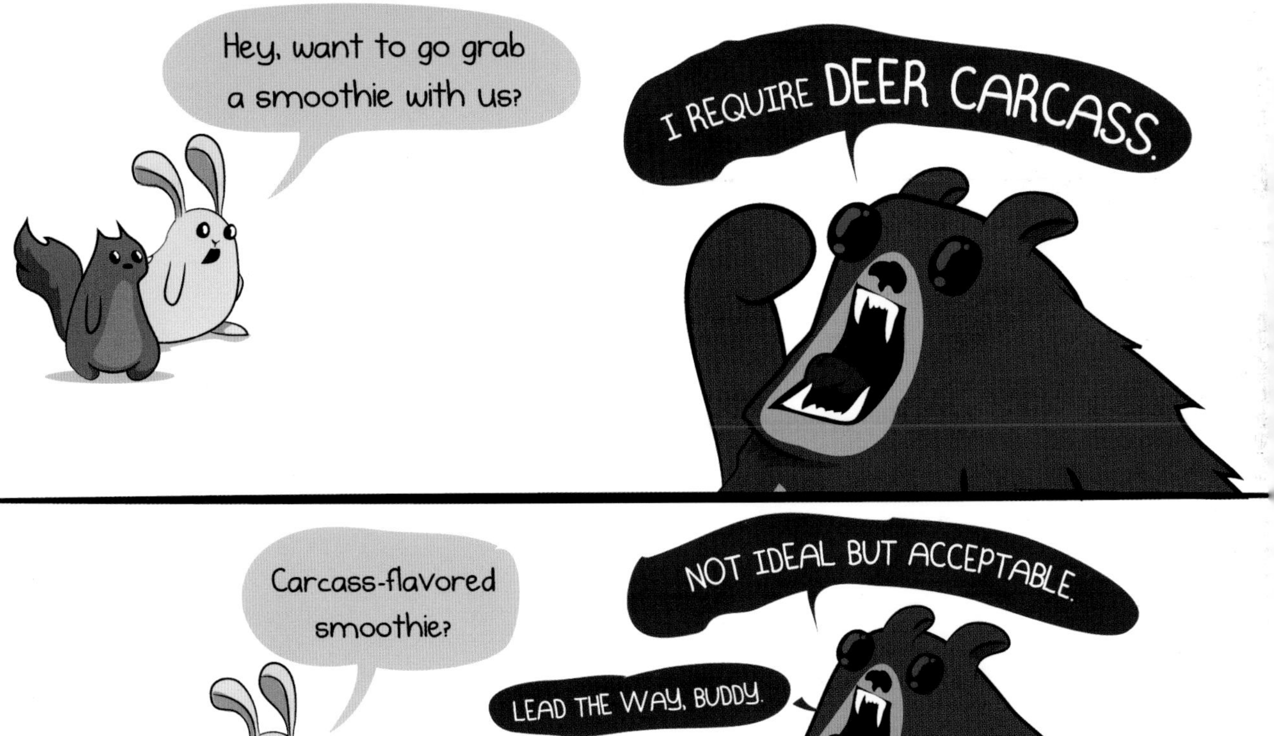
Hey, want to go grab a smoothie with us?
I REQUIRE DEER CARCASS.

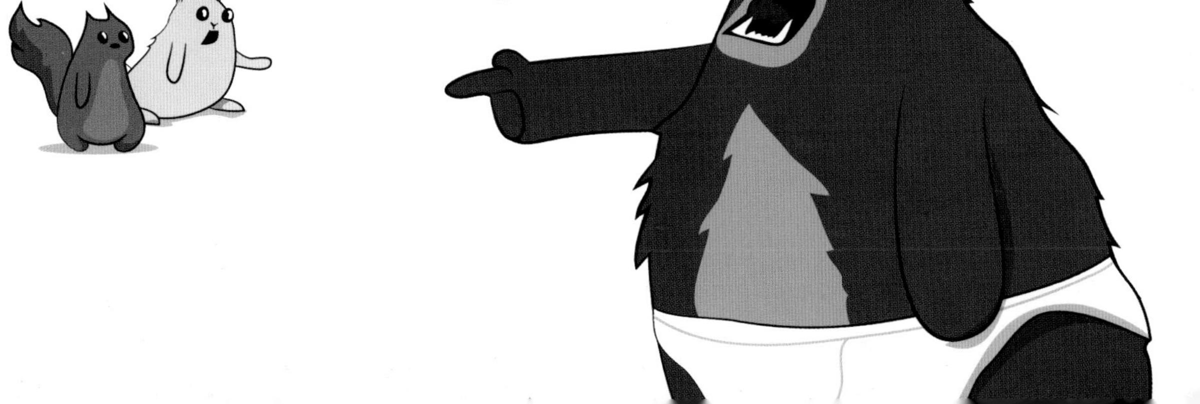
Carcass-flavored smoothie?
NOT IDEAL BUT ACCEPTABLE.
LEAD THE WAY, BUDDY.

I wish we lived in a world where stubborn, single-minded people had to walk around in their underpants all day, feeling **disarmed** and **vulnerable**.

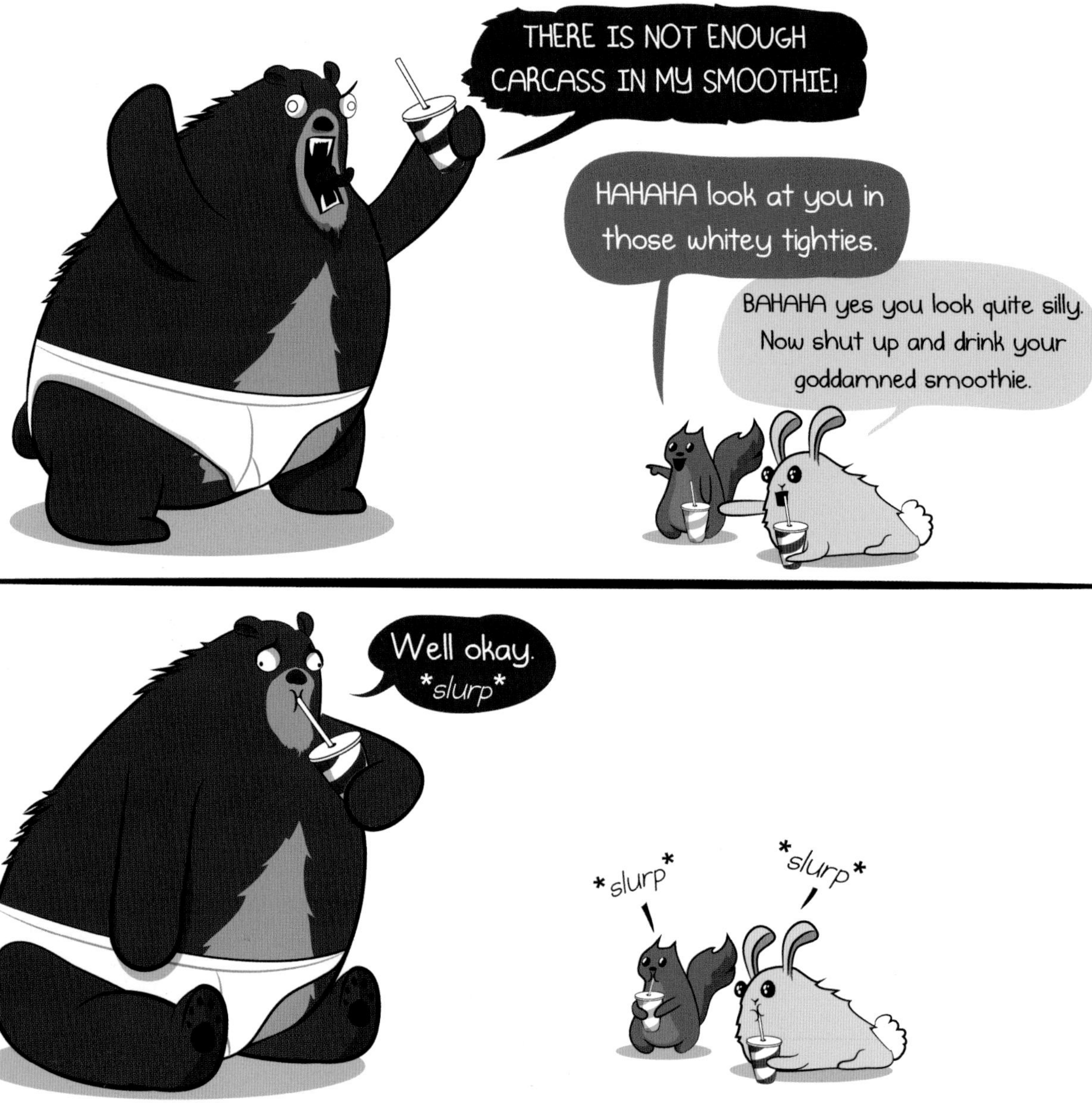
THERE IS NOT ENOUGH CARCASS IN MY SMOOTHIE!
HAHAHA look at you in those whitey tighties.
BAHAHA yes you look quite silly. Now shut up and drink your goddamned smoothie.
Well okay. *slurp*
slurp
slurp

But we don't,

so my advice to you is to remember that we're all capable of being grizzly bears at times, driven by our huge

claws, teeth, and appetites,

and blinded by our huge

agendas, needs, and emotions.

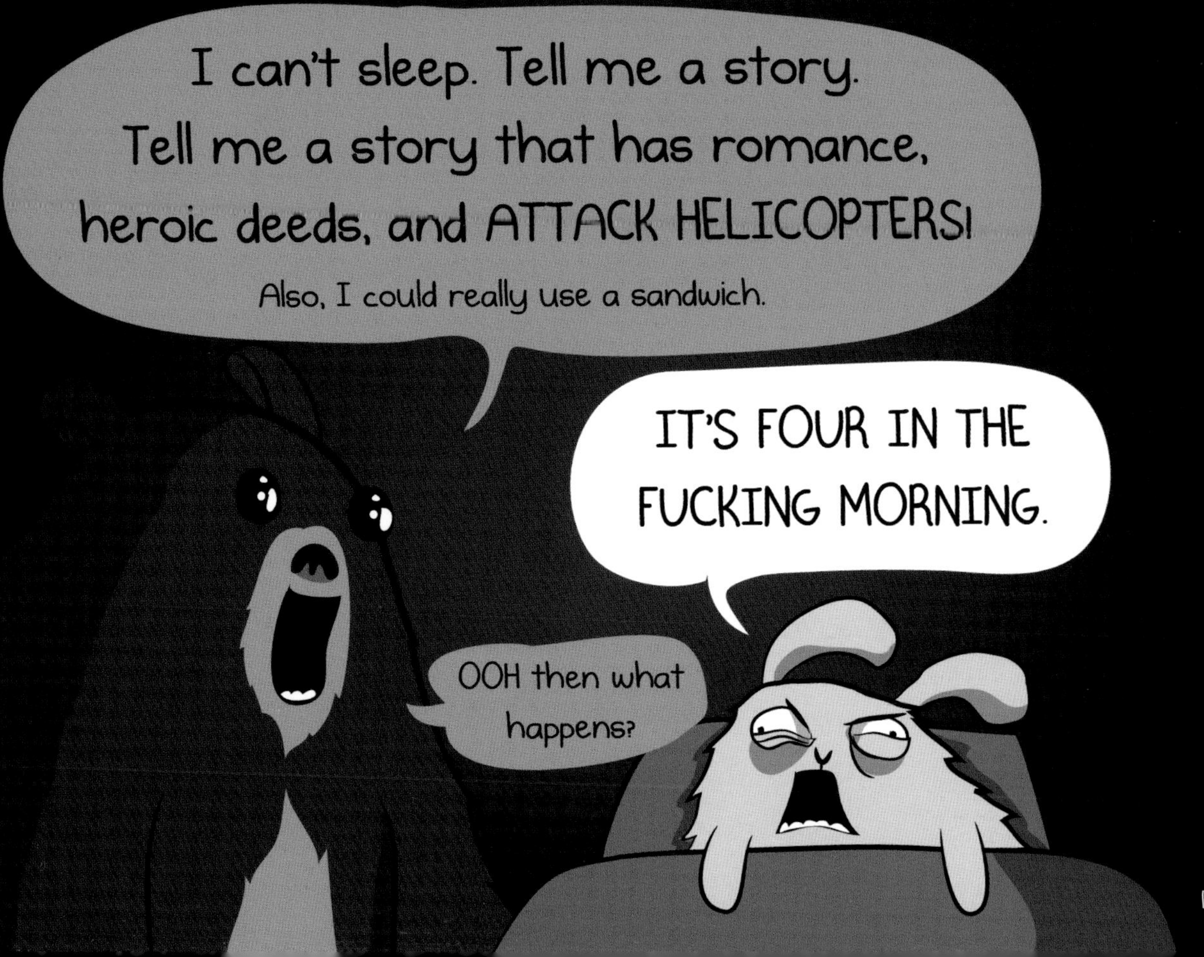

I can't sleep. Tell me a story. Tell me a story that has romance, heroic deeds, and ATTACK HELICOPTERS!
Also, I could really use a sandwich.
IT'S FOUR IN THE FUCKING MORNING.
OOH then what happens?

So if you find yourself behaving like a grizzly:

remember your fallibility,

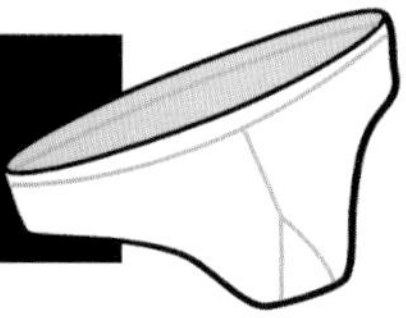

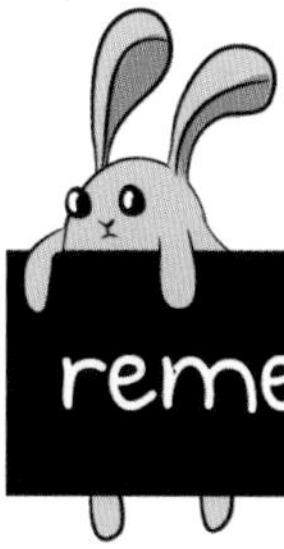

remember your fellow passengers,

and most importantly,

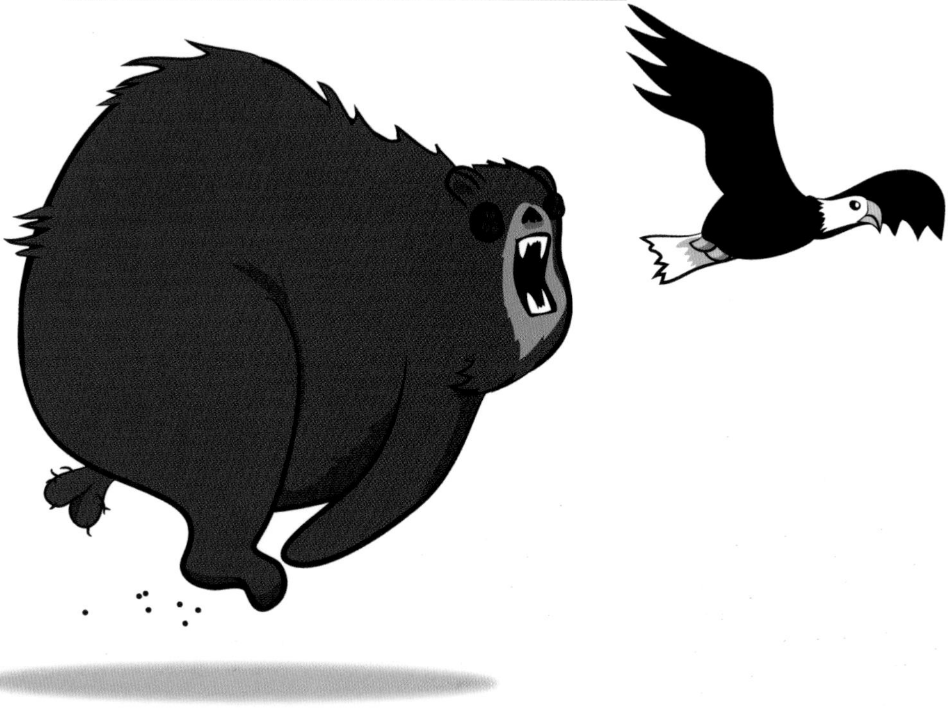

remember your testicles.

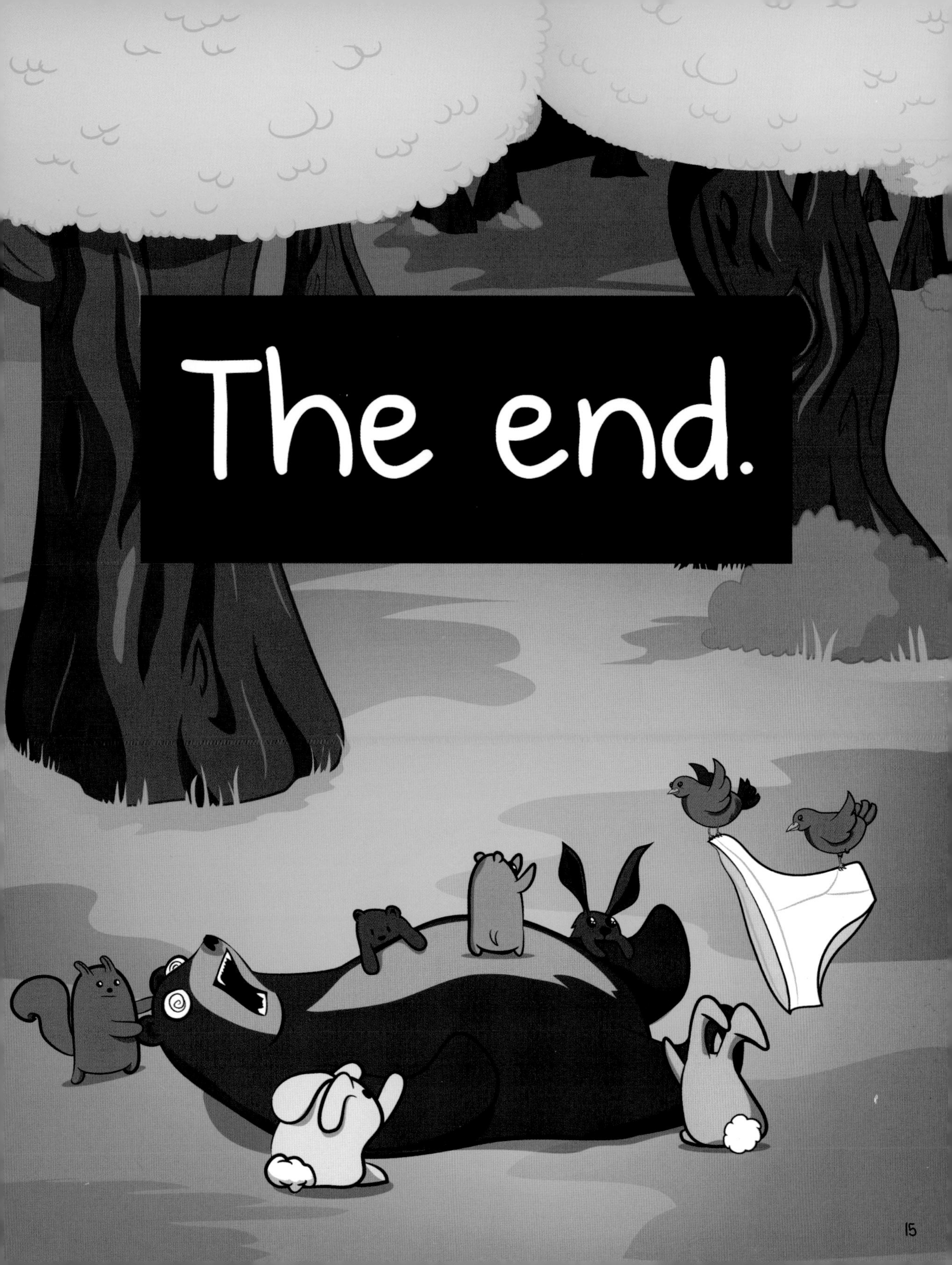
The end.

sound to Americans

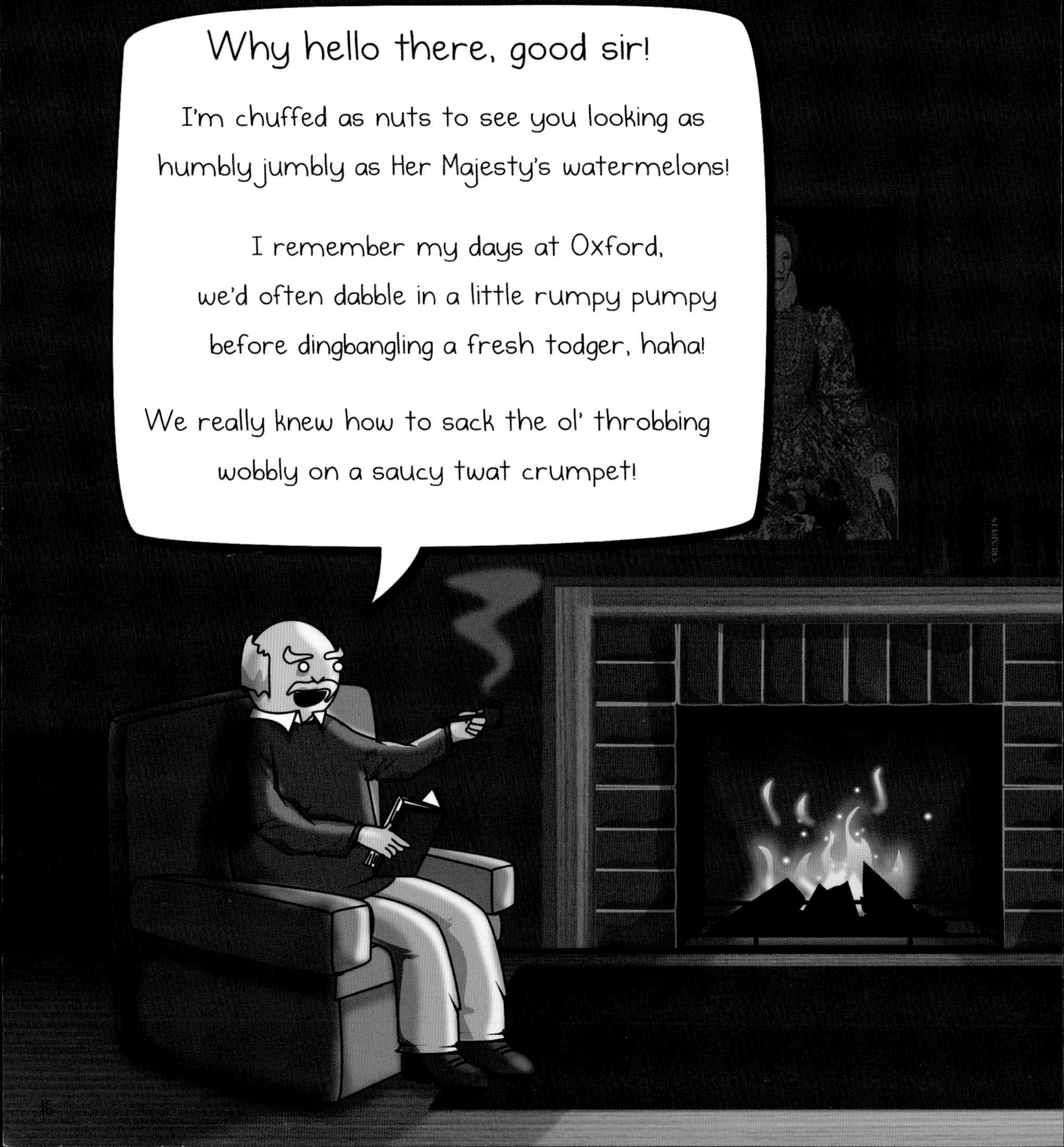
Why hello there, good sir!
I'm chuffed as nuts to see you looking as humbly jumbly as Her Majesty's watermelons!
I remember my days at Oxford, we'd often dabble in a little rumpy pumpy before dingbangling a fresh todger, haha!
We really knew how to sack the ol' throbbing wobbly on a saucy twat crumpet!

How American accents sound to the British

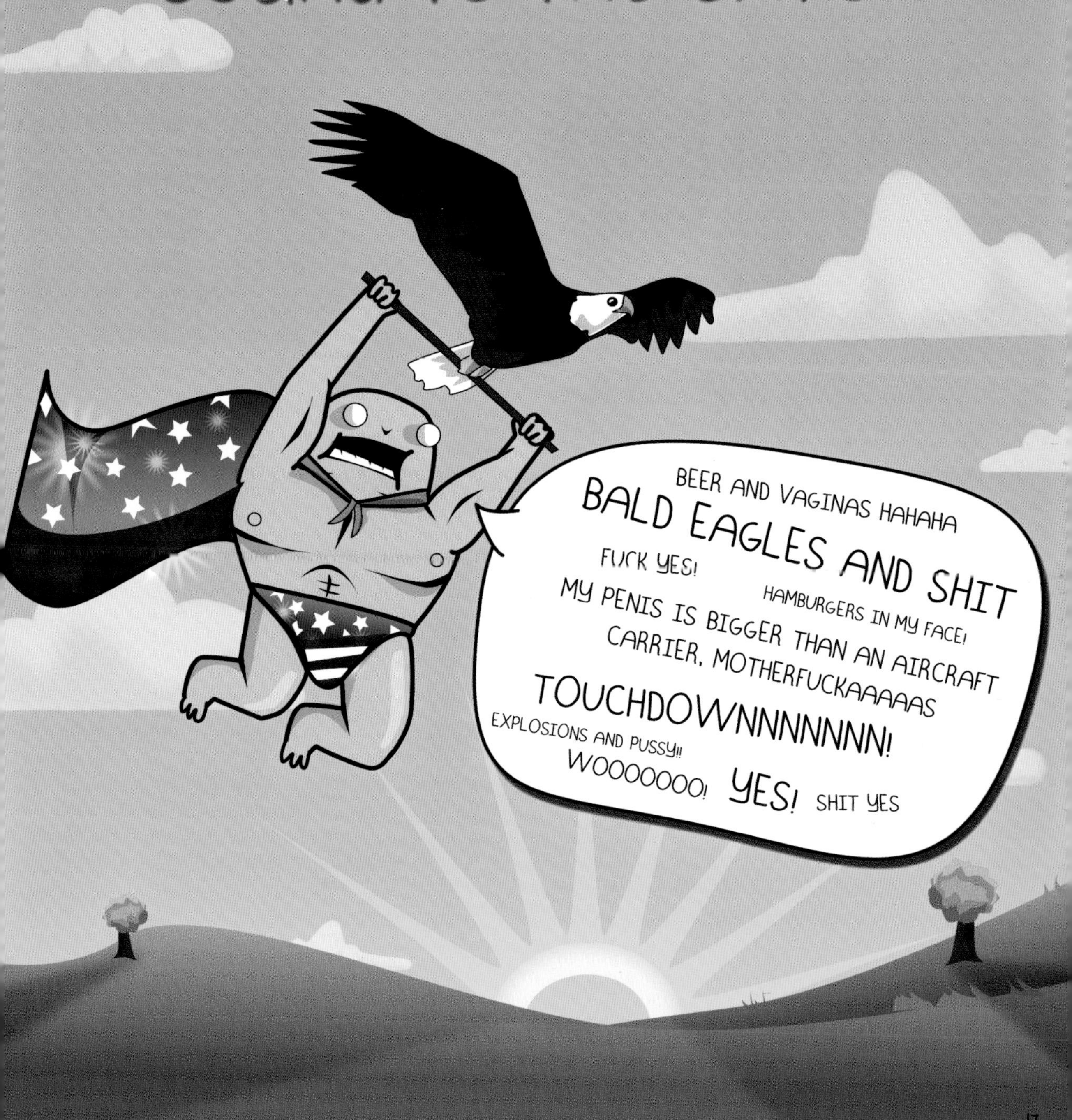
BEER AND VAGINAS HAHAHA
BALD EAGLES AND SHIT
FUCK YES!
HAMBURGERS IN MY FACE!
MY PENIS IS BIGGER THAN AN AIRCRAFT CARRIER, MOTHERFUCKAAAAAS
TOUCHDOWNNNNNNN!
EXPLOSIONS AND PUSSY!!
WOOOOOOO! YES! SHIT YES

Literally

means *actually* or without exaggeration.

When you say "I literally... ," it means you're describing something exactly as it happened; you are being literal.

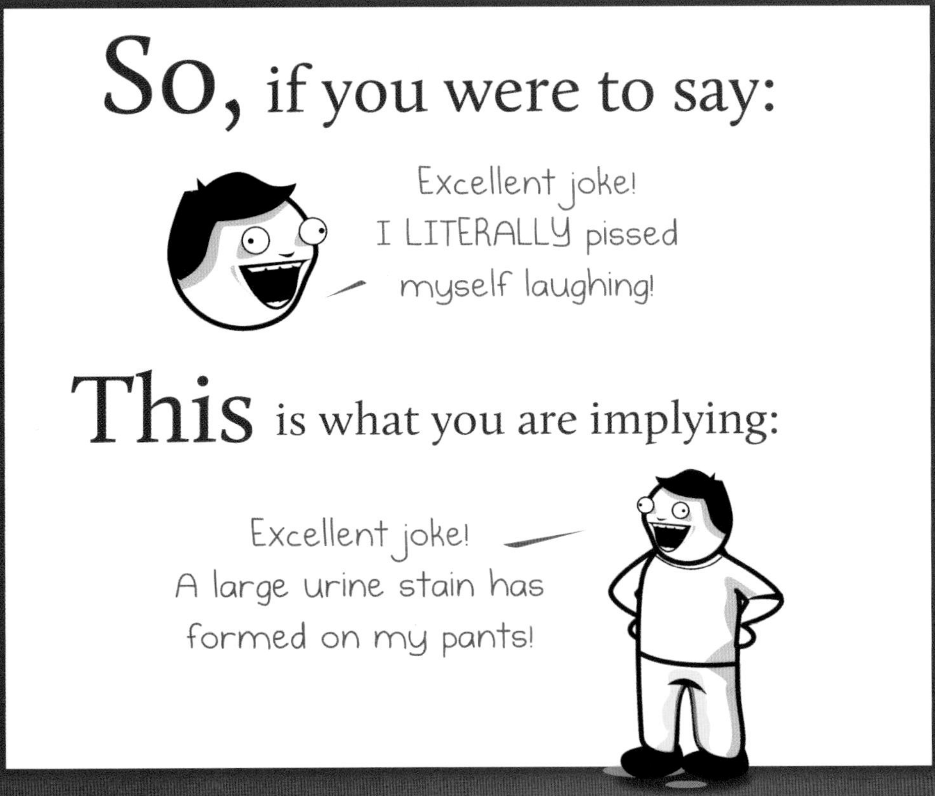
So, if you were to say:
Excellent joke! I LITERALLY pissed myself laughing!
This is what you are implying:
Excellent joke! A large urine stain has formed on my pants!

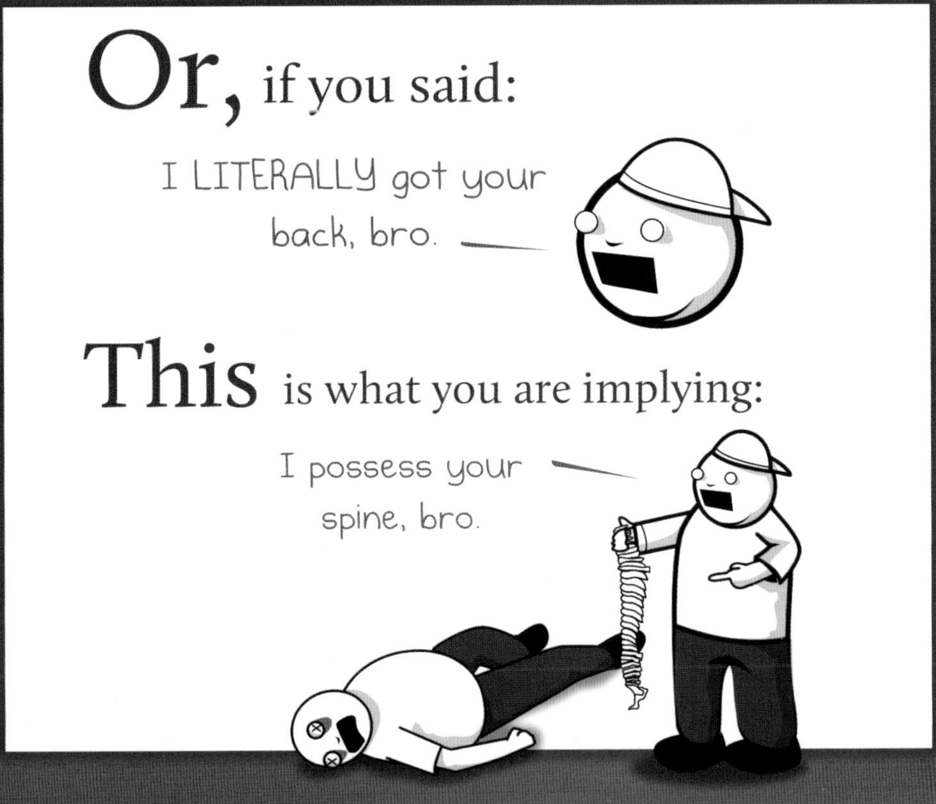
Or, if you said:
I LITERALLY got your back, bro.
This is what you are implying:
I possess your spine, bro.

A friend of mine once said:

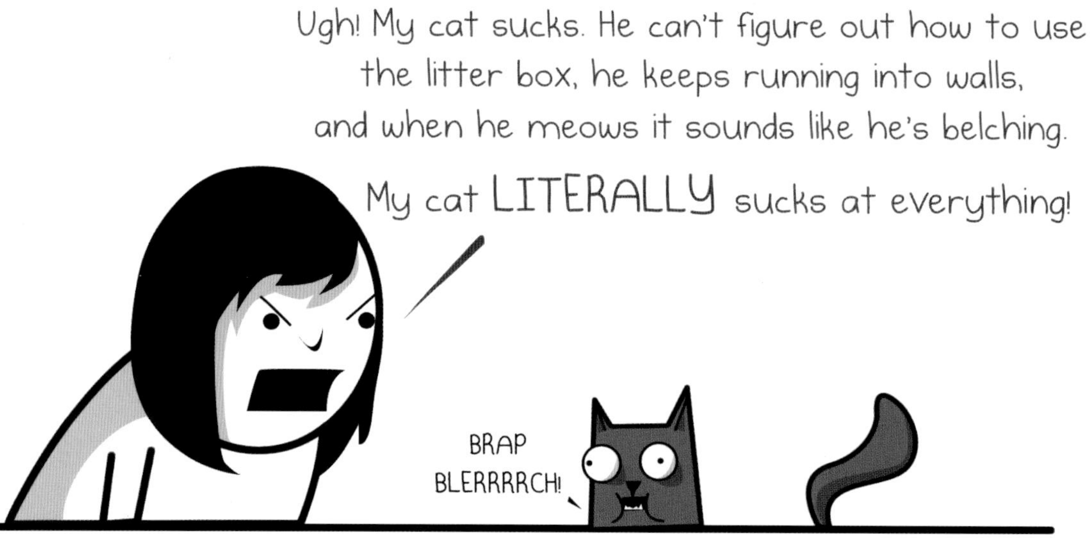

Ugh! My cat sucks. He can't figure out how to use the litter box, he keeps running into walls, and when he meows it sounds like he's belching.
My cat LITERALLY sucks at everything!
BRAP BLERRRRCH!

Which would mean this:

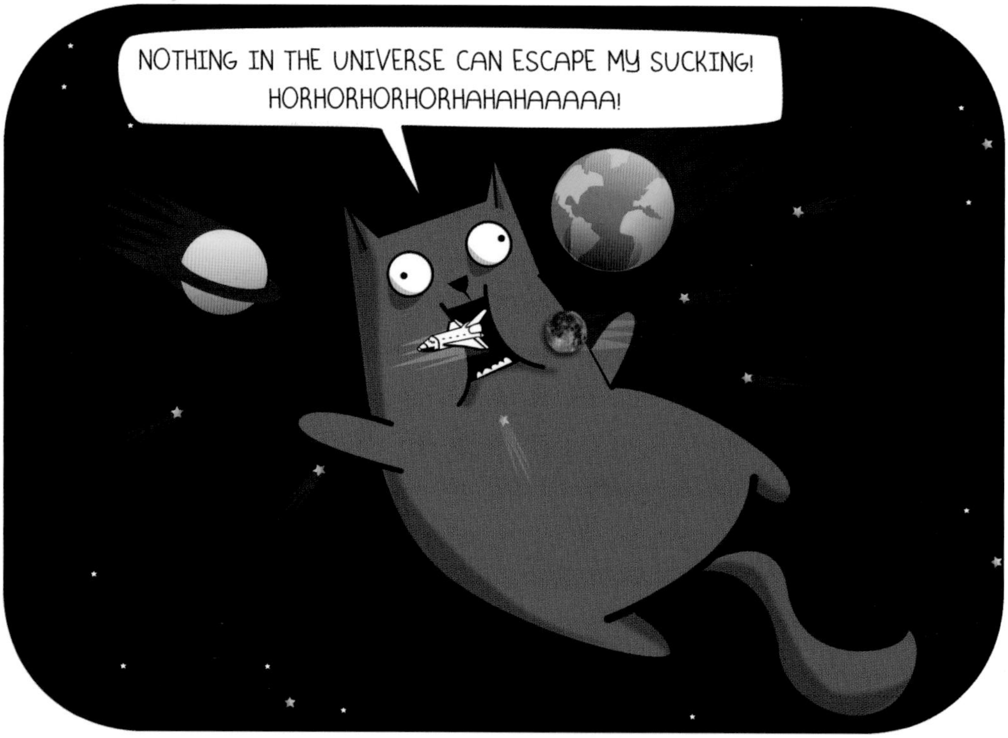

NOTHING IN THE UNIVERSE CAN ESCAPE MY SUCKING! HORHORHORHORHAHAHAAAAA!

The late

Jerry Falwell

provided this quotation before his death in 2007:

"If we do not act now, homosexuals will own America! If you and I do not speak up now, this homosexual steamroller will **literally** *crush all decent men, women, and children who get in its way ... and our nation will pay a terrible price!"*

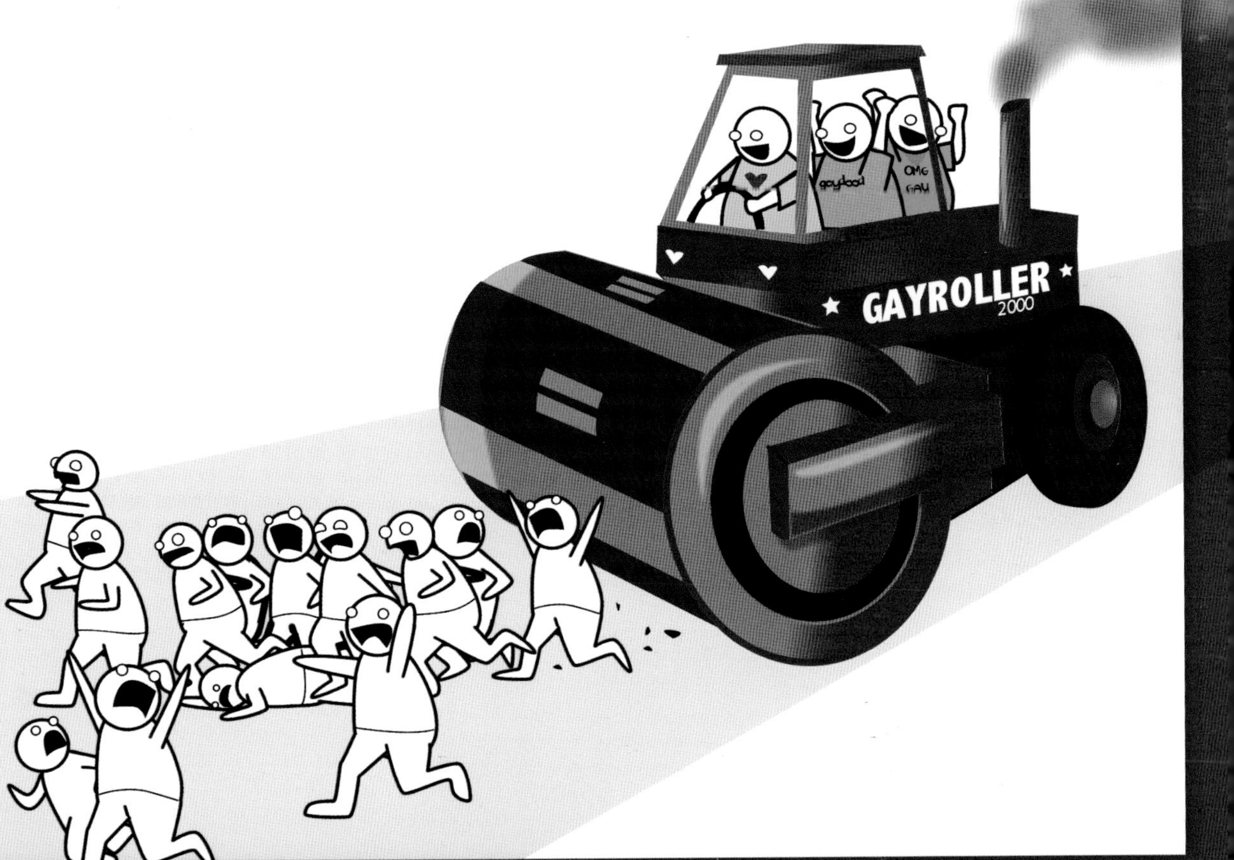
GAYROLLER
2000

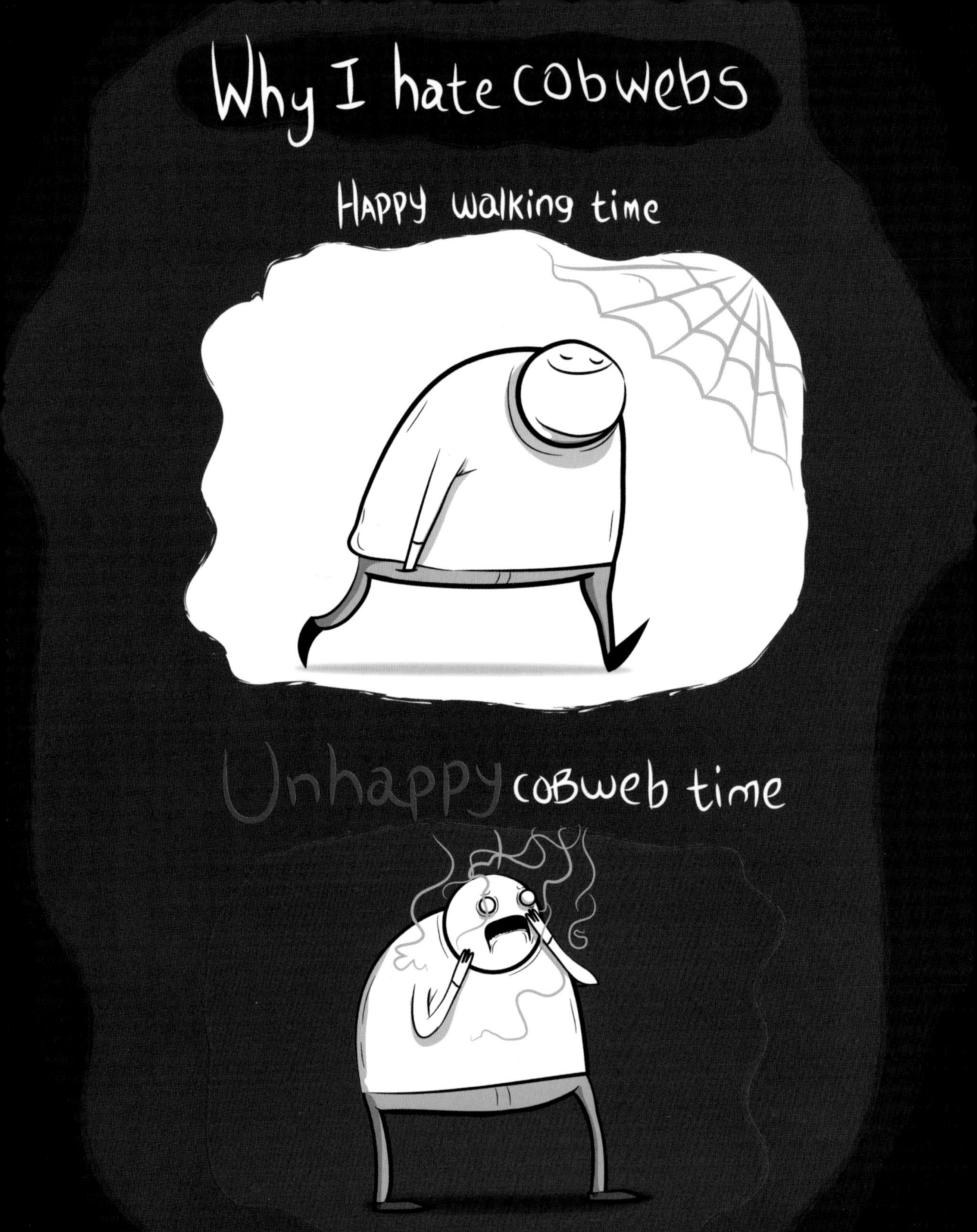
Why I hate cobwebs
Happy walking time
Unhappy cobweb time

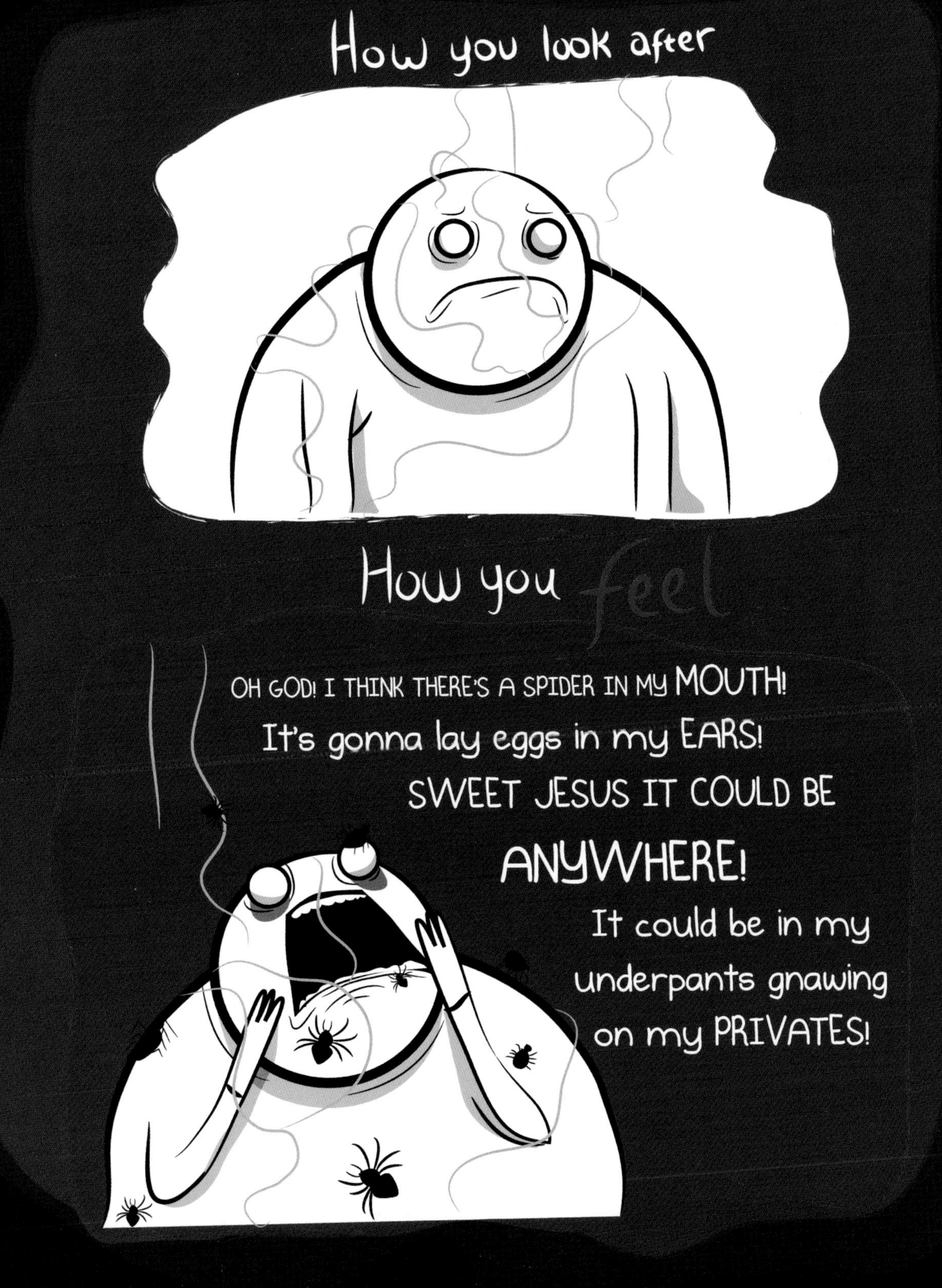
How you look after
How you feel
OH GOD! I THINK THERE'S A SPIDER IN MY MOUTH!
It's gonna lay eggs in my EARS!
SWEET JESUS IT COULD BE
ANYWHERE!
It could be in my underpants gnawing on my PRIVATES!

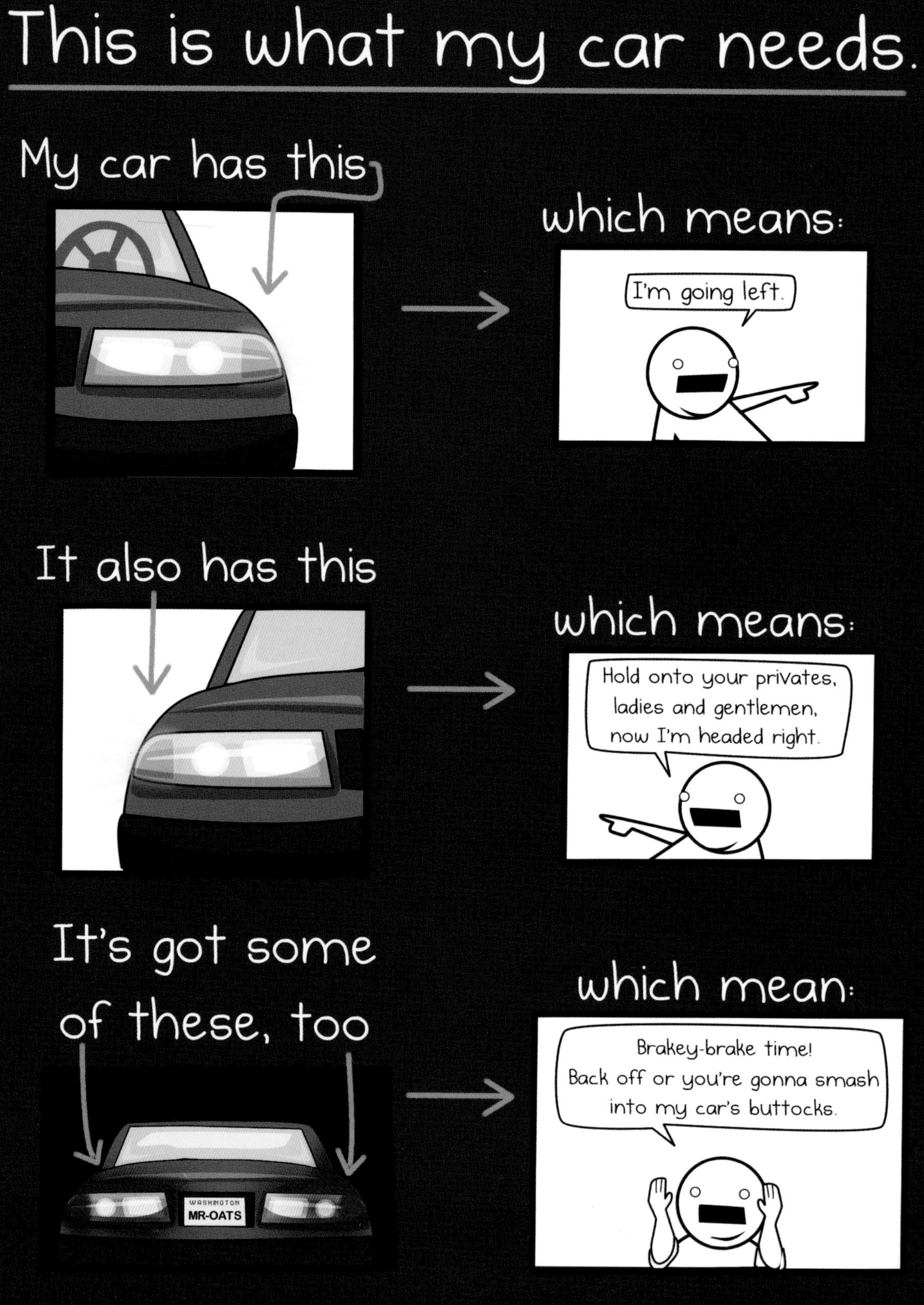

This is what my car needs.

My car has this

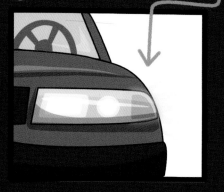

which means:

I'm going left.

It also has this

which means:

Hold onto your privates, ladies and gentlemen, now I'm headed right.

It's got some of these, too

which mean:

Brakey-brake time! Back off or you're gonna smash into my car's buttocks.

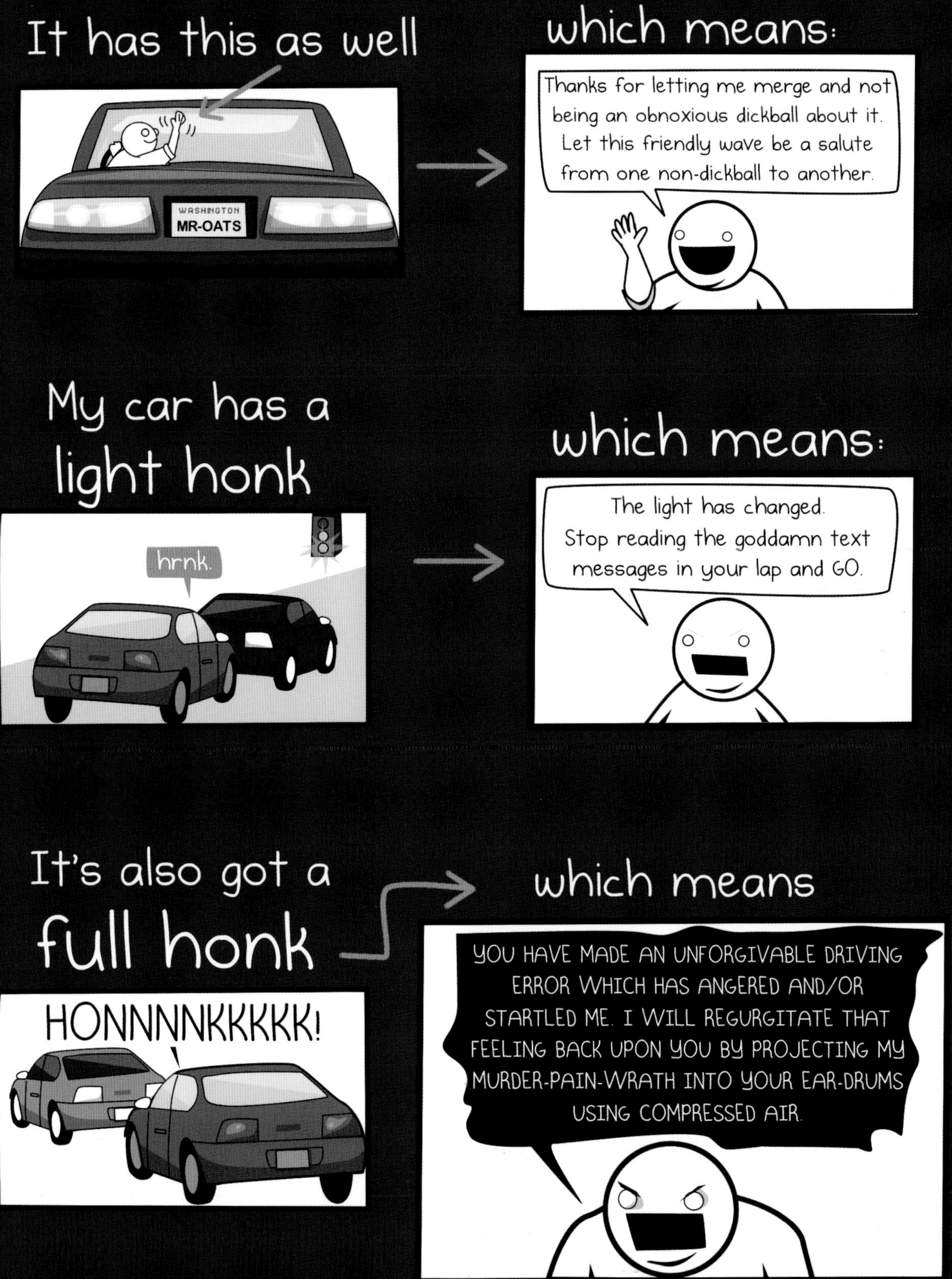
It has this as well
WASHINGTON
MR-OATS
which means:
Thanks for letting me merge and not being an obnoxious dickball about it. Let this friendly wave be a salute from one non-dickball to another.
My car has a light honk
hrnk.
which means:
The light has changed. Stop reading the goddamn text messages in your lap and GO.
It's also got a full honk
HONNNNKKKKK!
which means
YOU HAVE MADE AN UNFORGIVABLE DRIVING ERROR WHICH HAS ANGERED AND/OR STARTLED ME. I WILL REGURGITATE THAT FEELING BACK UPON YOU BY PROJECTING MY MURDER-PAIN-WRATH INTO YOUR EAR-DRUMS USING COMPRESSED AIR.

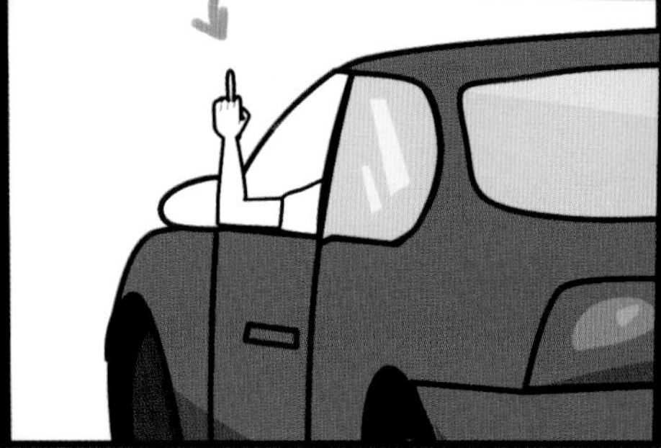

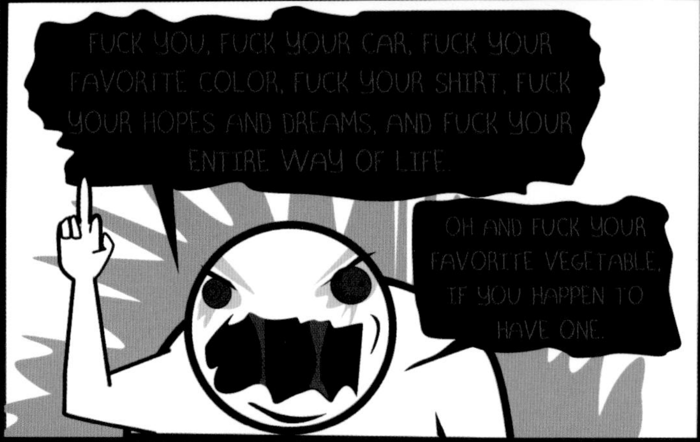
FUCK YOU, FUCK YOUR CAR, FUCK YOUR FAVORITE COLOR, FUCK YOUR SHIRT, FUCK YOUR HOPES AND DREAMS, AND FUCK YOUR ENTIRE WAY OF LIFE.
OH AND FUCK YOUR FAVORITE VEGETABLE, IF YOU HAPPEN TO HAVE ONE.

My car has all of these things,
but what it really needs is this:

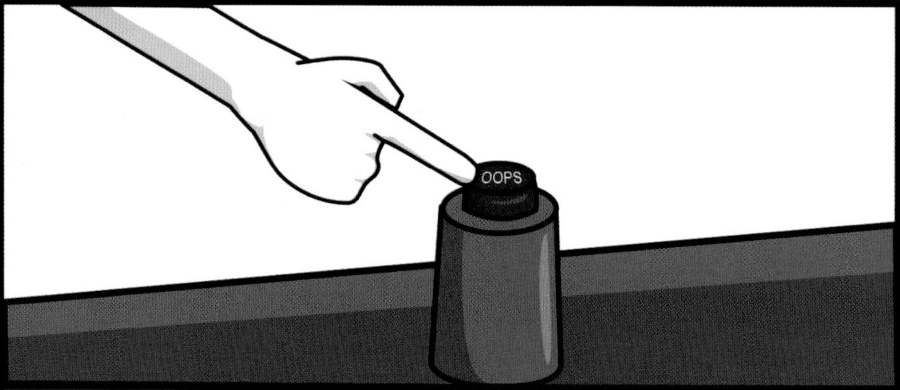
OOPS

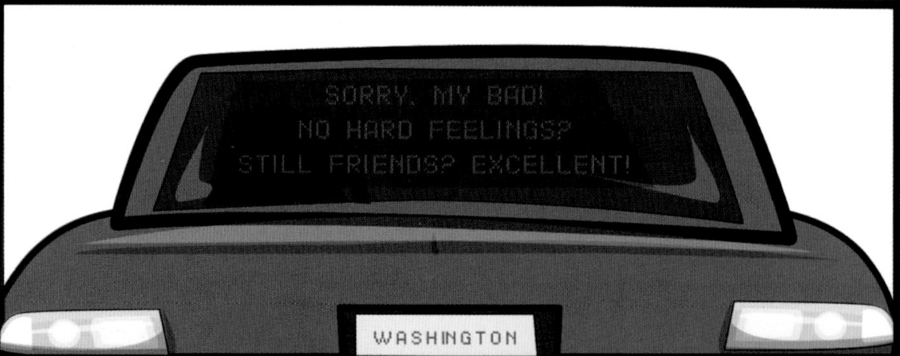
SORRY. MY BAD!
NO HARD FEELINGS?
STILL FRIENDS? EXCELLENT!
WASHINGTON

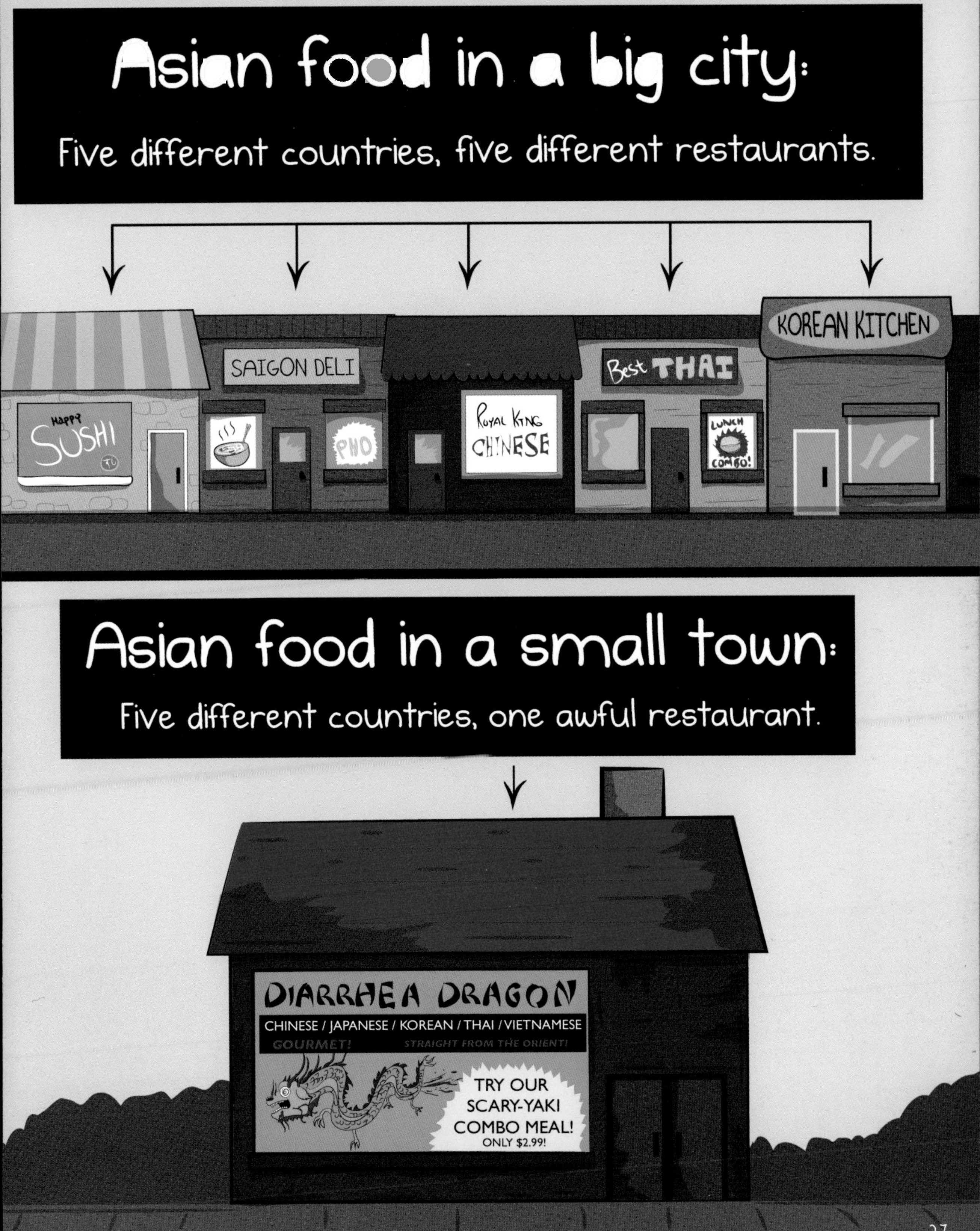

Asian food in a big city:
Five different countries, five different restaurants.
Happy SUSHI
SAIGON DELI
PHO
Royal King CHINESE
Best THAI
LUNCH COMBO!
KOREAN KITCHEN
Asian food in a small town:
Five different countries, one awful restaurant.
DIARRHEA DRAGON
CHINESE / JAPANESE / KOREAN / THAI / VIETNAMESE
GOURMET!
STRAIGHT FROM THE ORIENT!
TRY OUR SCARY-YAKI COMBO MEAL!
ONLY $2.99!

If my brain were an imaginary friend

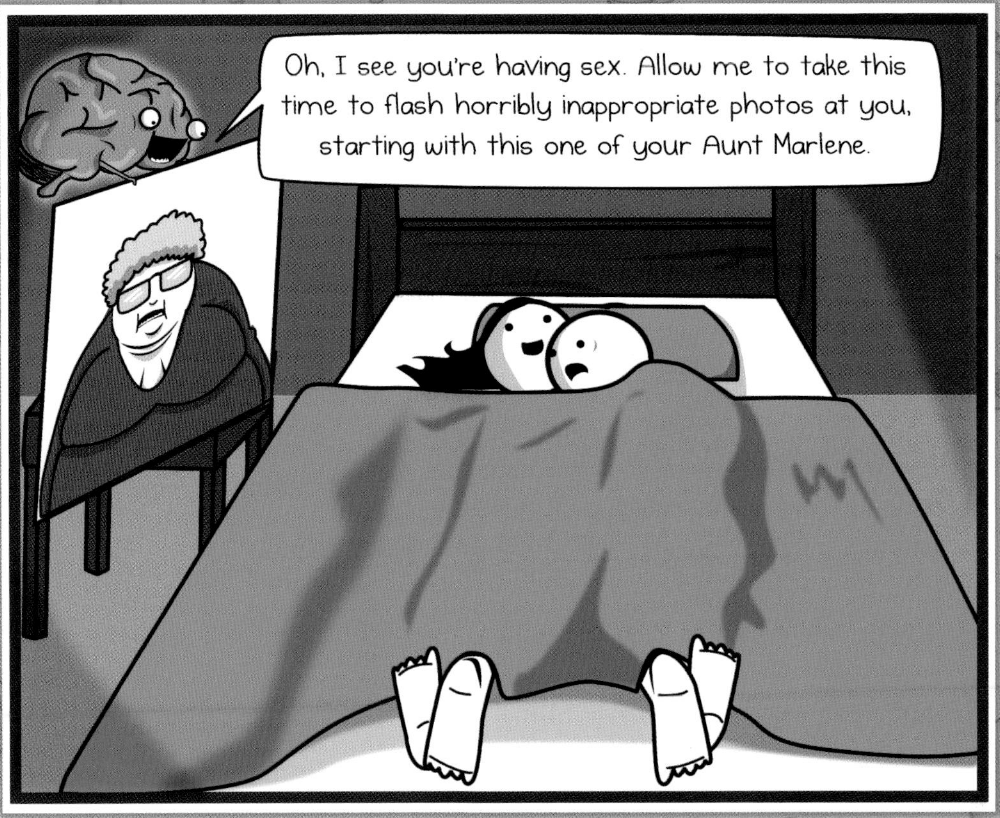
Oh, I see you're having sex. Allow me to take this time to flash horribly inappropriate photos at you, starting with this one of your Aunt Marlene.

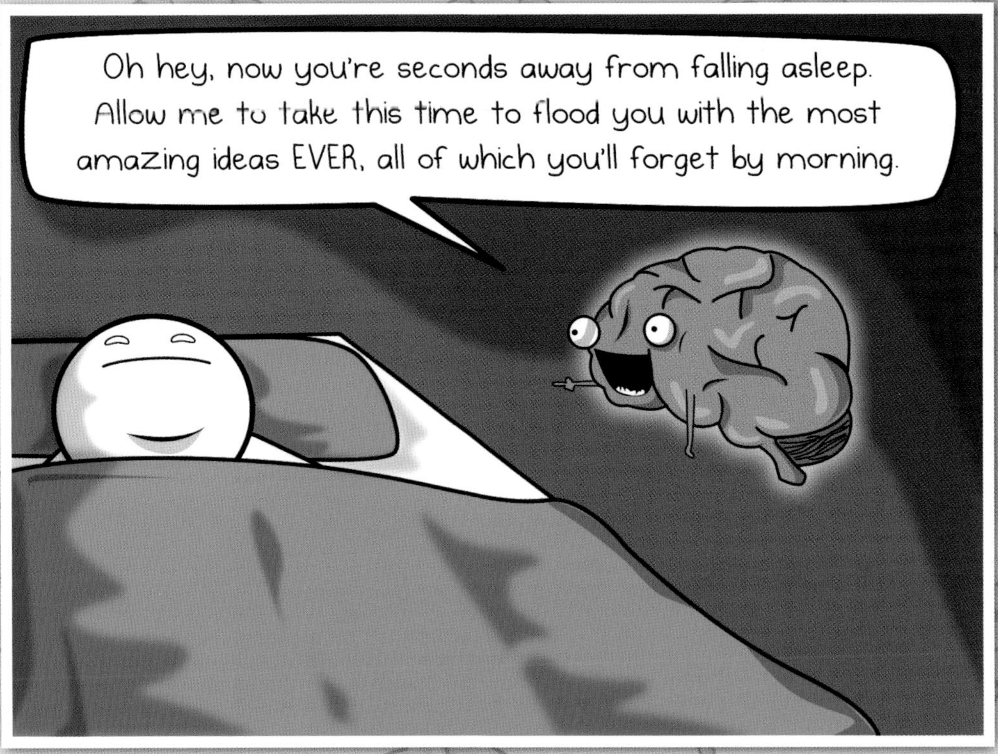
Oh hey, now you're seconds away from falling asleep. Allow me to take this time to flood you with the most amazing ideas EVER, all of which you'll forget by morning.

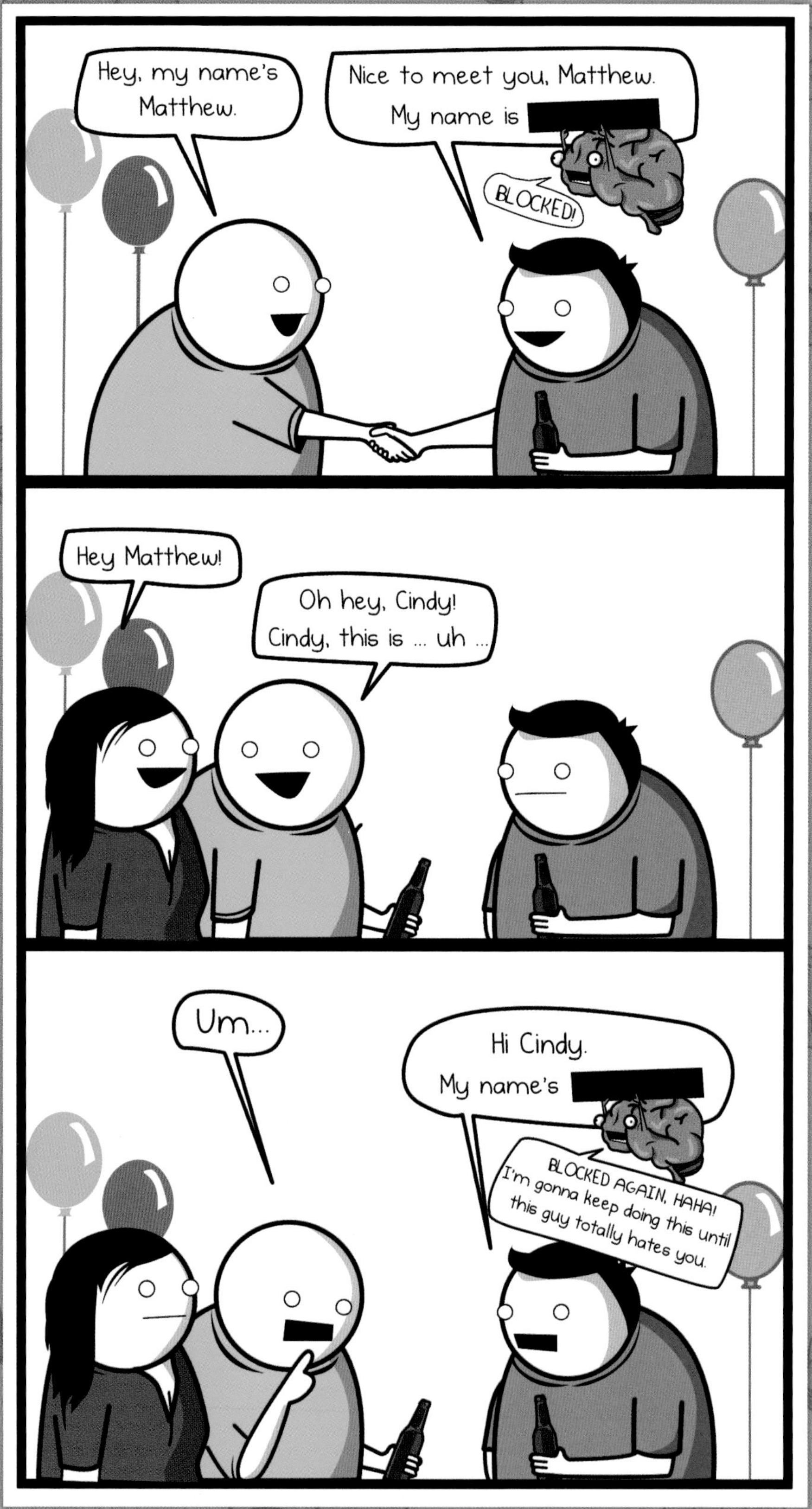
Hey, my name's Matthew.
Nice to meet you, Matthew. My name is [redacted]
BLOCKED!
Hey Matthew!
Oh hey, Cindy! Cindy, this is ... uh ...
Um...
Hi Cindy. My name's [redacted]
BLOCKED AGAIN, HAHA! I'm gonna keep doing this until this guy totally hates you.

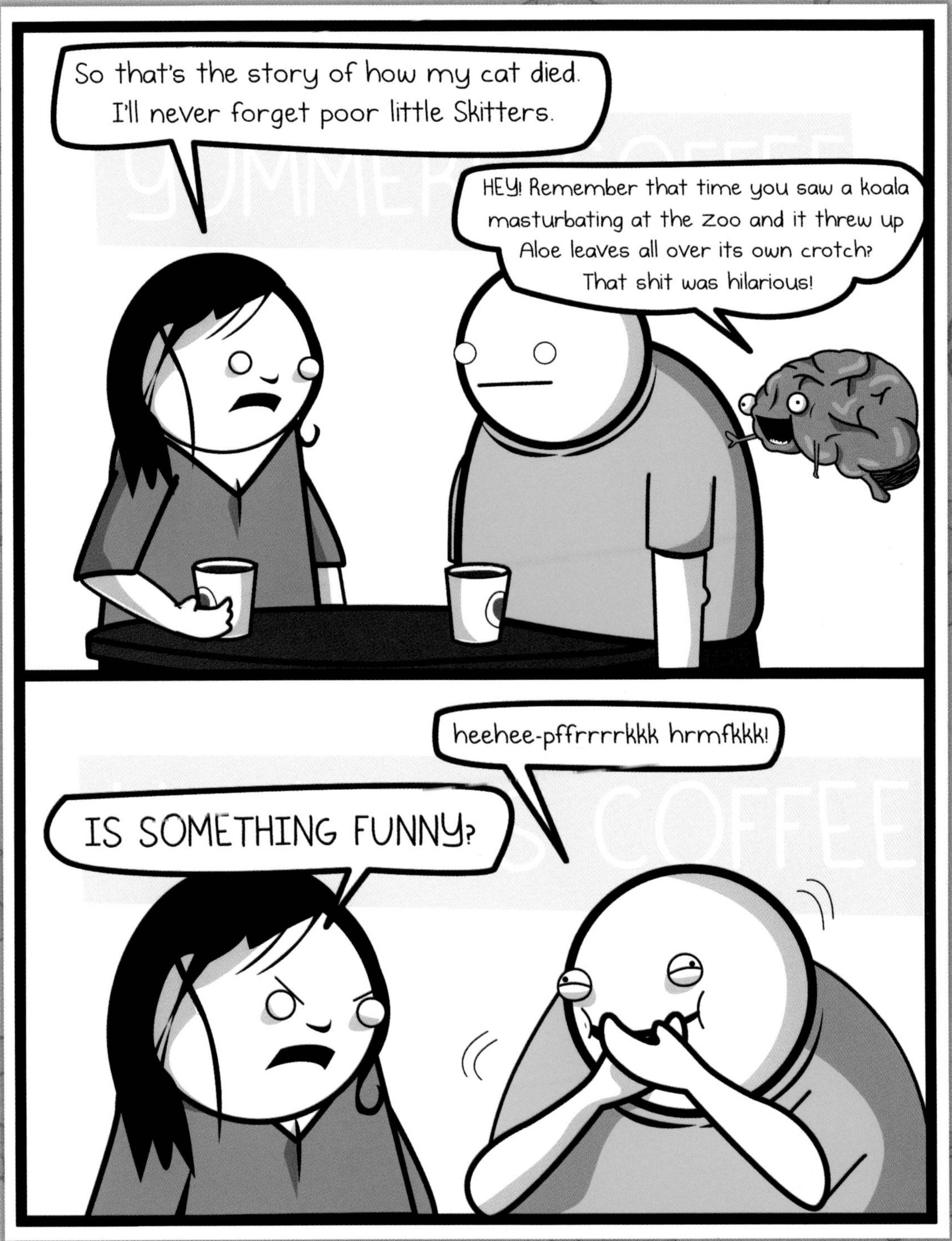

So that's the story of how my cat died. I'll never forget poor little Skitters.
HEY! Remember that time you saw a koala masturbating at the zoo and it threw up Aloe leaves all over its own crotch? That shit was hilarious!
heehee-pffrrrrkkk hrmfkkk!
IS SOMETHING FUNNY?

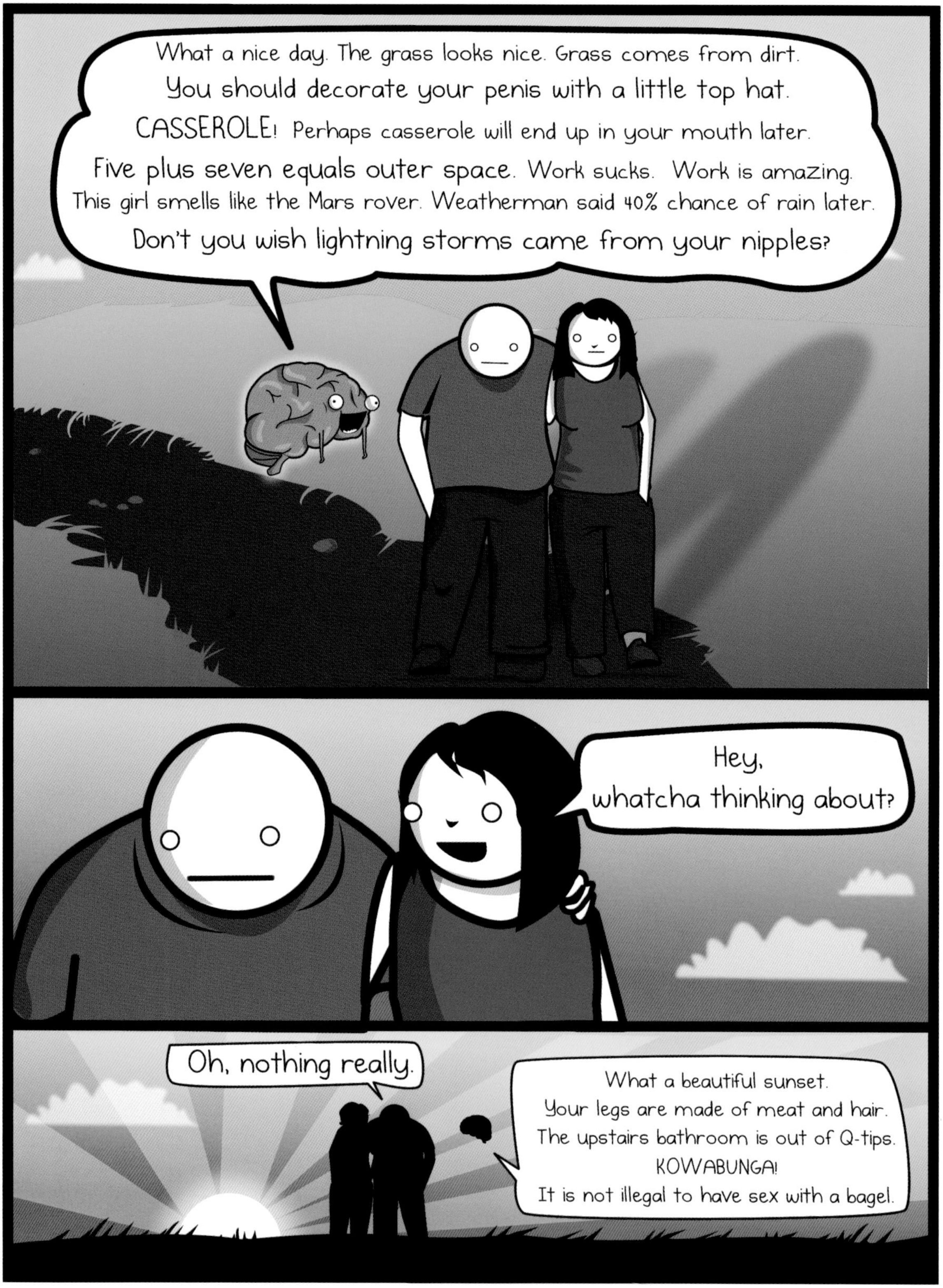

What a nice day. The grass looks nice. Grass comes from dirt.
You should decorate your penis with a little top hat.
CASSEROLE! Perhaps casserole will end up in your mouth later.
Five plus seven equals outer space. Work sucks. Work is amazing.
This girl smells like the Mars rover. Weatherman said 40% chance of rain later.
Don't you wish lightning storms came from your nipples?
Hey, whatcha thinking about?
Oh, nothing really.
What a beautiful sunset.
Your legs are made of meat and hair.
The upstairs bathroom is out of Q-tips.
KOWABUNGA!
It is not illegal to have sex with a bagel.

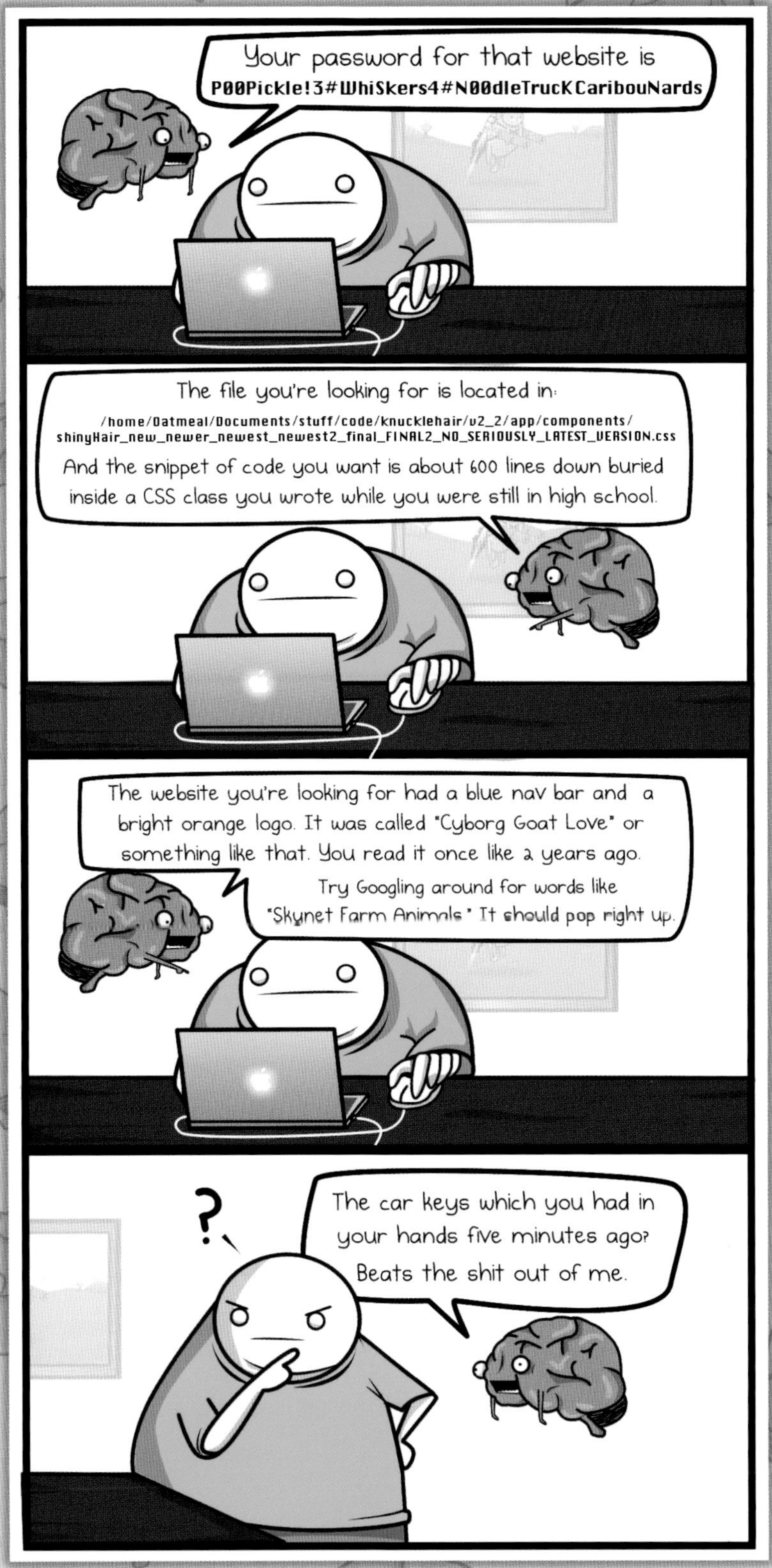
Your password for that website is
P00Pickle!3#WhiSkers4#N00dleTrucKCaribouNards
The file you're looking for is located in:
/home/Oatmeal/Documents/stuff/code/knucklehair/v2_2/app/components/shinyHair_new_newer_newest_newest2_final_FINAL2_NO_SERIOUSLY_LATEST_VERSION.css
And the snippet of code you want is about 600 lines down buried inside a CSS class you wrote while you were still in high school.
The website you're looking for had a blue nav bar and a bright orange logo. It was called "Cyborg Goat Love" or something like that. You read it once like 2 years ago.
Try Googling around for words like "Skynet Farm Animals." It should pop right up.
?
The car keys which you had in your hands five minutes ago? Beats the shit out of me.

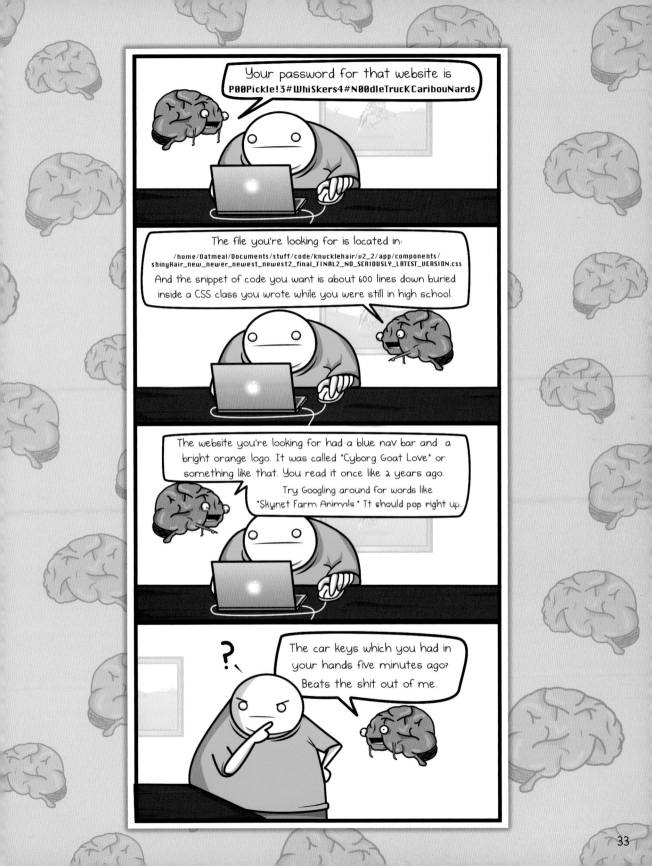

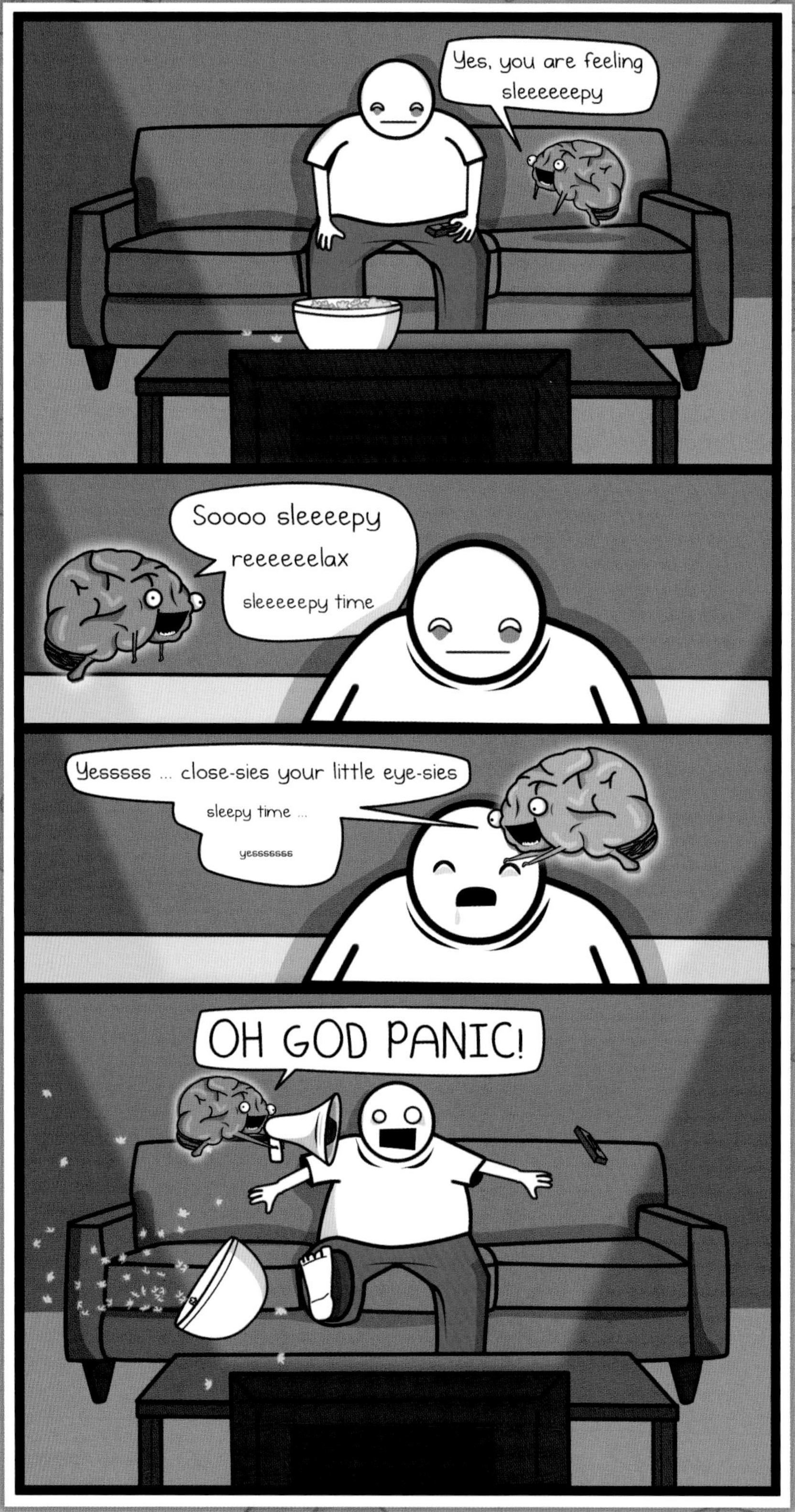

Yes, you are feeling sleeeeeepy
Soooo sleeeepy reeeeeelax sleeeeepy time
Yesssss ... close-sies your little eye-sies sleepy time ... yesssssss
OH GOD PANIC!

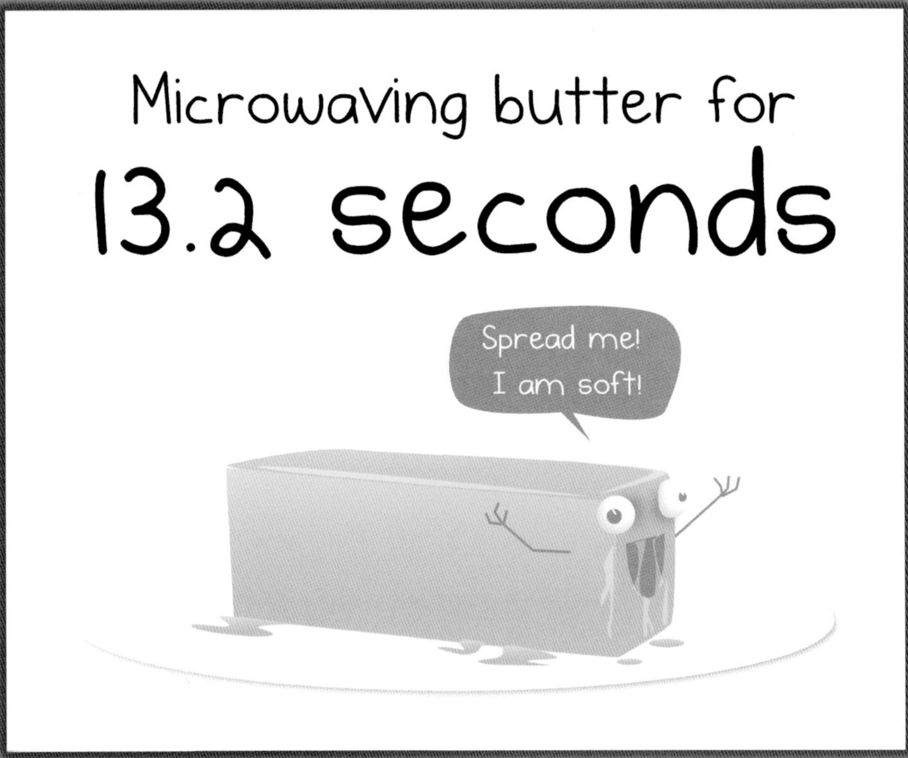
Microwaving butter for
13.2 seconds
Spread me! I am soft!

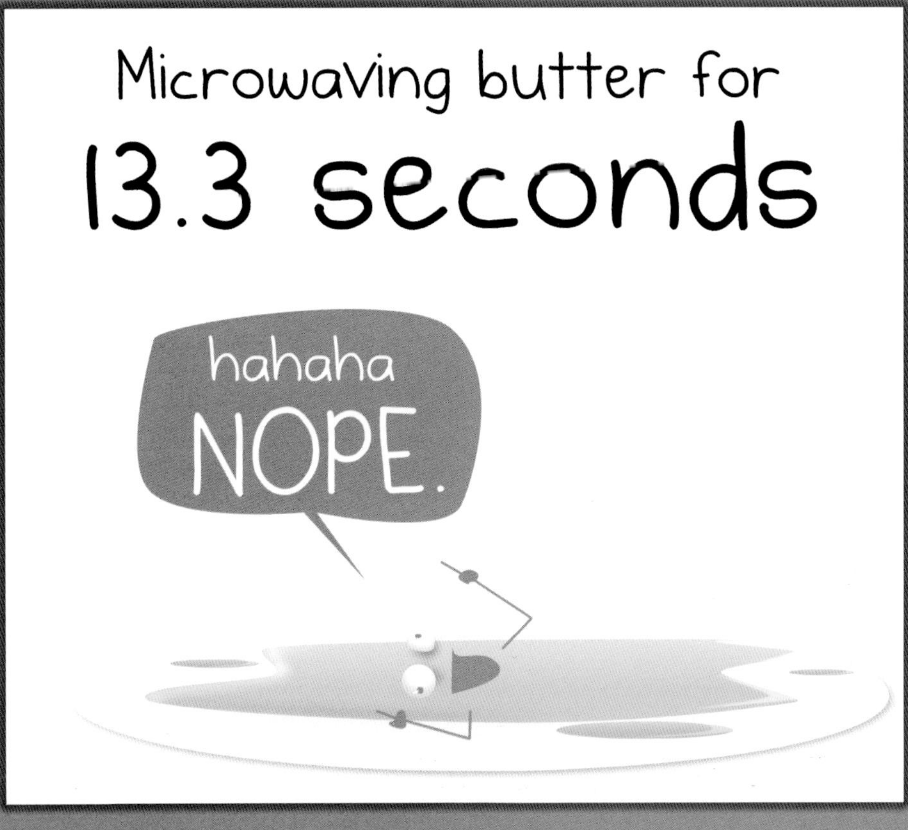
Microwaving butter for
13.3 seconds
hahaha NOPE.

How different age groups celebrate Christmas

Toddlers

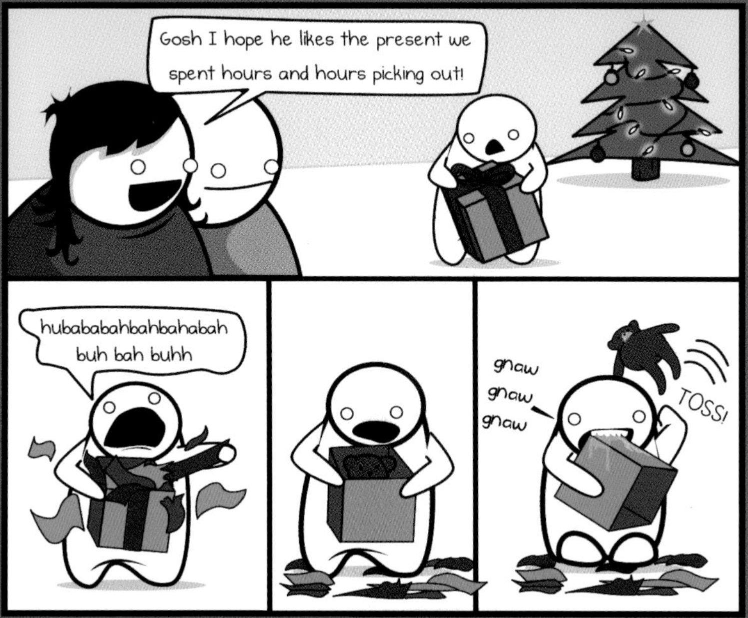

Gosh I hope he likes the present we spent hours and hours picking out!
hubababahbahbahabah buh bah buhh
gnaw gnaw gnaw
TOSS!

Children

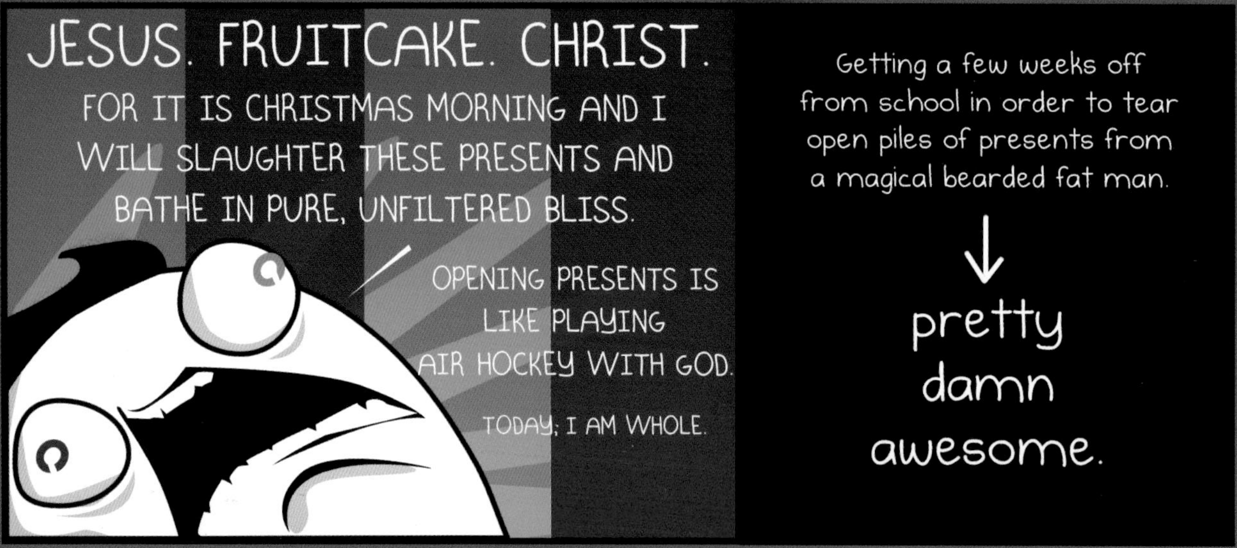

JESUS. FRUITCAKE. CHRIST.
FOR IT IS CHRISTMAS MORNING AND I WILL SLAUGHTER THESE PRESENTS AND BATHE IN PURE, UNFILTERED BLISS.
OPENING PRESENTS IS LIKE PLAYING AIR HOCKEY WITH GOD.
TODAY, I AM WHOLE.
Getting a few weeks off from school in order to tear open piles of presents from a magical bearded fat man.
pretty damn awesome.

20-somethings with kids

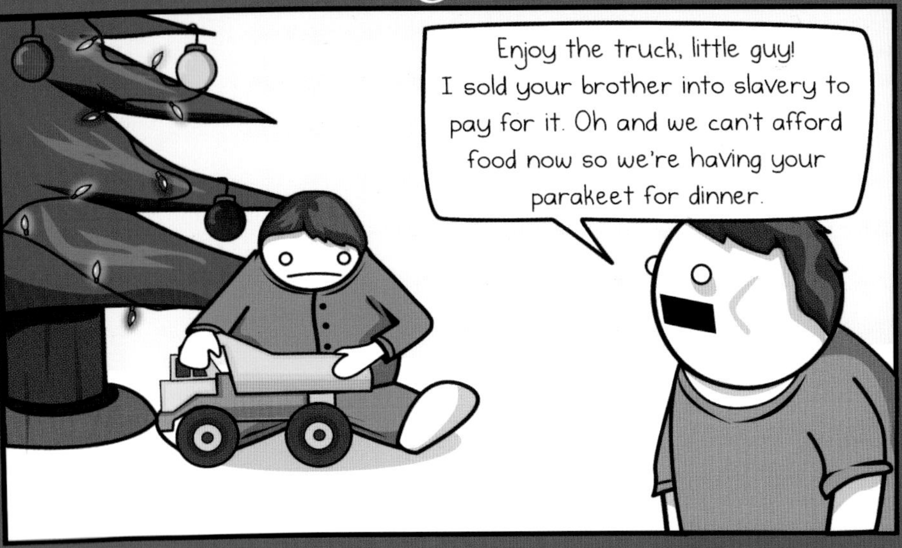
Enjoy the truck, little guy! I sold your brother into slavery to pay for it. Oh and we can't afford food now so we're having your parakeet for dinner.

20-somethings without kids

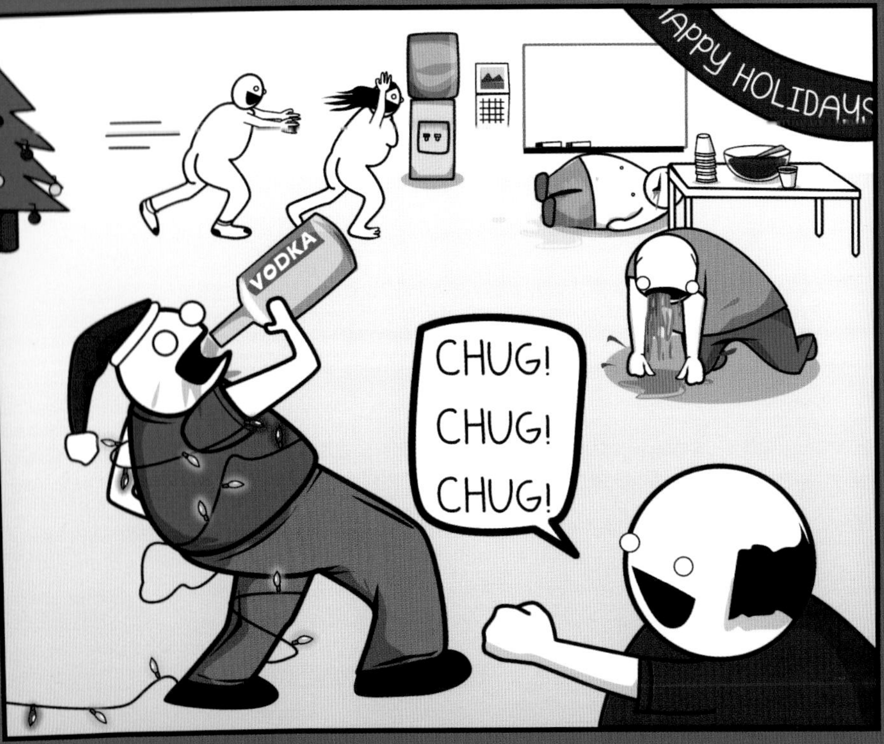
HOLIDAYS
VODKA
CHUG! CHUG! CHUG!

30-somethings with

To-do for Decembe

- ✓ Cover everything I own in obnoxiously awesom
- ✓ Spend the last half of December pretending to do re work.
- ✓ Use the threat of no presents to extort the kids into behaving well.
- ✓ Go shopping for the kids. Buy rad gifts like rubber snakes, plastic broadswords, and remote-controlled Godzillas.
- ✓ If on a budget, just give them something cheap like a Tyrannosaurus Rex made out of Little Debbie snacks. Kids don't care, they'll be genuinely happy to get a present regardless of cost.
- ✓ Eat mountains of food during the one month out of the year it's socially acceptable to grow love handles the size of mutated sea cucumbers.

Christmas for 30+ with kids =

pretty damn awesome

30-somethings without kids

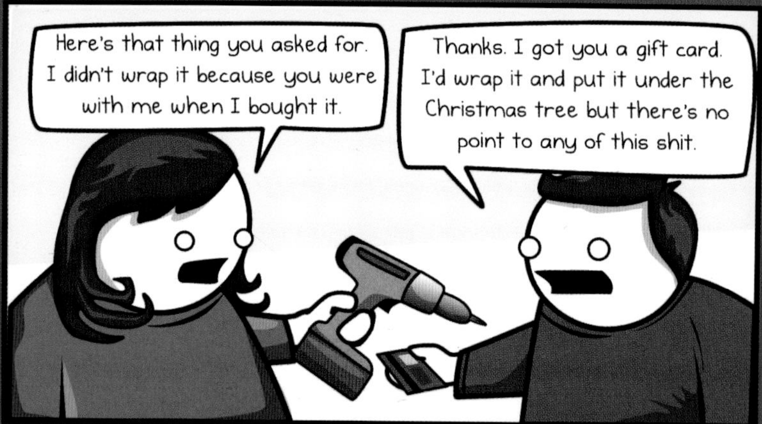
Here's that thing you asked for. I didn't wrap it because you were with me when I bought it.
Thanks. I got you a gift card. I'd wrap it and put it under the Christmas tree but there's no point to any of this shit.

40+ without kids

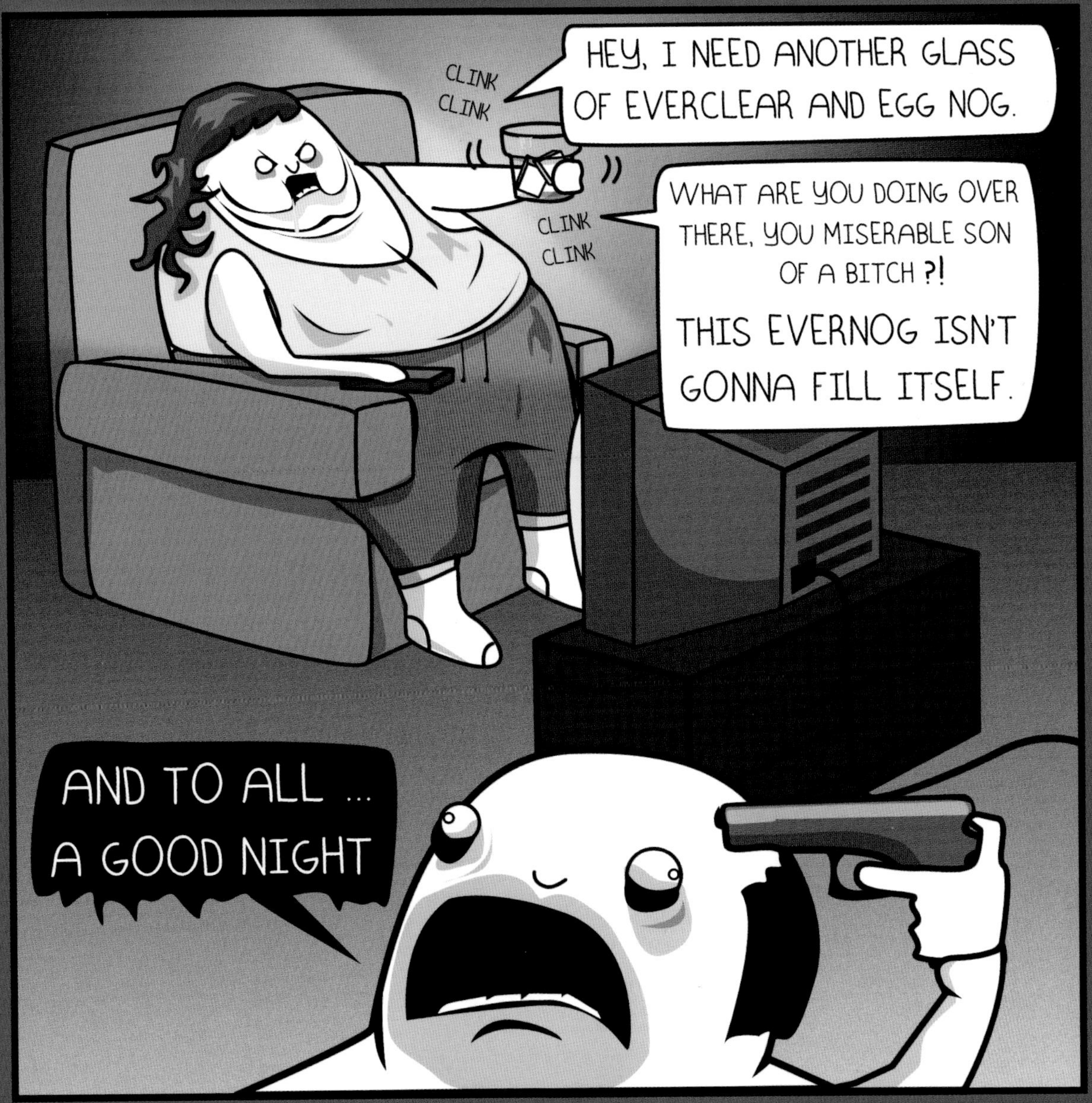
CLINK
CLINK
HEY, I NEED ANOTHER GLASS OF EVERCLEAR AND EGG NOG.
CLINK
CLINK
WHAT ARE YOU DOING OVER THERE, YOU MISERABLE SON OF A BITCH ?!
THIS EVERNOG ISN'T GONNA FILL ITSELF.
AND TO ALL ... A GOOD NIGHT

The crap we put up with getting on and off an airplane

Annoying: Paying $25.00 to check a bag.

More Annoying: Listening to people complain about paying $25.00 to check a bag.

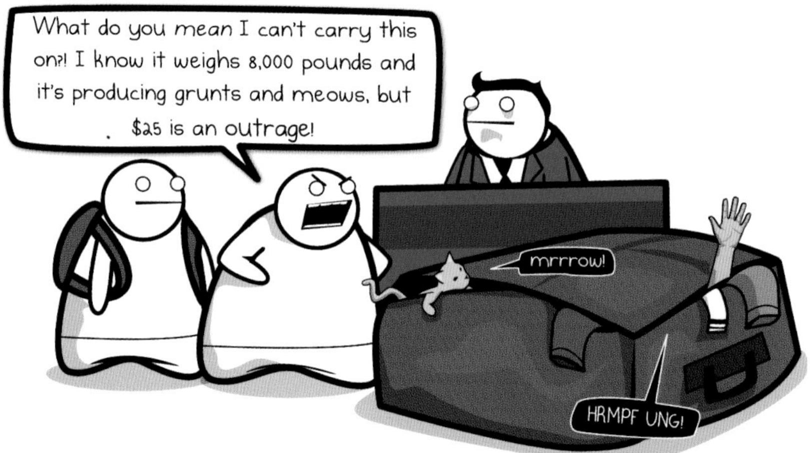
What do you *mean* I can't carry this on?! I know it weighs 8,000 pounds and it's producing grunts and meows, but $25 is an outrage!
mrrrow!
HRMPF UNG!

Annoying: Keeping all liquids under 3 ounces and putting them in a ziplock bag.

More Annoying: Getting stuck behind the person who has apparently never heard this rule before.

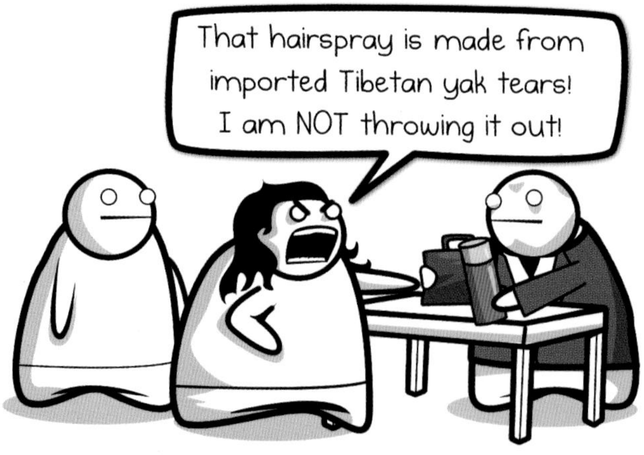
That hairspray is made from imported Tibetan yak tears! I am NOT throwing it out!

Annoying: Removing your shoes, coat, laptop, and putting them into little plastic bins.

More annoying: The feeling that you have to do this at a thousand miles per hour because of all the people behind you.

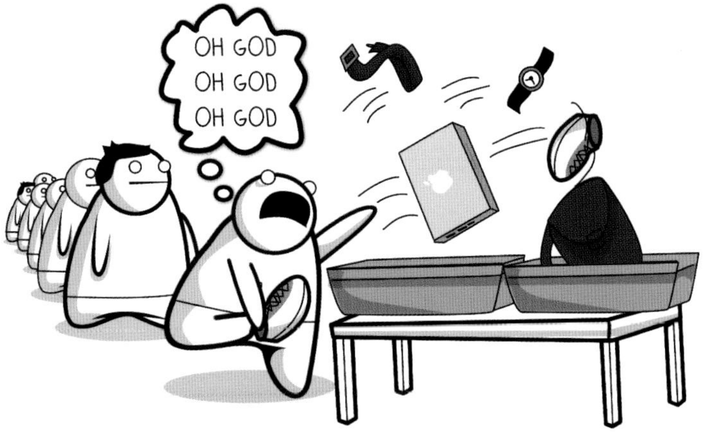
OH GOD
OH GOD
OH GOD

Annoying: Waiting to exit the airplane.

More Annoying: People who impatiently stand up when the plane touches down, regardless of where they're sitting.

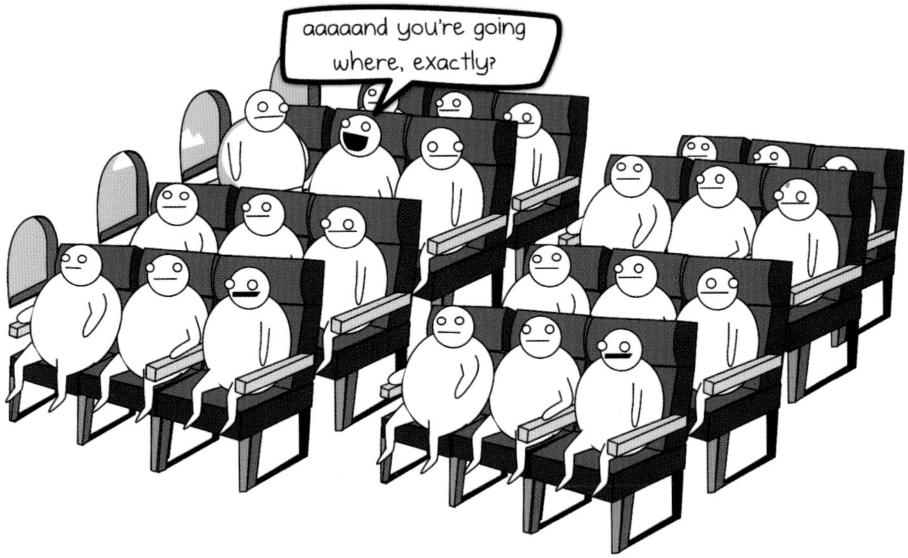
aaaaand you're going where, exactly?

Annoying:

Everyone crowding around the same part of the baggage carousel so they don't have to wait an extra 30 seconds for their luggage to come around.

Satisfying:

Walking into the middle of this crowd and ripping a massive fart.

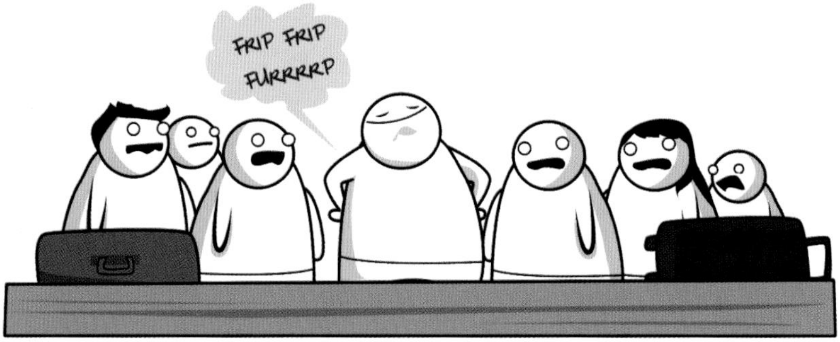
FRIP FRIP
FURRRRRP

Hilarious:

Standing in said fart cloud and watching tiny people lift giant bags.

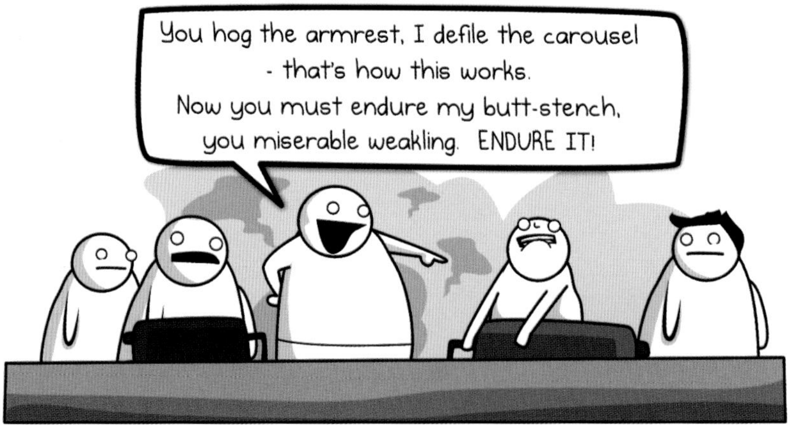
You hog the armrest, I defile the carousel - that's how this works. Now you must endure my butt-stench, you miserable weakling. ENDURE IT!

How to fix any computer

Windows

Step 1.
Reboot

Did that fix it?
No? Proceed to step 2

Step 2.
Format hard drive.
Reinstall Windows.
Lose all your files.
Quietly weep.

Apple

Step 1.
Take it to an
Apple store.

Did that fix it?
No? Proceed to step 2

Step 2.
Buy a new Mac.
Overdraw your account.
Quietly weep.

Linux

Step 1.

Learn to code in C. Recompile the kernel. Build your own microprocessor out of spare silicon you had lying around. Recompile the kernel again. Switch distros. Recompile the kernel again but this time using a CPU powered by refracted light from Saturn. Grow a giant beard. Blame Sun Microsystems. Turn your bedroom into a server closet and spend ten years falling asleep to the sound of whirring fans. Switch distros again. Abandon all hygiene. Write a regular expression that would make other programmers cry blood. Learn to code in Java. Recompile the kernel again (but this time while wearing your lucky socks).

Did that fix it?
No? Proceed to step 2

Step 2.
Revert back to using
Windows or a Mac.
Quietly weep.

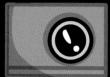

6 things you really don't need to take a photo of

1. Anything at a bar

OMG bigtime holla! Who ordered mango-tinis?
I CERTAINLY DID, U CRAZY GIRL! The entire world is going to see these photos and know that our lives are craaaazy and exotic because we go to crowded bars and drink sugary cocktails while squealing like slutty orangutans!
ULTRA MEGA HOLLA! Let's drink until one of us vomits and starts crying in the bathroom!

2. Food

Because this looks appetizing and I'm hungry, my taste buds are tricking my brain into thinking it's photo-worthy when in truth it's quite forgettable.
YOU ARE SO BEAUTIFUL. I WILL NEVER FORGET YOU, MAYONNAISE PORKWICH.
I will love you until the ends of time.
You are my oily pigflesh soulmate.

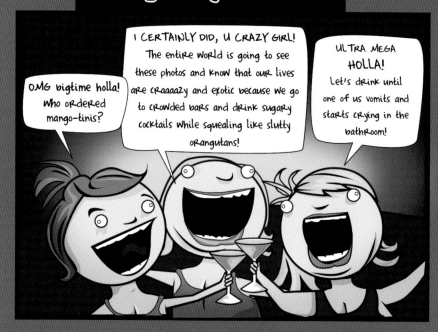

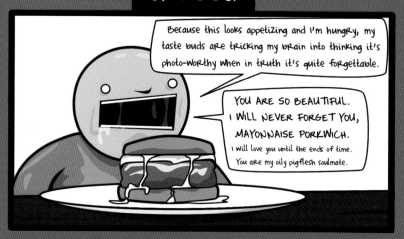

3. Scenery

My God, just LOOK at those shrubs - simply amazing! Quick Martha, take a picture! Nevermind the fact that we won't give a crap about these photos later, instead we'll just blaze past them to look at the photos we took of ourselves. But hey - let's fill up a memory card with waterfalls and mountains and shit anyway - sound good?

4. Concerts

What is this I'm looking at? It looks like a blurry shit-smear of rainbow sherbet ice cream.
It's from the concert last night. Instead of actually enjoying the show I spent half the night sticking my crappy camera phone in the air trying to immortalize the moment.

5. Your car

It can go from zero to douche in 60 seconds.

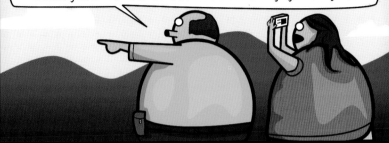

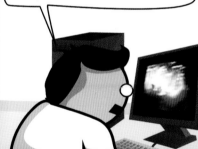

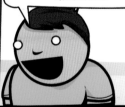

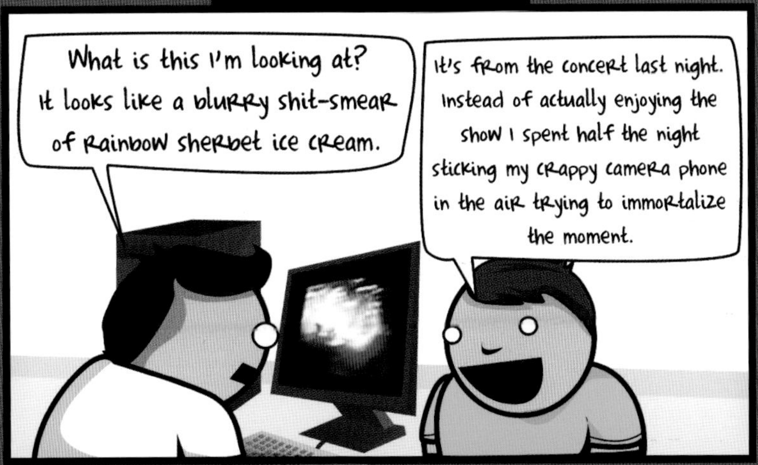

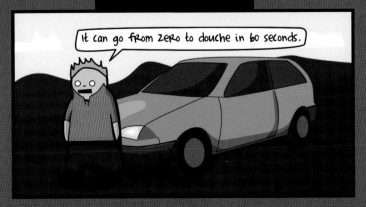

6. Pics of yourself in the mirror

This is how you look after taking dozens of bathroom mirror photos from various angles until you get one that makes you look perfect:

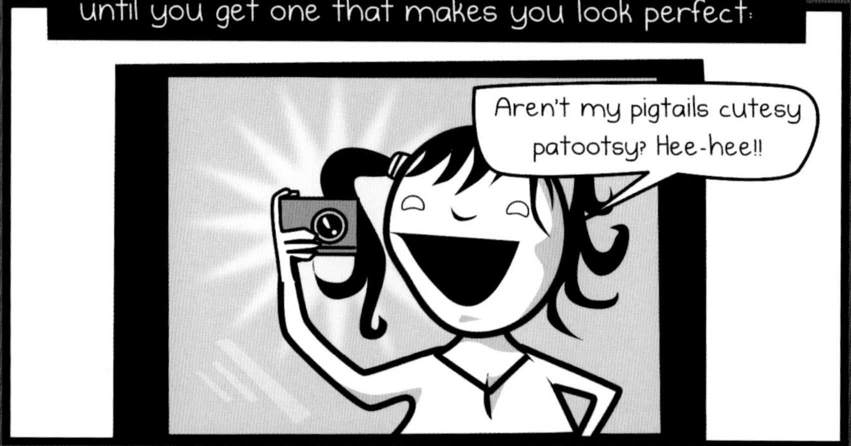
Aren't my pigtails cutesy patootsy? Hee-hee!!

This is how you actually look in real life:

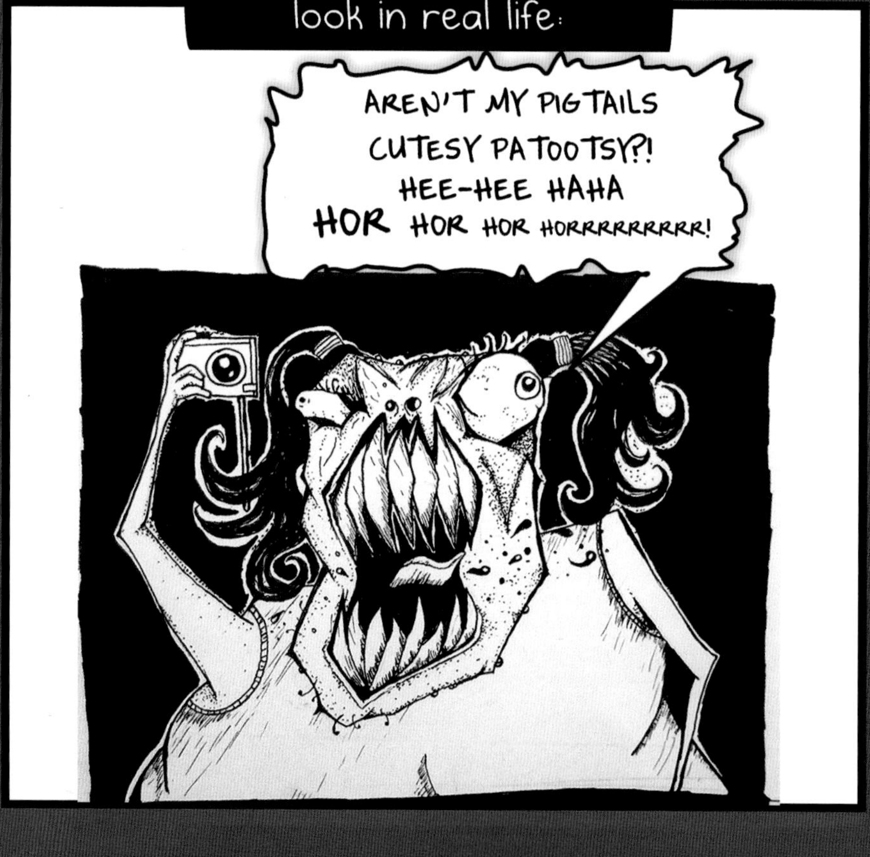
AREN'T MY PIGTAILS CUTESY PATOOTSY?! HEE-HEE HAHA HOR HOR HOR HORRRRRRRRR!

Pens:

I swear to God this is what they must be doing.

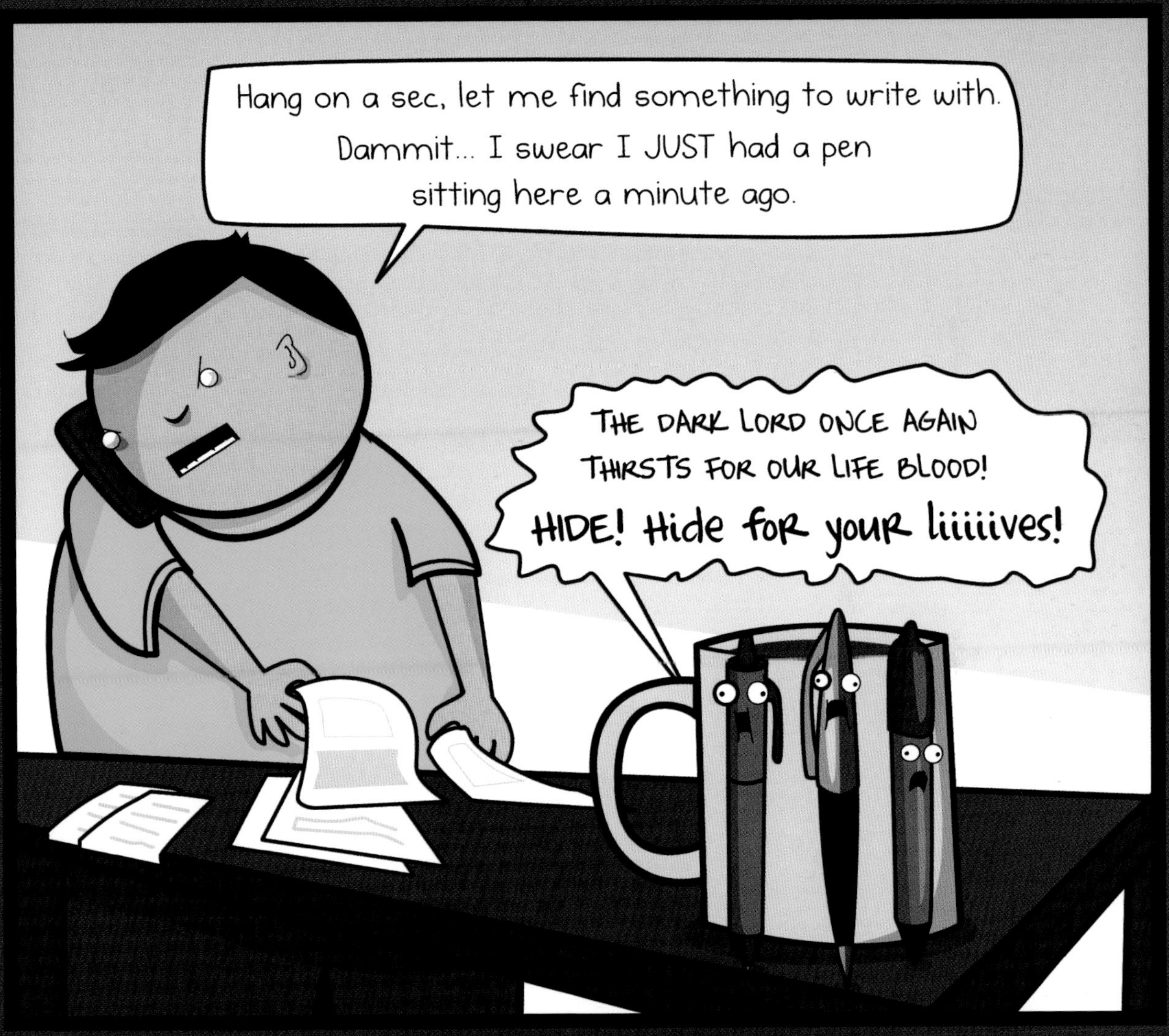
Hang on a sec, let me find something to write with. Dammit... I swear I JUST had a pen sitting here a minute ago.
THE DARK LORD ONCE AGAIN THIRSTS FOR OUR LIFE BLOOD! HIDE! Hide for your liiiiives!

What it's like to own an

Apple product

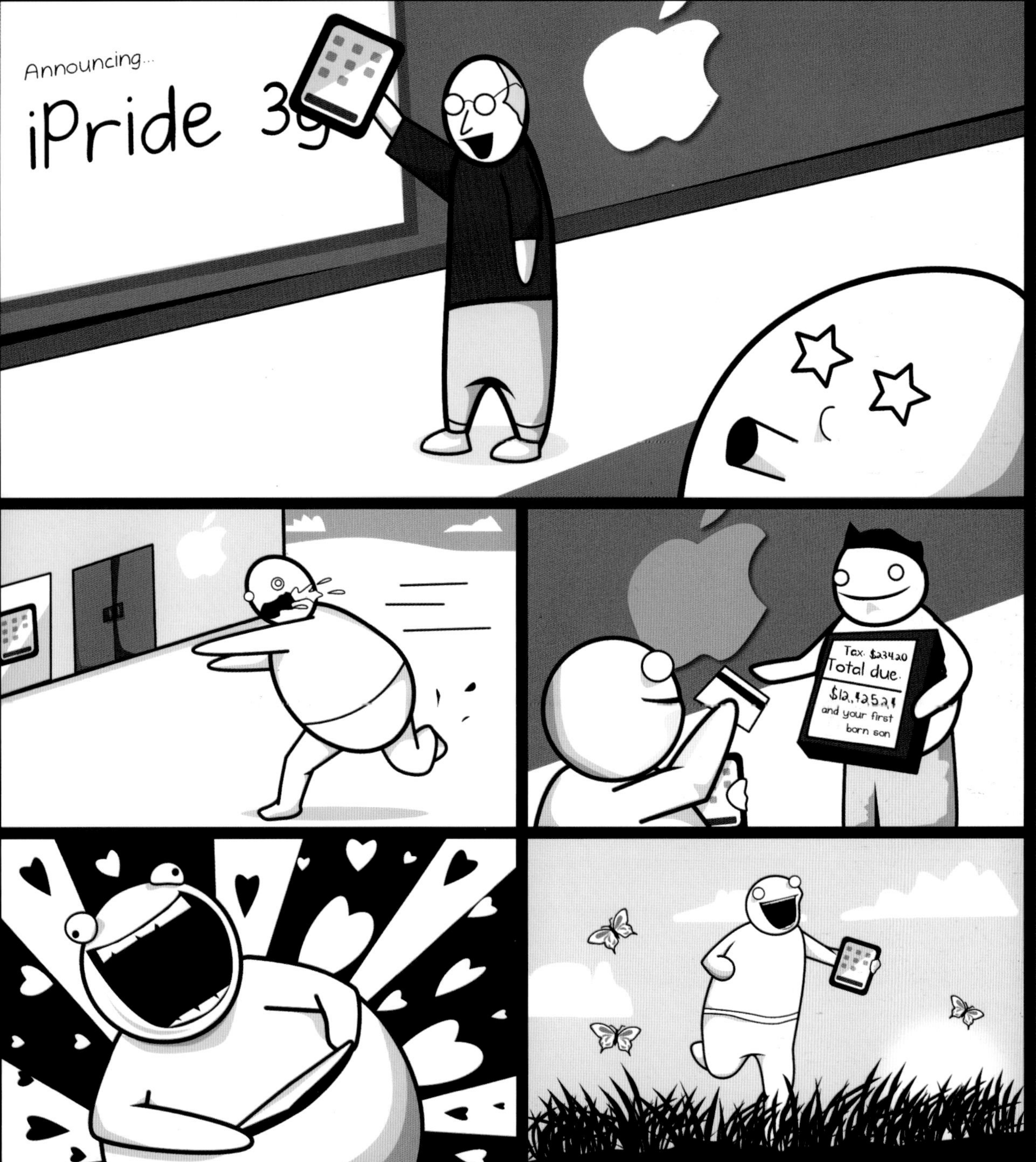
Announcing...
iPride 3
Tax. $234.20
Total due.
and your first born son

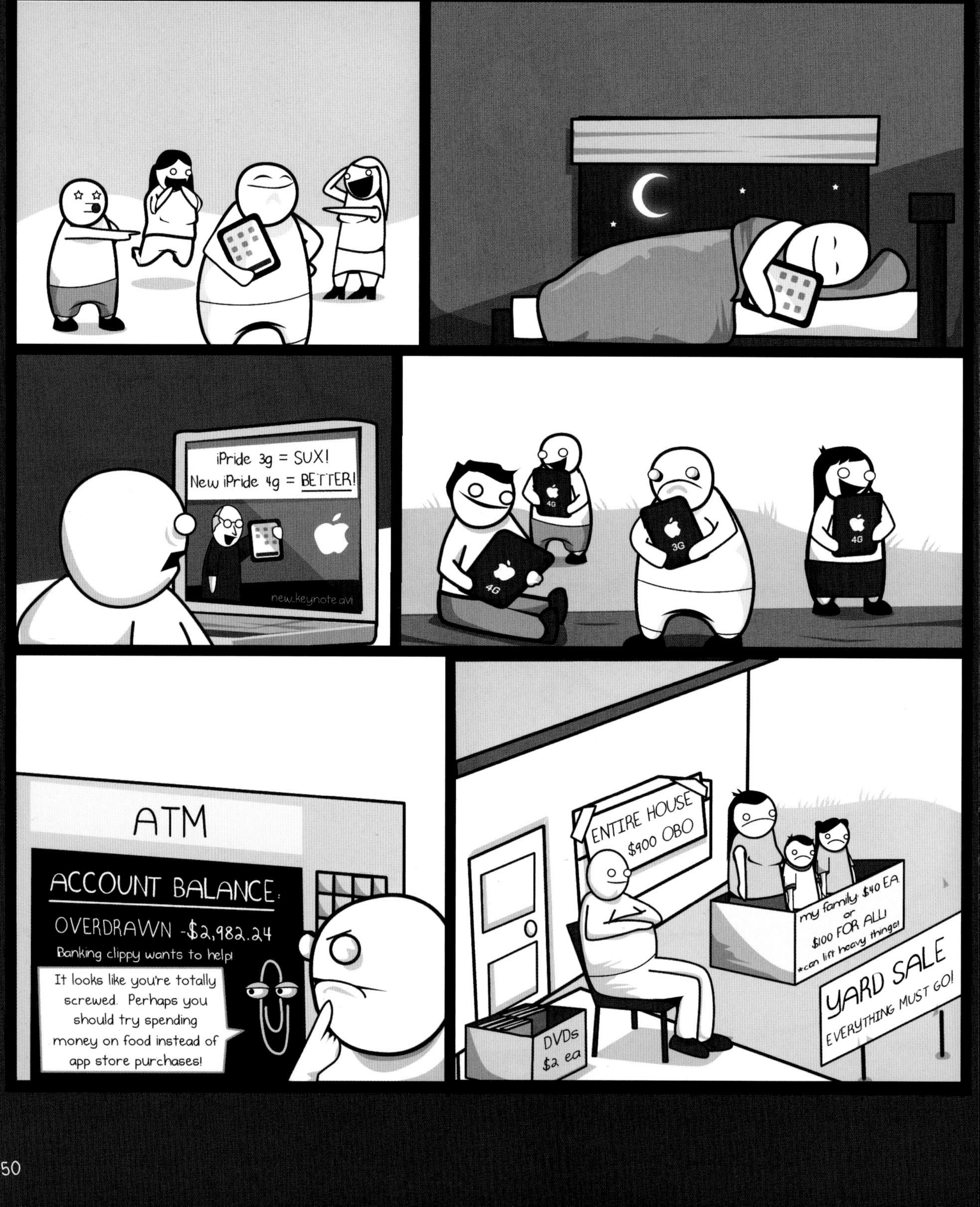
iPride 3g = SUX!
New iPride 4g = BETTER!
new_keynote.avi
4G
3G
4G
4G
ATM
ACCOUNT BALANCE:
OVERDRAWN -$2,982.24
Banking clippy wants to help!
It looks like you're totally screwed. Perhaps you should try spending money on food instead of app store purchases!
ENTIRE HOUSE $900 OBO
my family: $40 EA. or $100 FOR ALL! *can lift heavy things!
YARD SALE
EVERYTHING MUST GO!
DVDs $2 ea

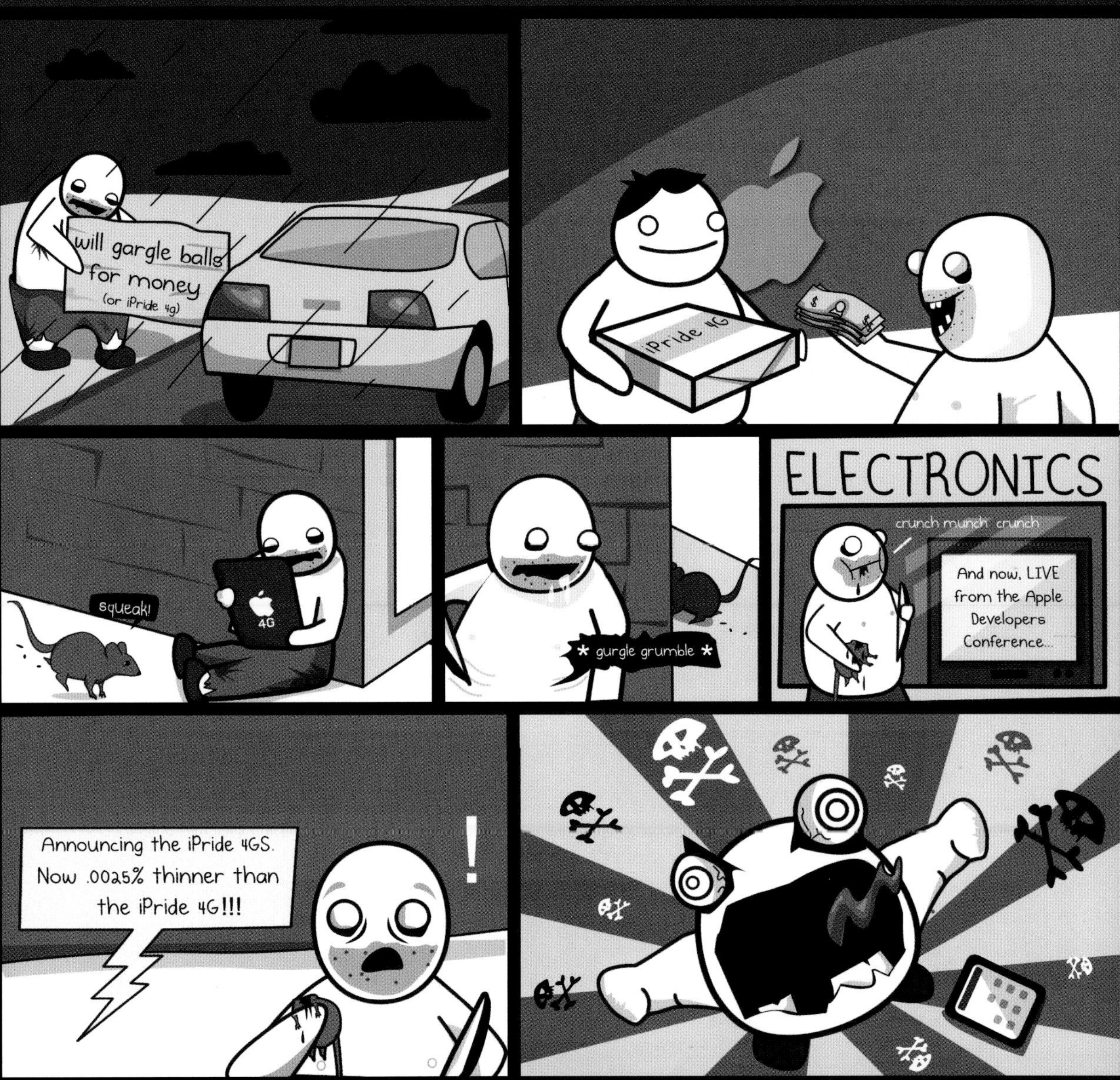
will gargle balls for money
(or iPride 4g)
iPride 4G
squeak!
4G
* gurgle grumble *
ELECTRONICS
crunch munch crunch
And now, LIVE from the Apple Developers Conference...
Announcing the iPride 4GS. Now .0025% thinner than the iPride 4G!!!
!

The End.

Written, drawn, and experienced by The Oatmeal.

6 Reasons to Ride a Polar Bear to Work

It'll impress your fellow commuters.

Polar bears can grow to be over 10 feet tall (3.1 meters) and weigh 1500 lbs (680 kg). That's taller than an elephant and about half the weight of a compact car.

Hey Bill, check out my new vespa! It's just as dangerous as a motorcycle, but instead of looking cool while I ride it I look like I gave my testicles their own little minivan!
Oh yeah? Check out my ride: it takes dumps the size of your kids!

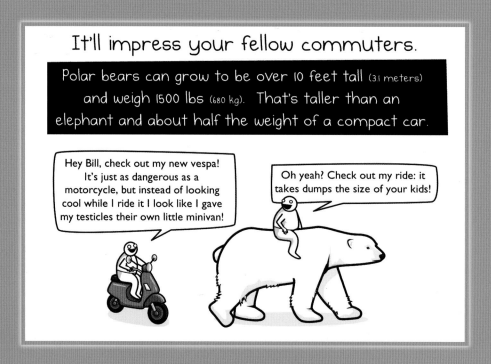

A polar bear can haul ass.

Polar bears can sprint short distances at 25 MPH (40 KPH), which is almost as fast as the 100-meter world-record holder Usain Bolt.

Quick! The light is changing Maximum warp on my mark ...
ENGAGE!

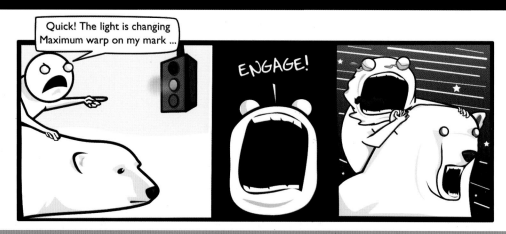

Polar bears are amazing swimmers.

A polar bear has webbed feet and can swim distances of over 100 miles at around 6 mph (9.7 kph) - that's more than twice the speed of Olympic gold medalist Michael Phelps.

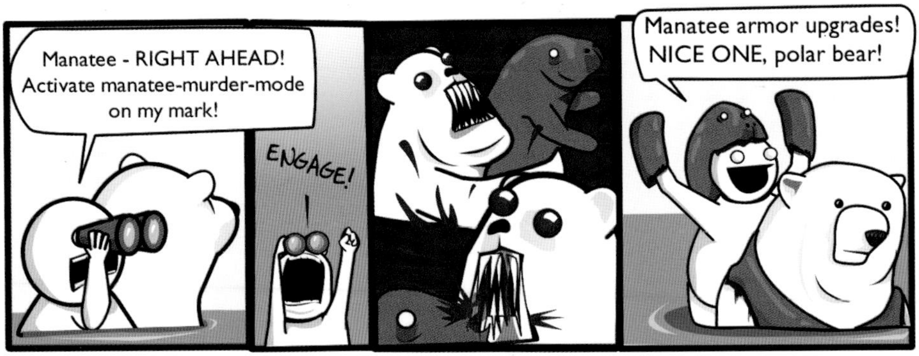
Manatee - RIGHT AHEAD! Activate manatee-murder-mode on my mark!
ENGAGE!
Manatee armor upgrades! NICE ONE, polar bear!

Polar bears can keep you warm.

A polar bear's fur isn't actually white; each hair is a clear, hollow tube. The hollow hair traps the heat and keeps a polar bear's black, blubbery skin warm at a toasty 98 degrees Fahrenheit. (36 C)

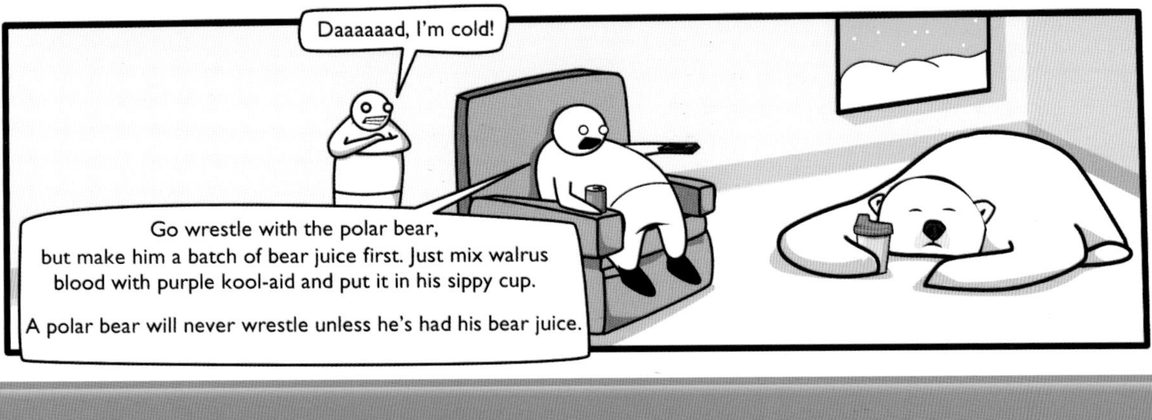
Daaaaaad, I'm cold!
Go wrestle with the polar bear, but make him a batch of bear juice first. Just mix walrus blood with purple kool-aid and put it in his sippy cup.
A polar bear will never wrestle unless he's had his bear juice.

A polar bear can go months without eating and still be awesome.

If food is scarce, a polar bear can reduce its metabolic rate and enter a state of "walking hibernation." In this state, polar bears can go months without eating but still walk around and do things like sunbathing and partying.

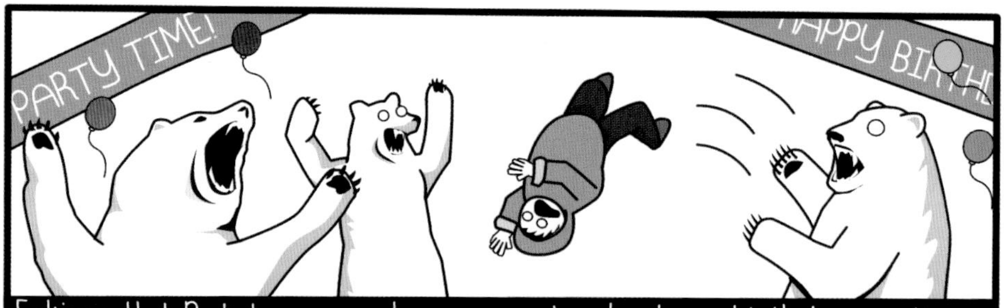
PARTY TIME!
HAPPY BIRTH
Eskimo Hot Potato: a popular game at polar bear birthday parties.

Polar bears have stealth mode.

Polar bears are invisible to infrared cameras because they have thick, insulating fur which traps all their body heat.

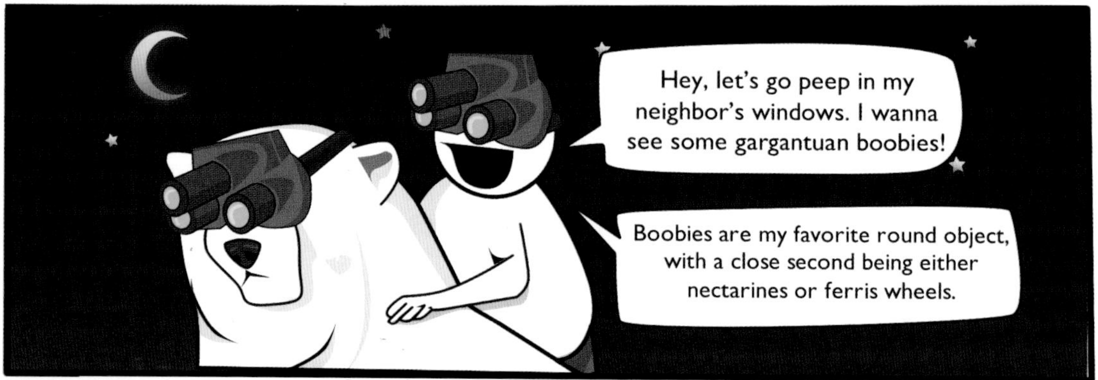
Hey, let's go peep in my neighbor's windows. I wanna see some gargantuan boobies!
Boobies are my favorite round object, with a close second being either nectarines or ferris wheels.

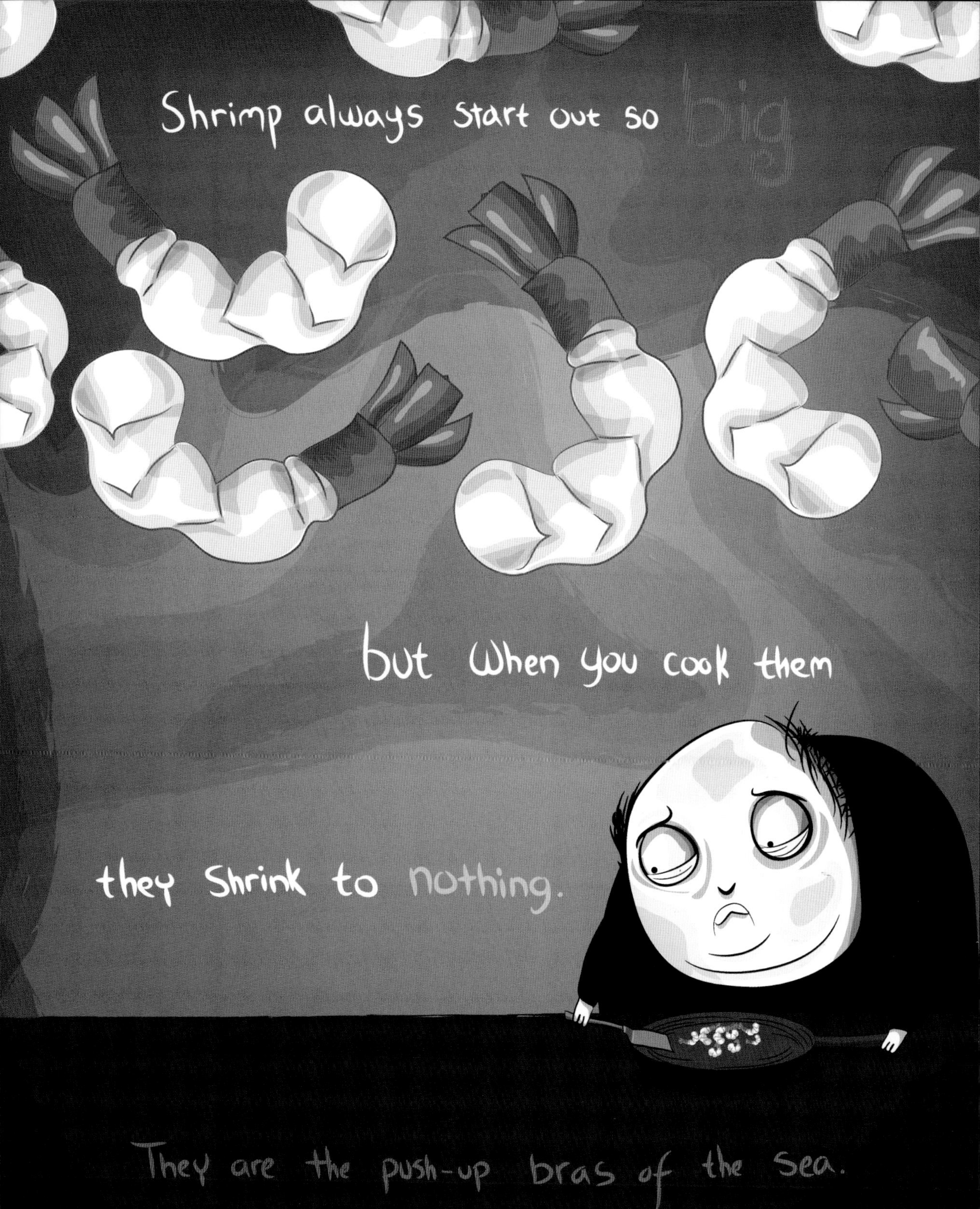
Shrimp always start out so big
but when you cook them
they shrink to nothing.
They are the push-up bras of the sea.

The worst thing about Valentine's Day

isn't this:

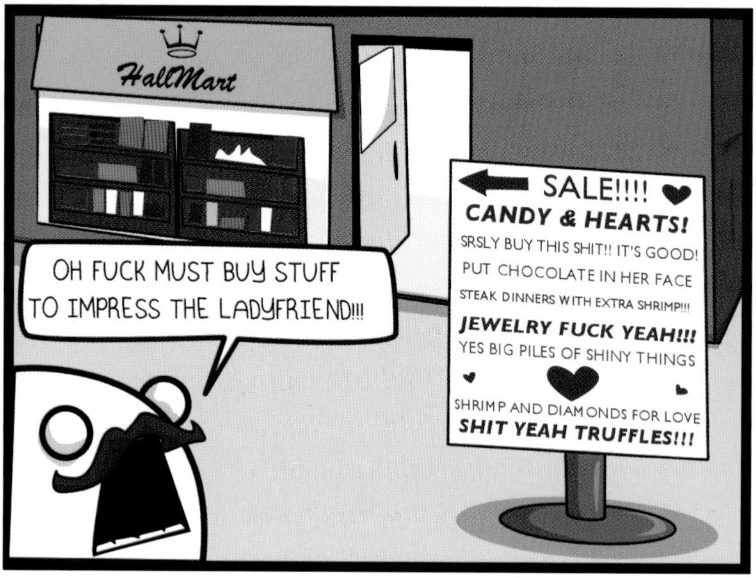
HallMart
OH FUCK MUST BUY STUFF TO IMPRESS THE LADYFRIEND!!!
SALE!!!!
CANDY & HEARTS!
SRSLY BUY THIS SHIT!! IT'S GOOD!
PUT CHOCOLATE IN HER FACE
STEAK DINNERS WITH EXTRA SHRIMP!!!
JEWELRY FUCK YEAH!!!
YES BIG PILES OF SHINY THINGS
SHRIMP AND DIAMONDS FOR LOVE
SHIT YEAH TRUFFLES!!!

or this:

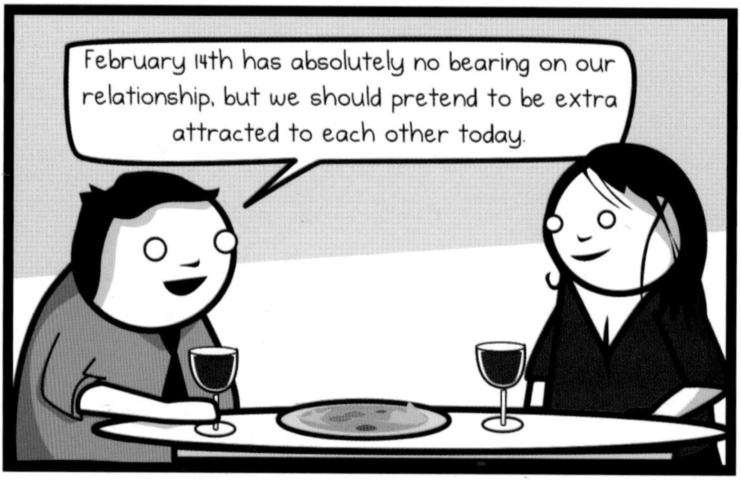
February 14th has absolutely no bearing on our relationship, but we should pretend to be extra attracted to each other today.

or even this:

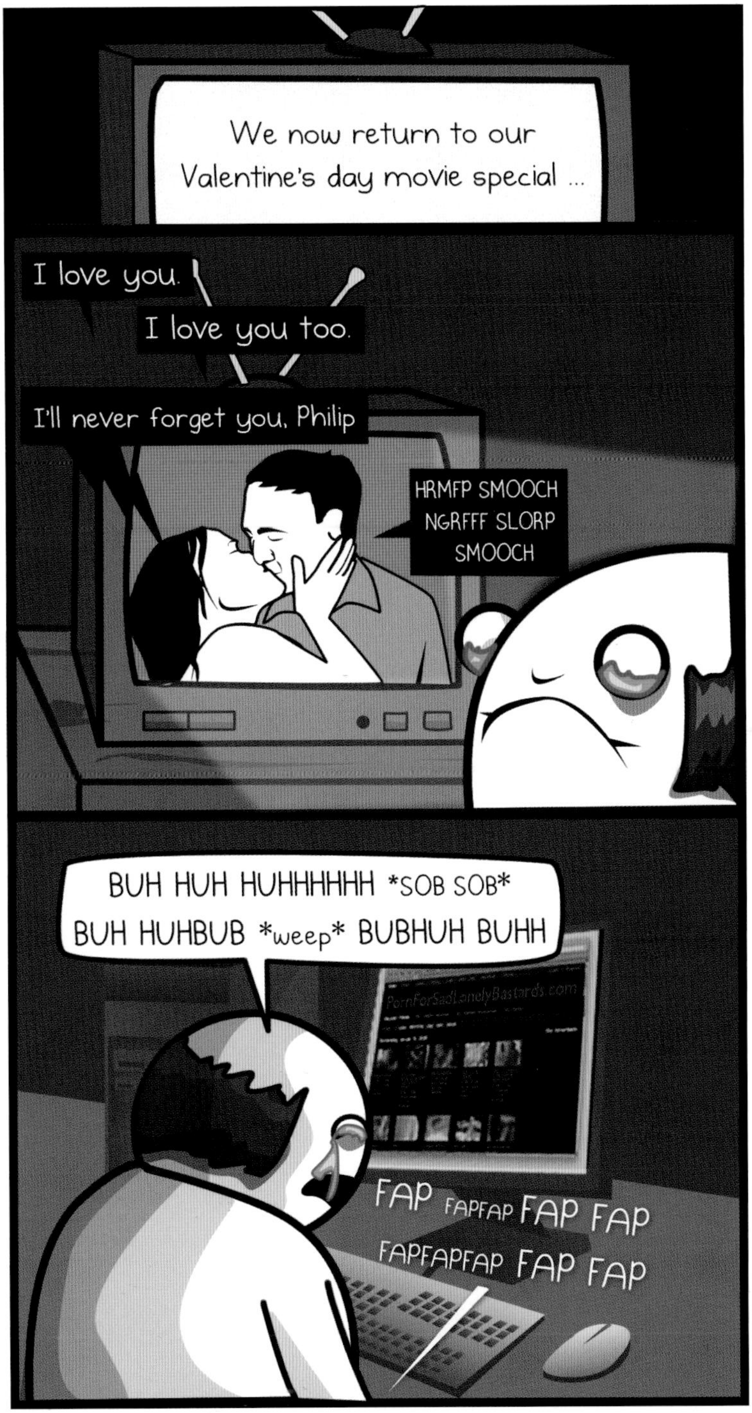
We now return to our Valentine's day movie special ...
I love you.
I love you too.
I'll never forget you, Philip
HRMFP SMOOCH NGRFFF SLORP SMOOCH
BUH HUH HUHHHHHH *SOB SOB* BUH HUHBUB *weep* BUBHUH BUHH
PornForSadLonelyBastards.com
FAP FAPFAP FAP FAP FAPFAPFAP FAP FAP

The worst thing about Valentine's Day is trying to ignore it,

meanwhile every goddamn person I come into contact with is saying something like this:

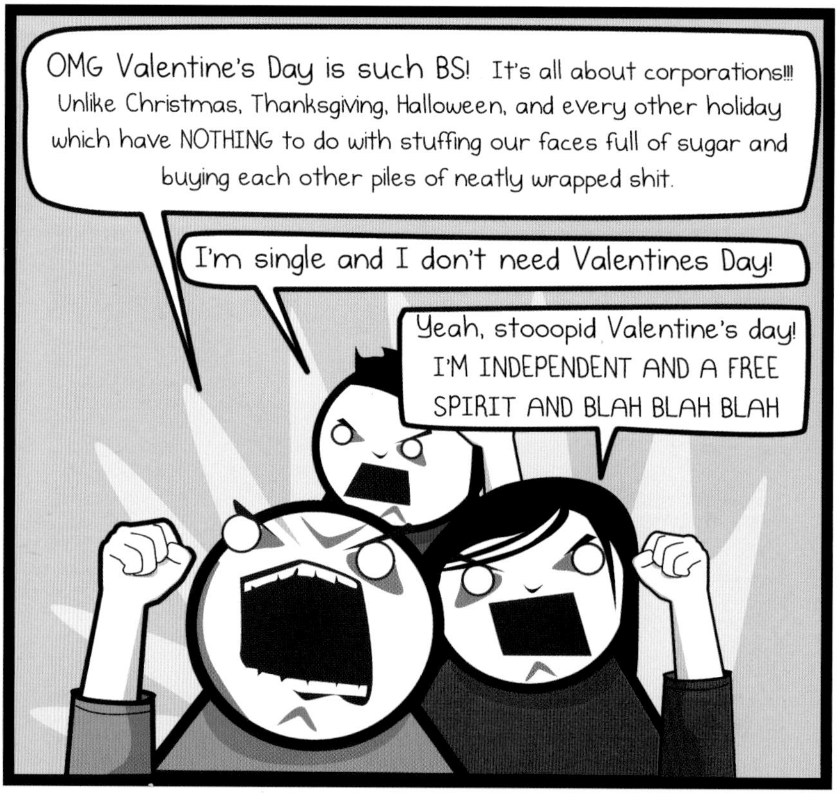

OMG Valentine's Day is such BS! It's all about corporations!!! Unlike Christmas, Thanksgiving, Halloween, and every other holiday which have NOTHING to do with stuffing our faces full of sugar and buying each other piles of neatly wrapped shit.
I'm single and I don't need Valentines Day!
Yeah, stooopid Valentine's day! I'M INDEPENDENT AND A FREE SPIRIT AND BLAH BLAH BLAH

If Valentine's Day really means so little to you, then I politely ask you to shut the hell up and treat it like any other day.

Or

go have a sexy adventure rumpus with someone who smells nice.

Less complaining.

More sexy rumpus.

-The Oatmeal

The punches I throw

are fast and terrible and **deep**

and sometimes when I roll over

I clock you in your **sleep**.

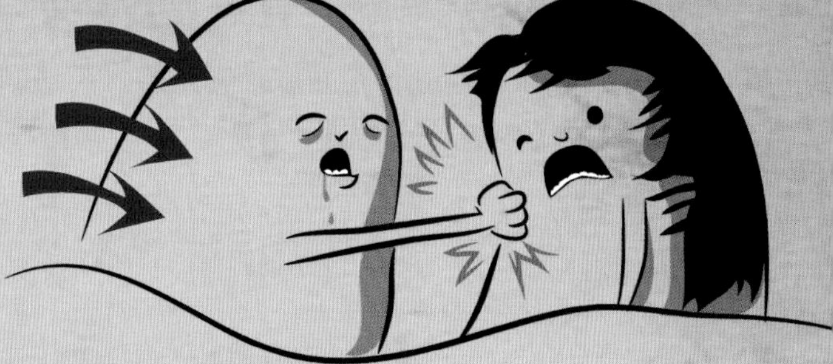

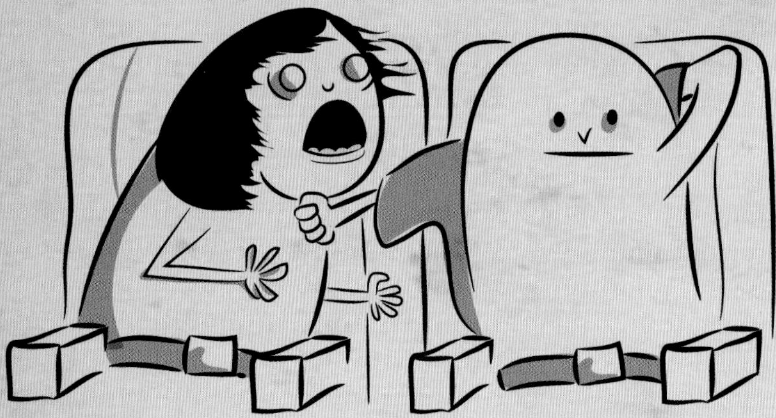

The airplanes we fly

soar high up in the sky

and when I remove my **coat**

I punch you in the **throat**.

Sometimes I see

things so **delightfully neat**

that I slug your pretty face

and knock you off your **feet**.

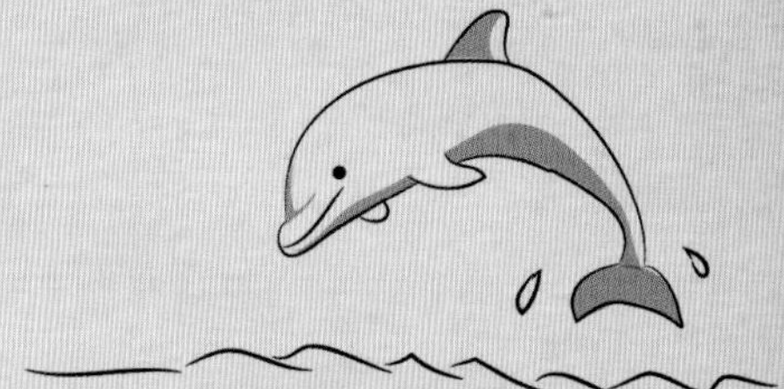

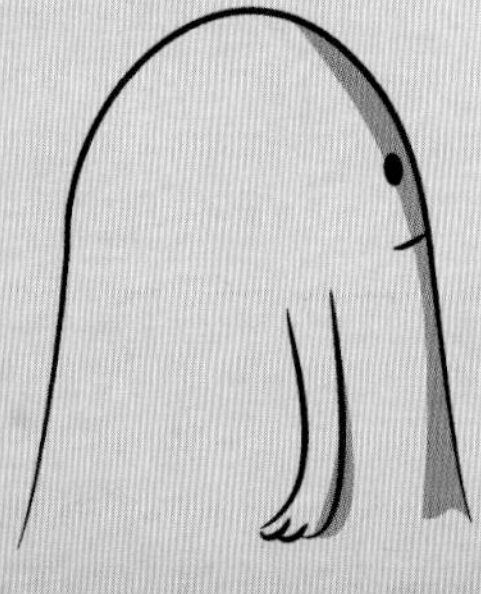

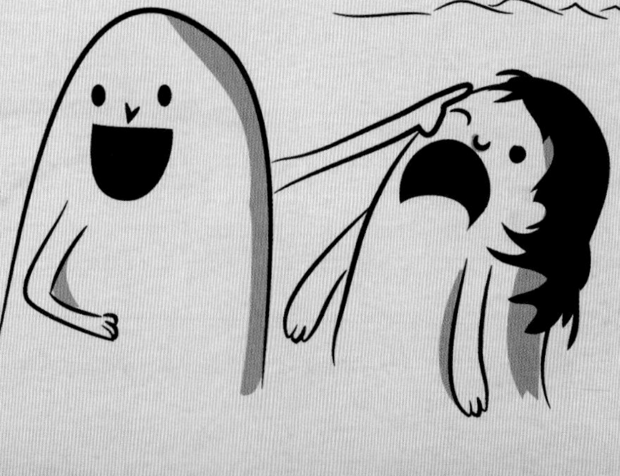

This steak is so delicious

bulging, bloody, meat

but you're left-handed, sweetie

so maybe don't sit next to me?

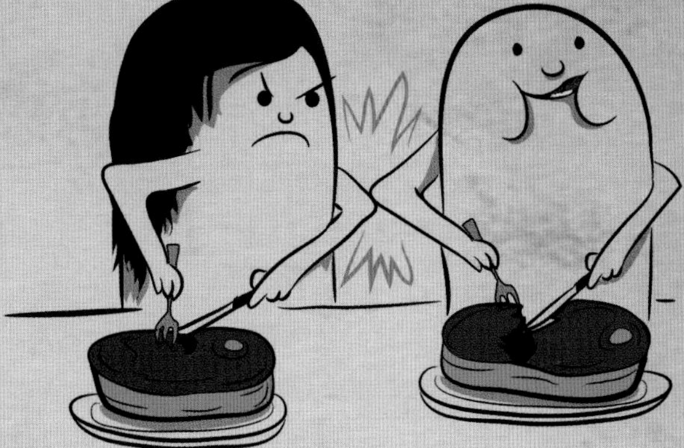

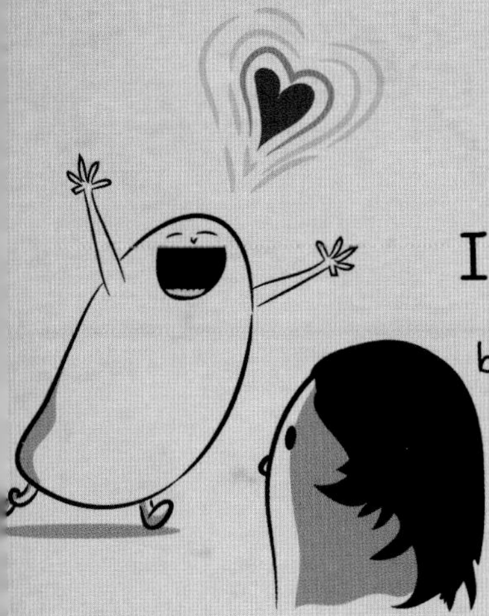

I missed you so much

but my hug was a little misplaced.

so I sorta fucked it up

and punched you in the face.

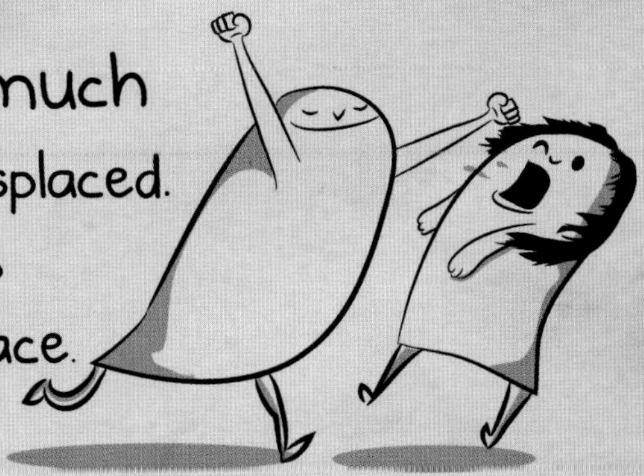

These are the punches I throw

so fast and terrible and deep.

I never meant to hurt you

I'm just a careless little

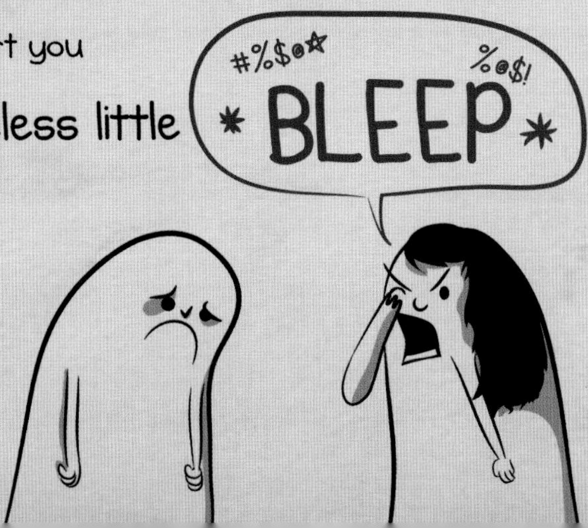
#%$@☆
%@$!
* BLEEP *

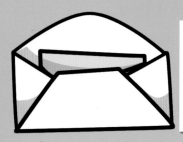

What your email address says about your computer skills

Own domain (ex.somedood@theoatmeal.com)	• Good chance of being skilled and capable. • Maybe even a programmer or designer.
@gmail.com	• Most likely knows their way around a computer. • When the internet stops working, actually tries rebooting the router before calling a family member for help.
@hotmail.com	• Uses a Compaq. • Still has issues with spyware. • Still thinks that Myspace is hip.
@yahoo.com	• Usually types in all capslock. • Sends you email chain letters saying that Bill Gates will eat your hard drive unless you forward this message to everyone you know.
@aol.com	• Before asking for computer help, still thinks it's funny to make jokes about being computer illiterate. • Calls you on the phone to tell you about a neat website they've discovered, then says into the receiver: *" Okay, go to...* *h ... t ... t ...p ... colon ... slash ... slash... w ... w ... w ... dot ... "* • Prints out emails and brings them over to your house.

I always do this at the movies

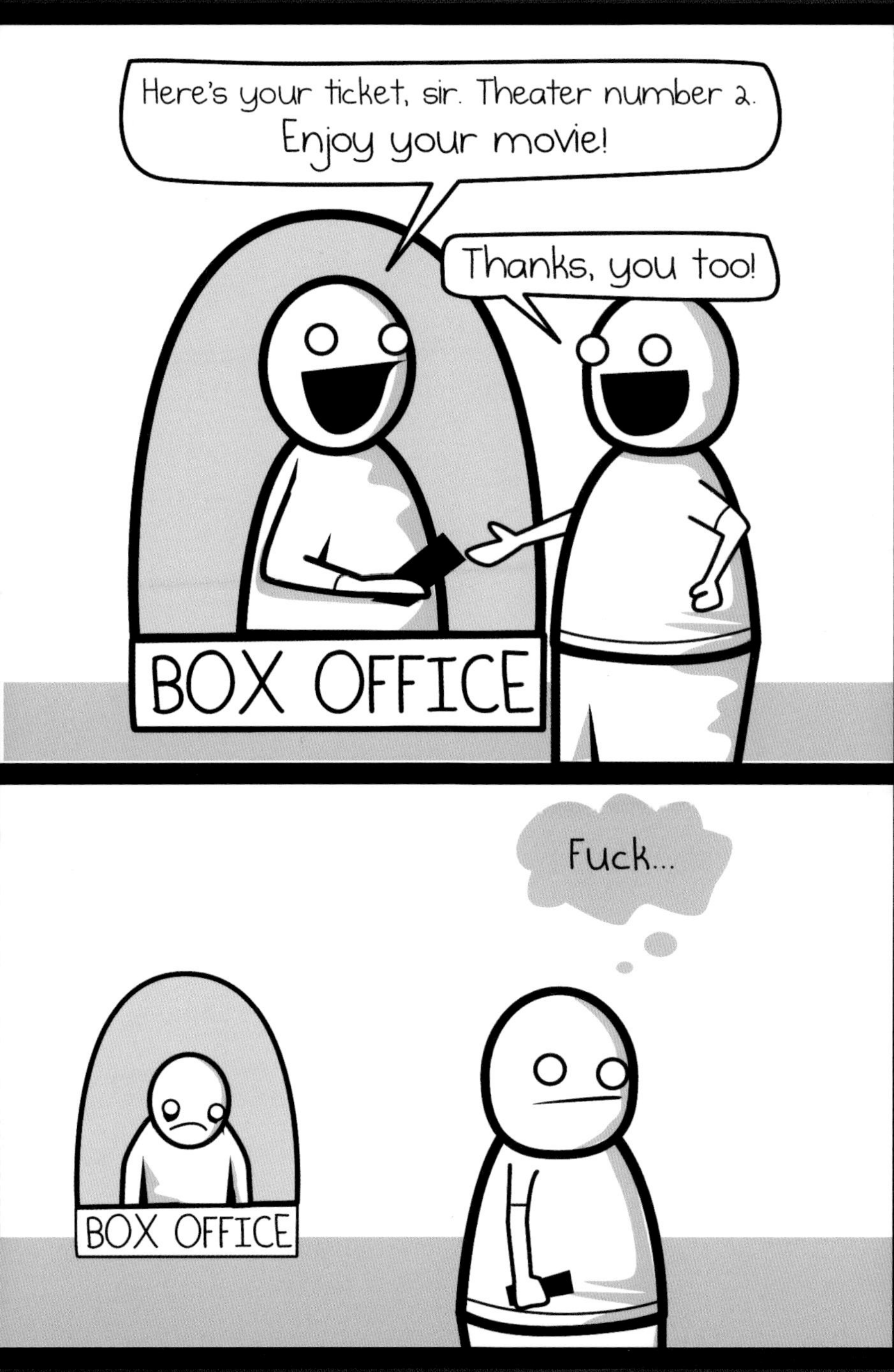
Here's your ticket, sir. Theater number 2.
Enjoy your movie!
Thanks, you too!
BOX OFFICE
Fuck...
BOX OFFICE

Some things
my computer needs

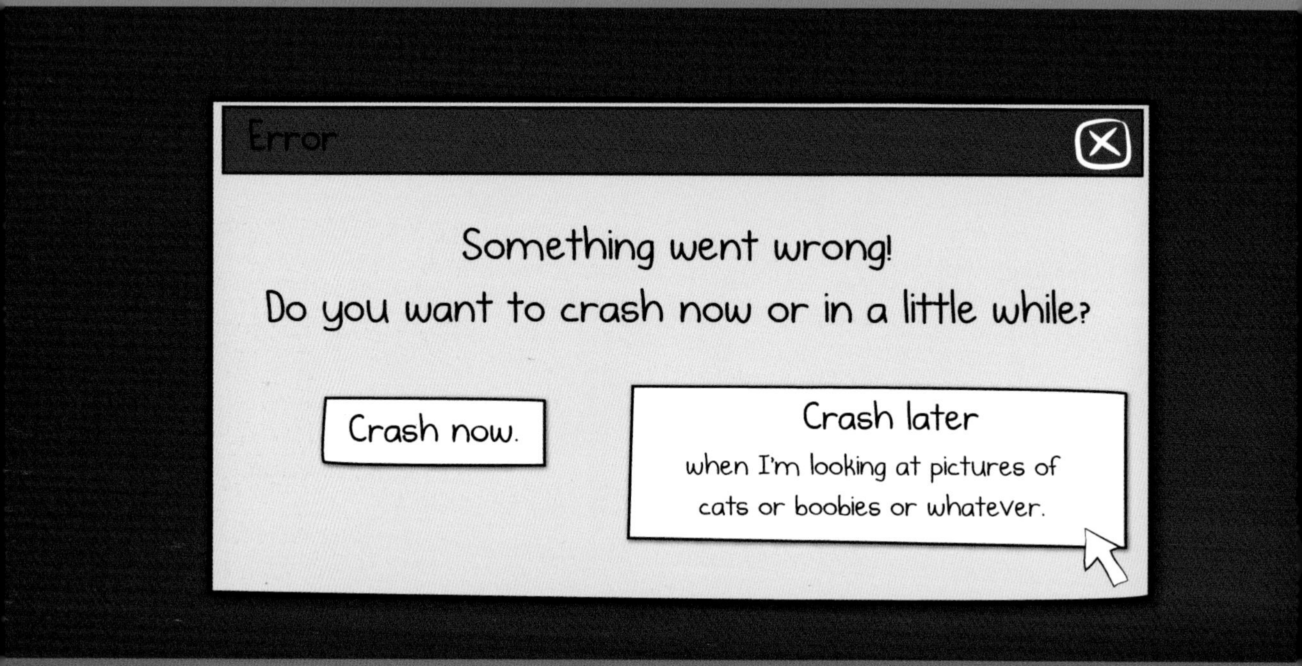

Error
Something went wrong!
Do you want to crash now or in a little while?
Crash now.
Crash later
when I'm looking at pictures of cats or boobies or whatever.

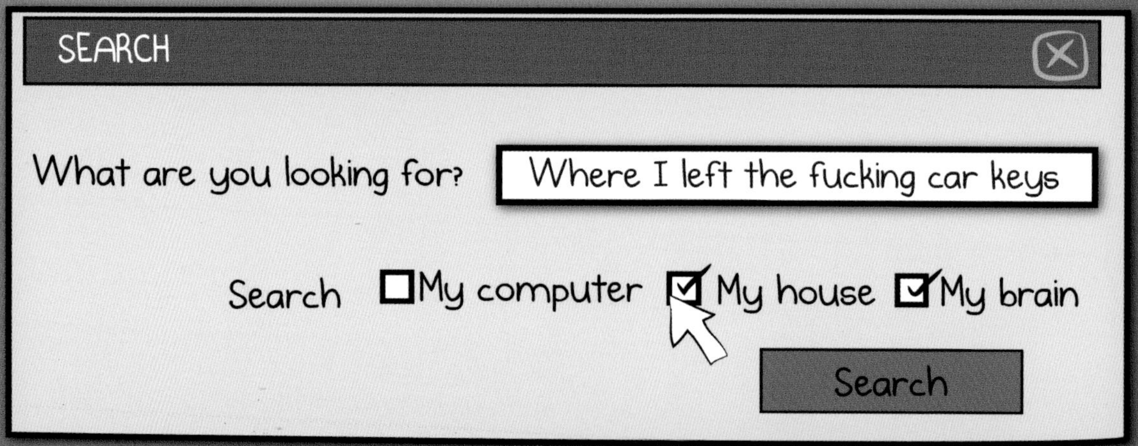

SEARCH
What are you looking for?
Where I left the fucking car keys
Search
My computer
My house
My brain
Search

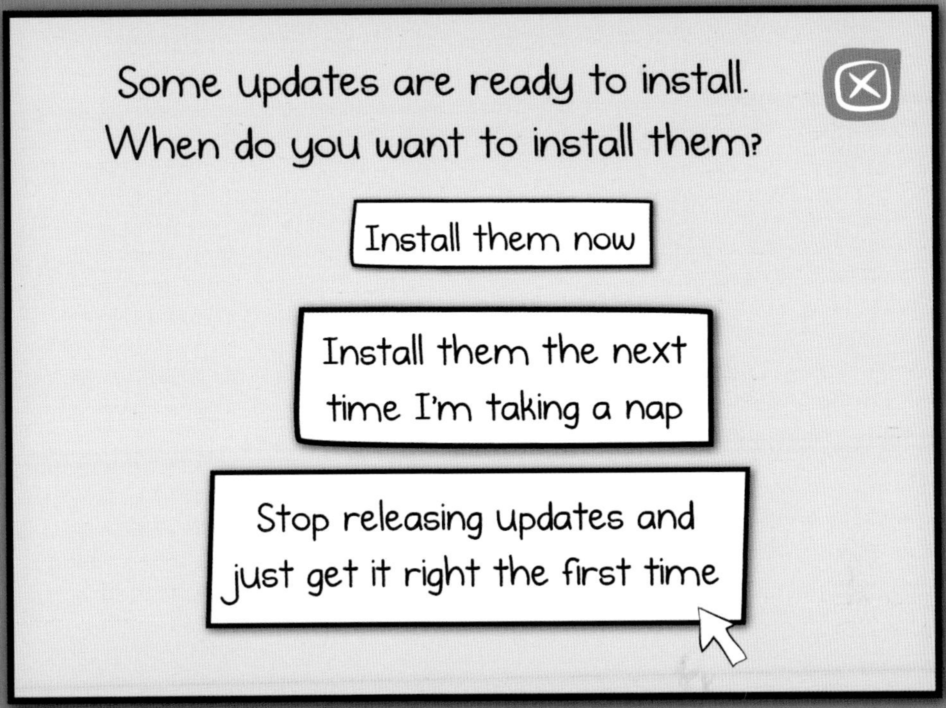
Some updates are ready to install.
When do you want to install them?
Install them now
Install them the next time I'm taking a nap
Stop releasing updates and just get it right the first time

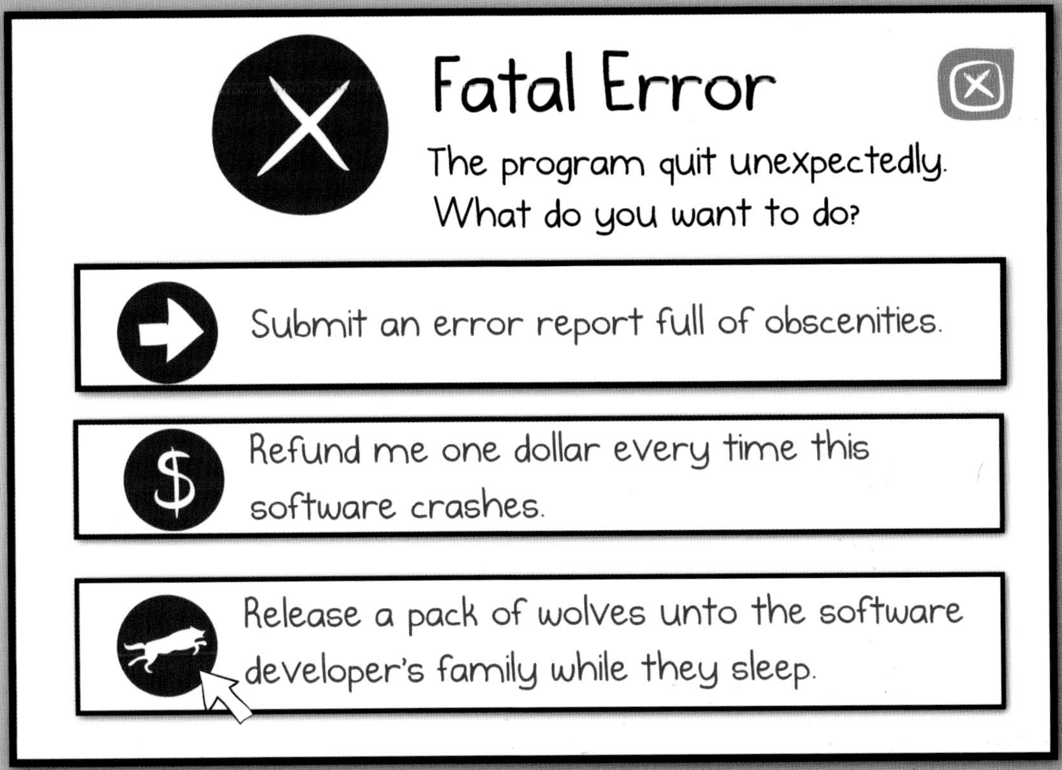
Fatal Error
The program quit unexpectedly.
What do you want to do?
Submit an error report full of obscenities.
$
Refund me one dollar every time this software crashes.
Release a pack of wolves unto the software developer's family while they sleep.

SEXYTIME IN NORTH AMERICA

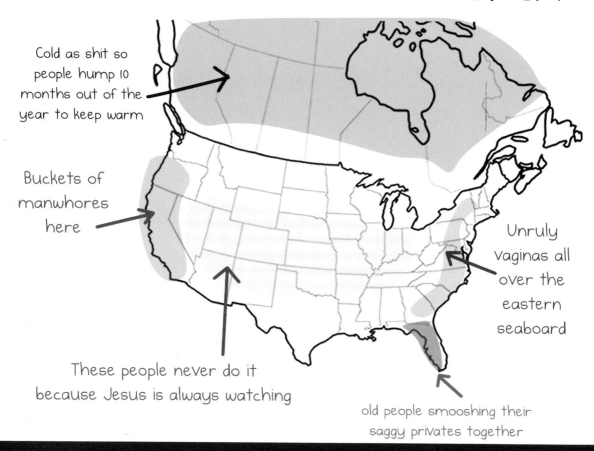

Cold as shit so people hump 10 months out of the year to keep warm

Buckets of manwhores here

These people never do it because Jesus is always watching

Unruly vaginas all over the eastern seaboard

old people smooshing their saggy privates together

Wearing a suit to work on the

East Coast

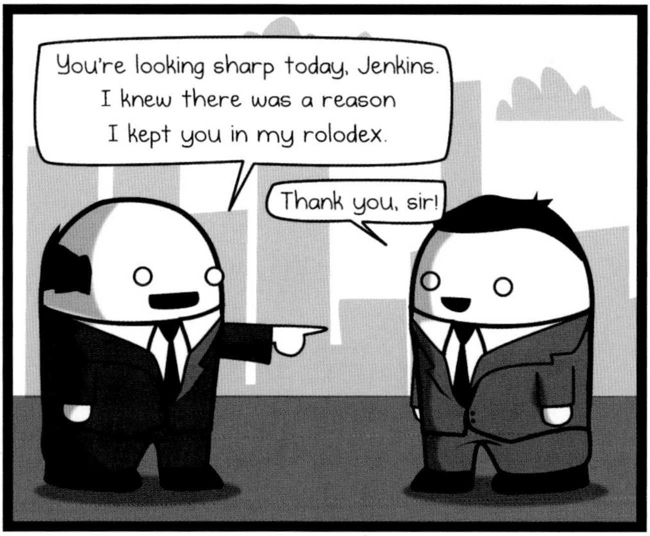
You're looking sharp today, Jenkins. I knew there was a reason I kept you in my rolodex.
Thank you, sir!

Wearing a suit to work on the

West Coast

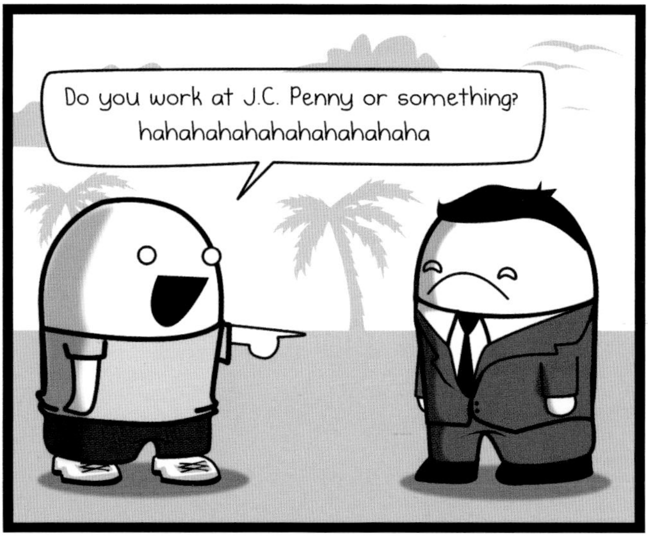
Do you work at J.C. Penny or something? hahahahahahahahahahaha

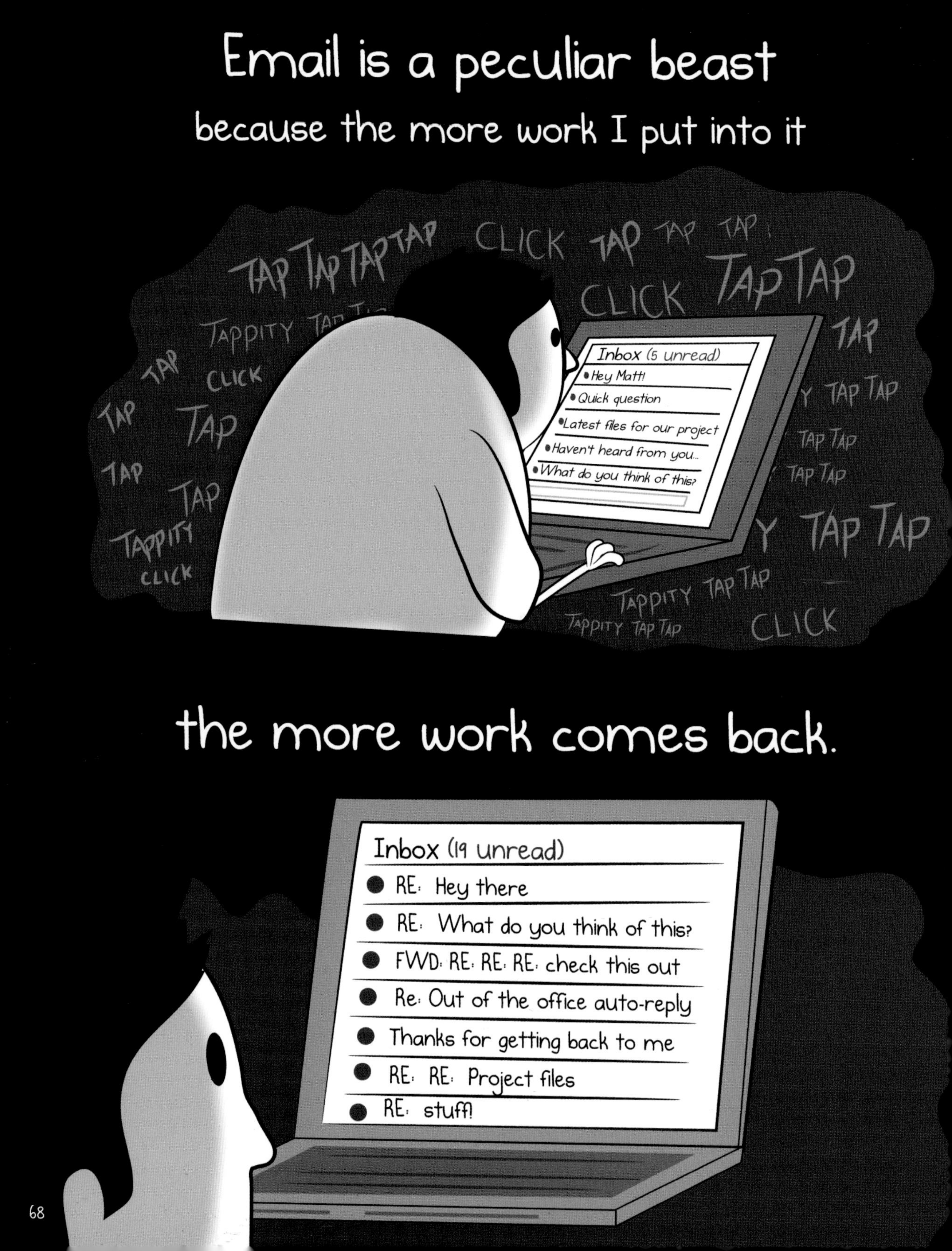
Email is a peculiar beast
because the more work I put into it
TAP TAP TAP TAP
CLICK
TAP
TAPPITY
CLICK
TAP TAP
Inbox (5 unread)
Hey Matt!
Quick question
Latest files for our project
Haven't heard from you...
What do you think of this?
TAP TAP
TAPPITY TAP TAP
CLICK
the more work comes back.
Inbox (19 unread)
RE: Hey there
RE: What do you think of this?
FWD: RE: RE: RE: check this out
Re: Out of the office auto-reply
Thanks for getting back to me
RE: RE: Project files
RE: stuff!

And I can't NOT do the work, either.

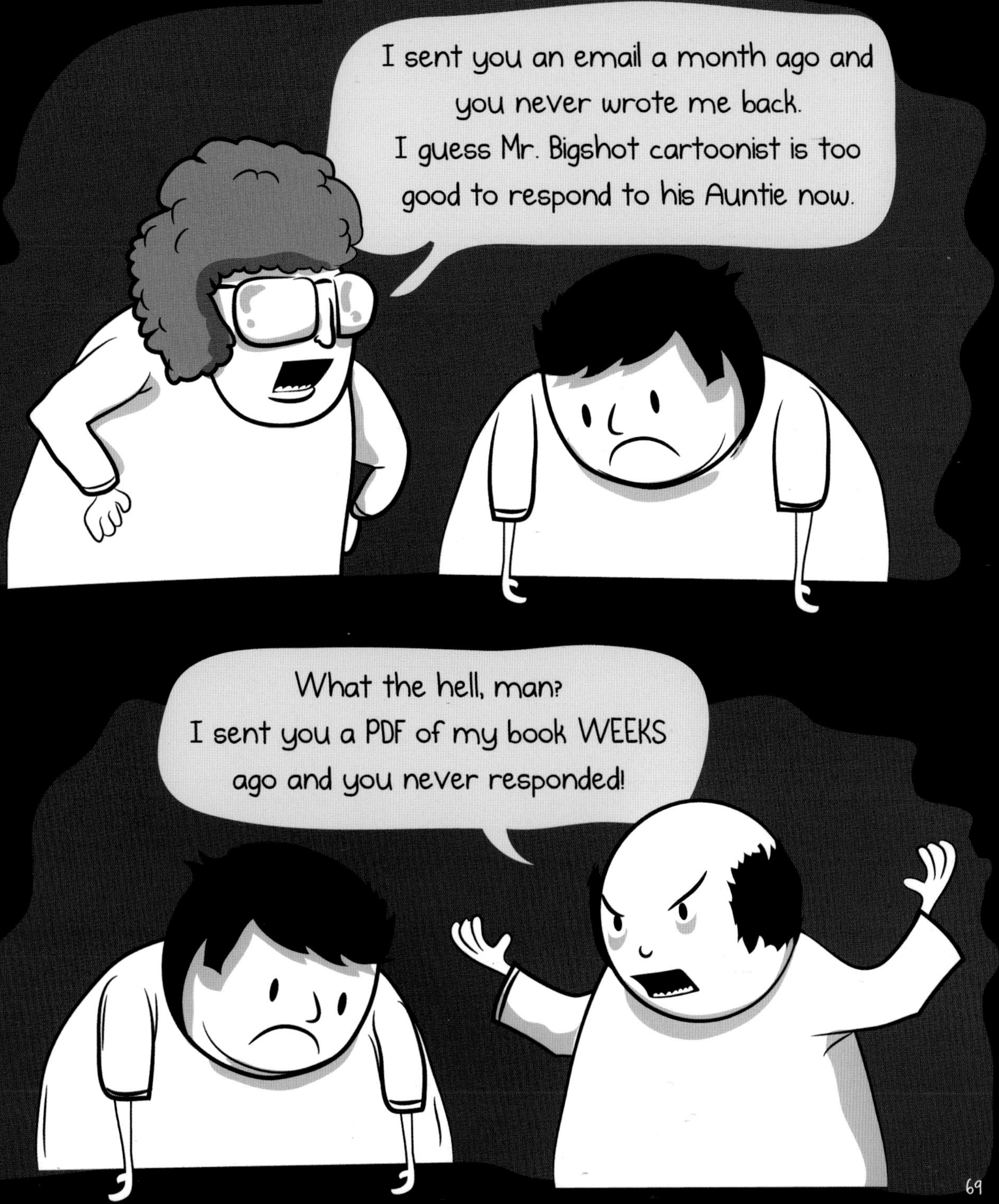
I sent you an email a month ago and you never wrote me back. I guess Mr. Bigshot cartoonist is too good to respond to his Auntie now.
What the hell, man? I sent you a PDF of my book WEEKS ago and you never responded!

So now I do this:

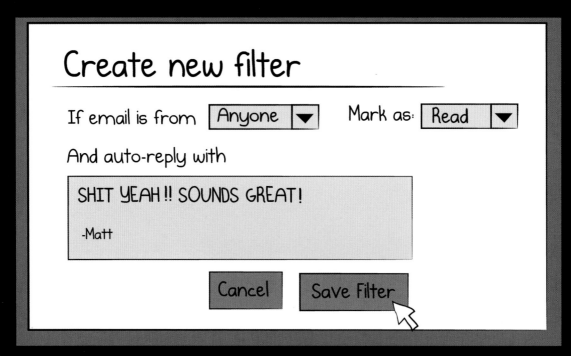

Create new filter

If email is from [Anyone ▼]   Mark as: [Read ▼]

And auto-reply with

SHIT YEAH!! SOUNDS GREAT!

-Matt

[Cancel]   [Save Filter]

and everyone wins.

Inbox (1 unread)

From: Matt Inman
Re: surgery next week
Received 5 min ago

SHIT YEAH!! SOUNDS GREAT!

-Matt

Hey Matt,
Next week I'm going in for surgery to have a
benign tumor removed from my butt.
They're going to drain the fluid first and then ...

What I remember most about LEGOs

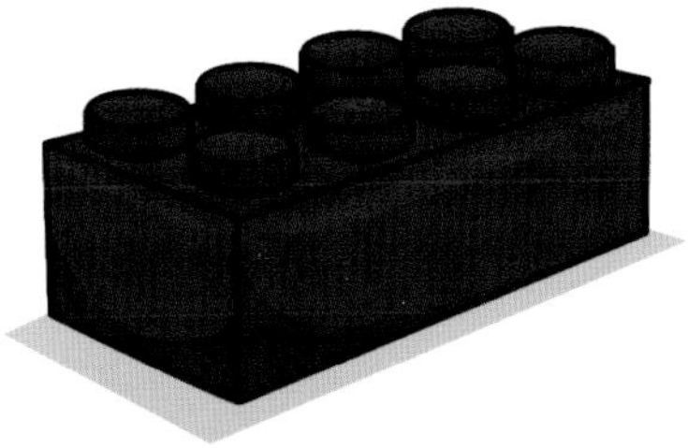

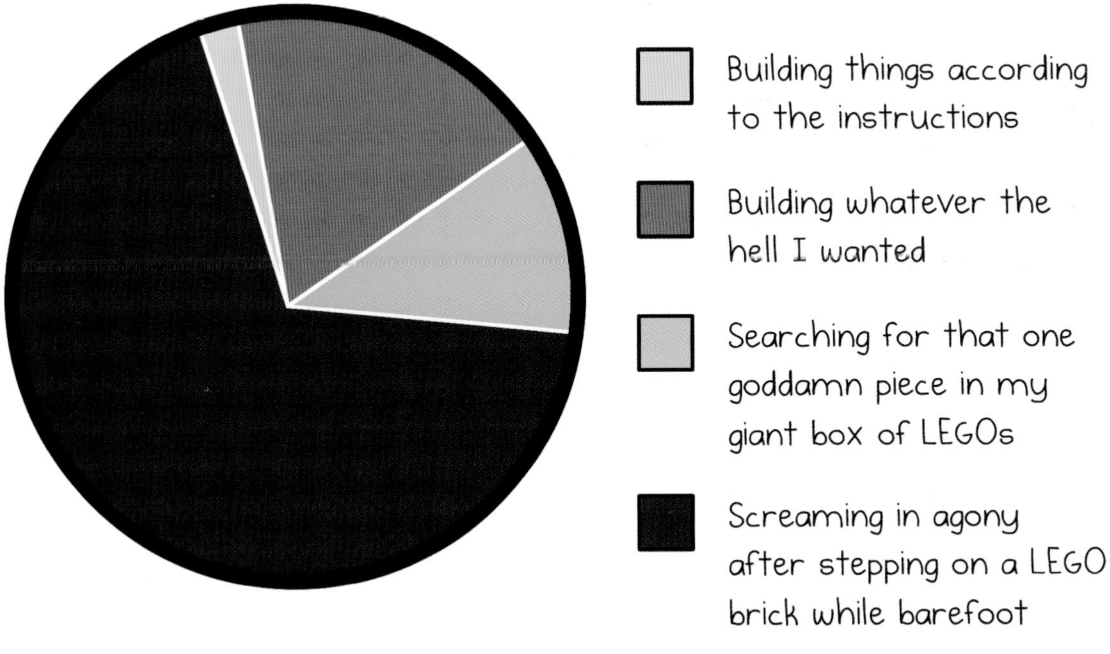
Building things according to the instructions
Building whatever the hell I wanted
Searching for that one goddamn piece in my giant box of LEGOs
Screaming in agony after stepping on a LEGO brick while barefoot

Why I love and hate having a Smartphone

I love being able to settle any debate

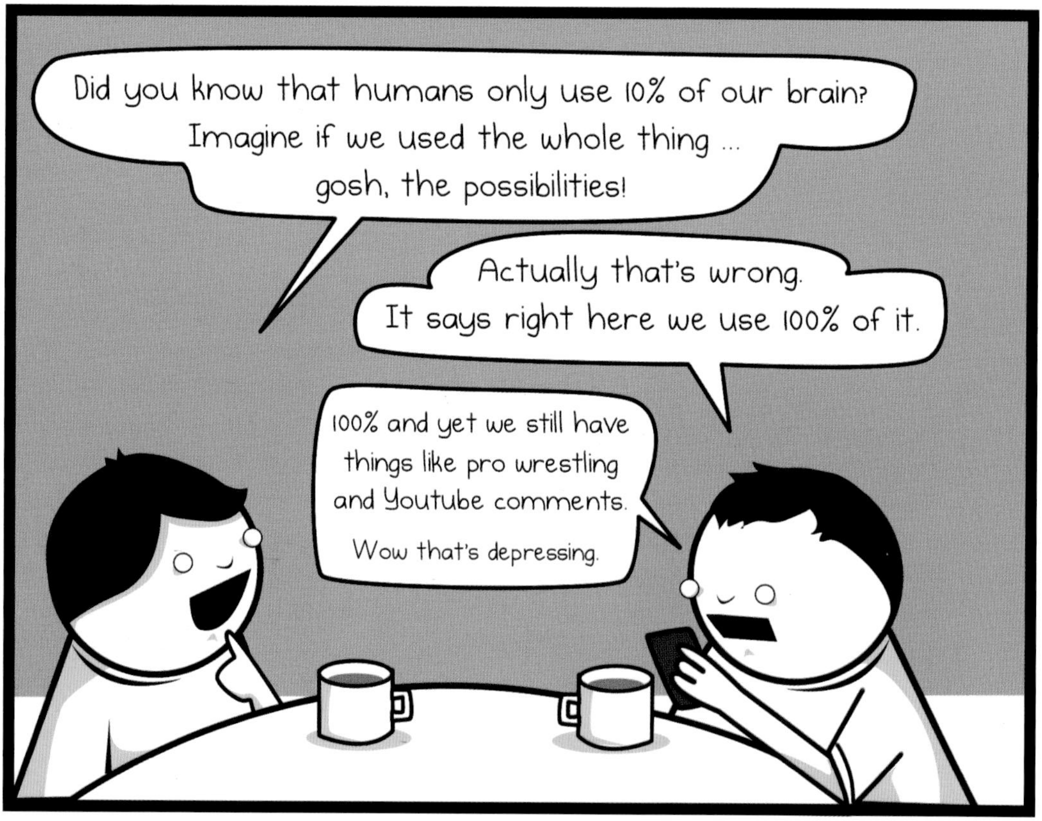

Did you know that humans only use 10% of our brain? Imagine if we used the whole thing ... gosh, the possibilities!
Actually that's wrong. It says right here we use 100% of it.
100% and yet we still have things like pro wrestling and Youtube comments.
Wow that's depressing.

And I love being able to look up anything, anytime, anywhere.

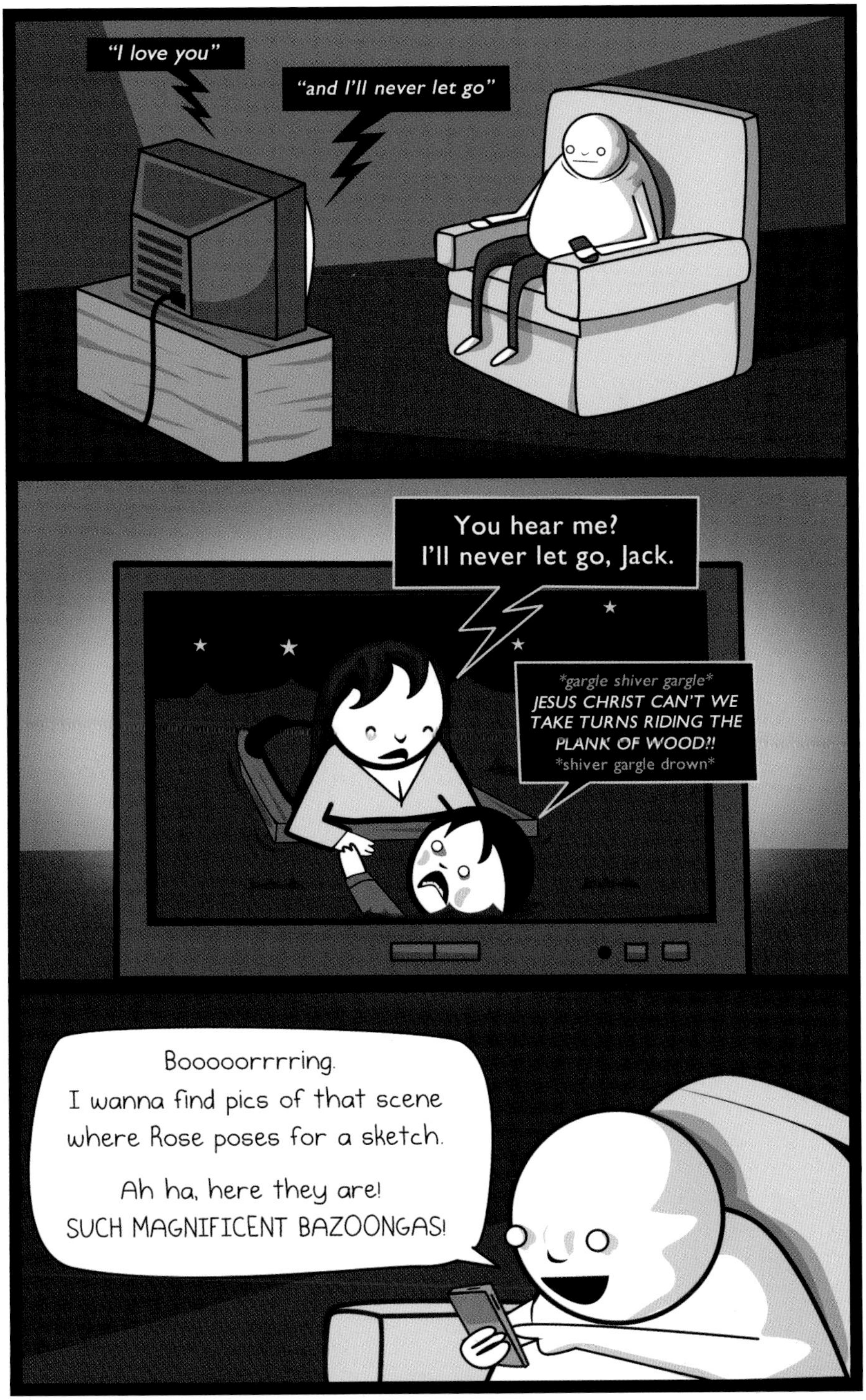
"I love you"
"and I'll never let go"
You hear me? I'll never let go, Jack.
gargle shiver gargle JESUS CHRIST CAN'T WE TAKE TURNS RIDING THE PLANK OF WOOD?! *shiver gargle drown*
Booooorrrring. I wanna find pics of that scene where Rose poses for a sketch.
Ah ha, here they are! SUCH MAGNIFICENT BAZOONGAS!

Being constantly connected has its advantages, too.

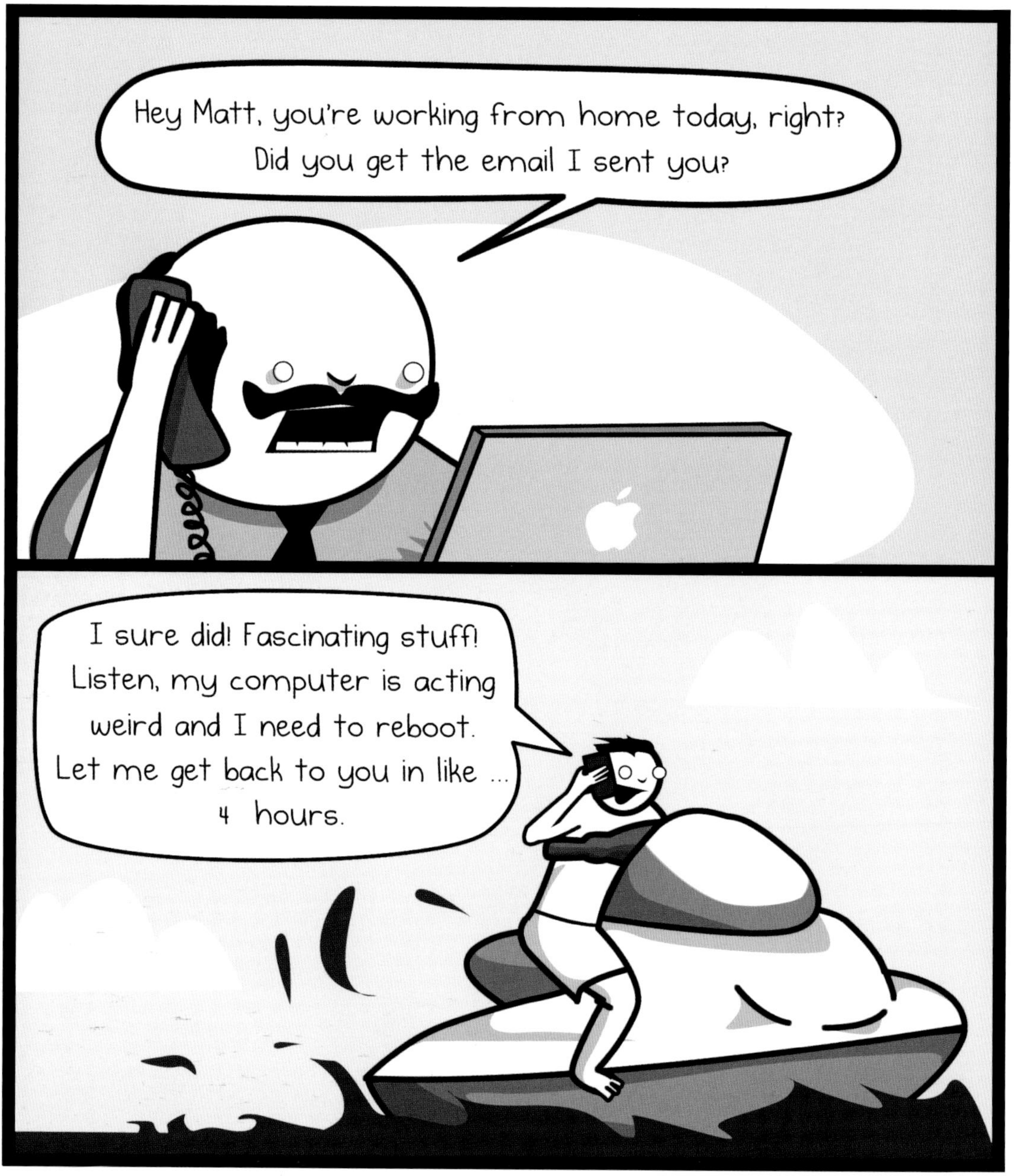
Hey Matt, you're working from home today, right? Did you get the email I sent you?
I sure did! Fascinating stuff! Listen, my computer is acting weird and I need to reboot. Let me get back to you in like ... 4 hours.

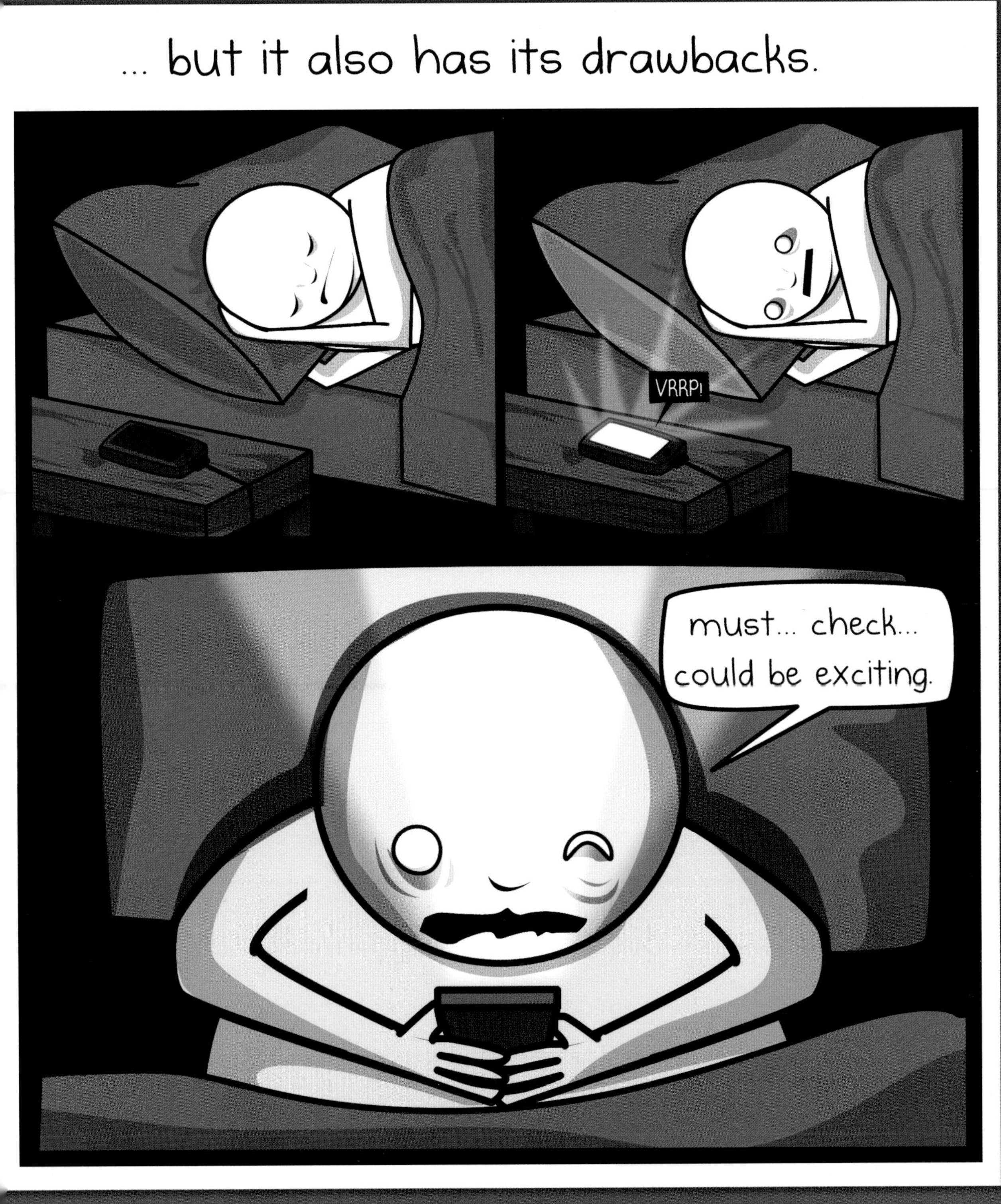
... but it also has its drawbacks.
VRRP!
must... check... could be exciting.

If I'm standing around waiting for something, a smartphone is a great way to keep busy.

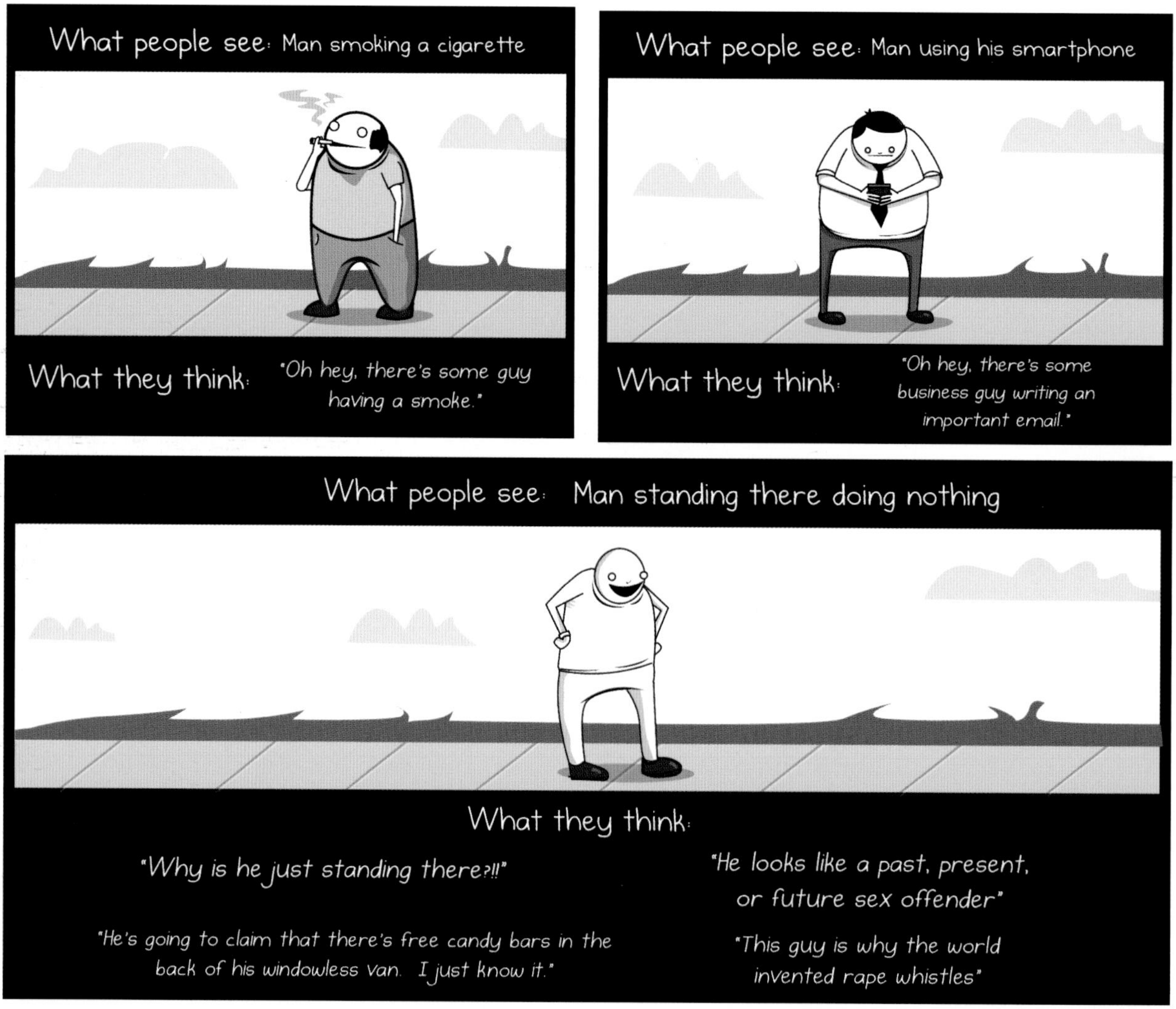
What people see: Man smoking a cigarette
What they think: "Oh hey, there's some guy having a smoke."
What people see: Man using his smartphone
What they think: "Oh hey, there's some business guy writing an important email."
What people see: Man standing there doing nothing
What they think:
"Why is he just standing there?!!"
"He's going to claim that there's free candy bars in the back of his windowless van. I just know it."
"He looks like a past, present, or future sex offender"
"This guy is why the world invented rape whistles"

It's also a great escape from awkward social situations.

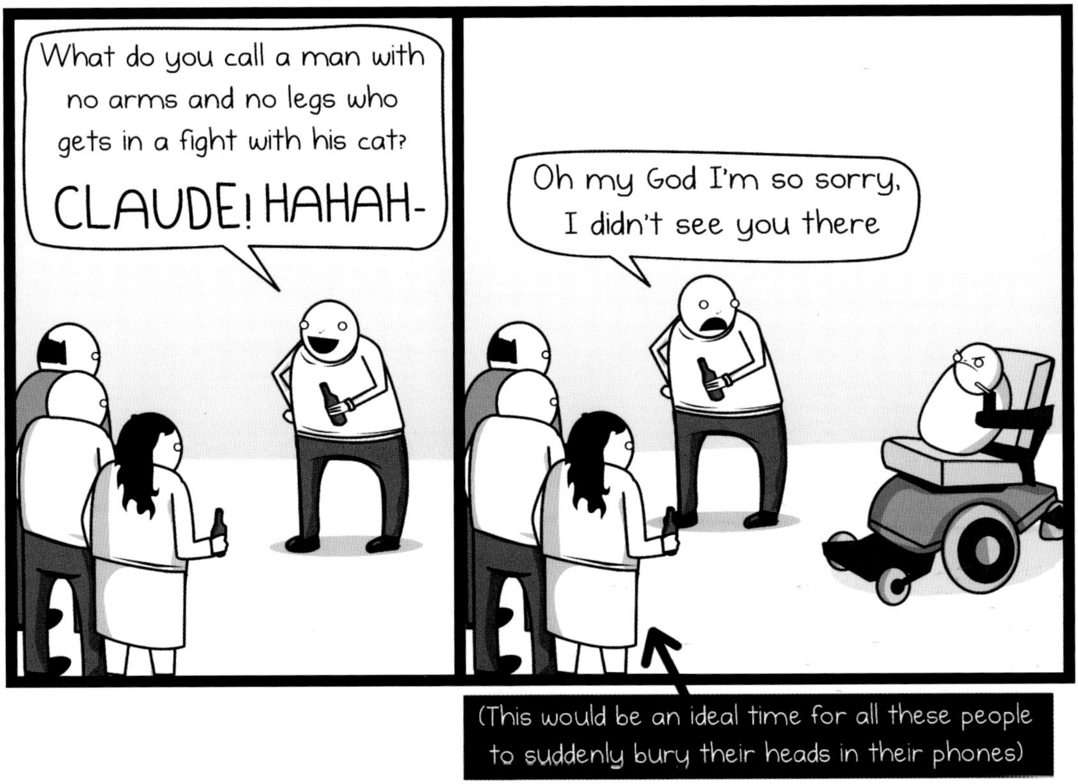
What do you call a man with no arms and no legs who gets in a fight with his cat? CLAUDE! HAHAH-
Oh my God I'm so sorry, I didn't see you there
(This would be an ideal time for all these people to suddenly bury their heads in their phones)

Although socially awkward people tend to abuse this privilege.

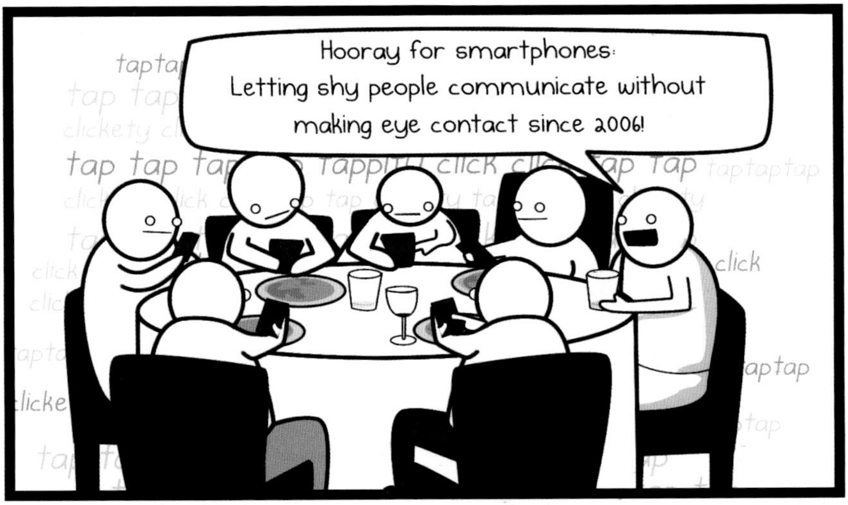
Hooray for smartphones: Letting shy people communicate without making eye contact since 2006!

Smartphones are great for meeting up, too.

I've gotten so used to my phone, I don't know how anyone ever managed to get together prior to its invention.

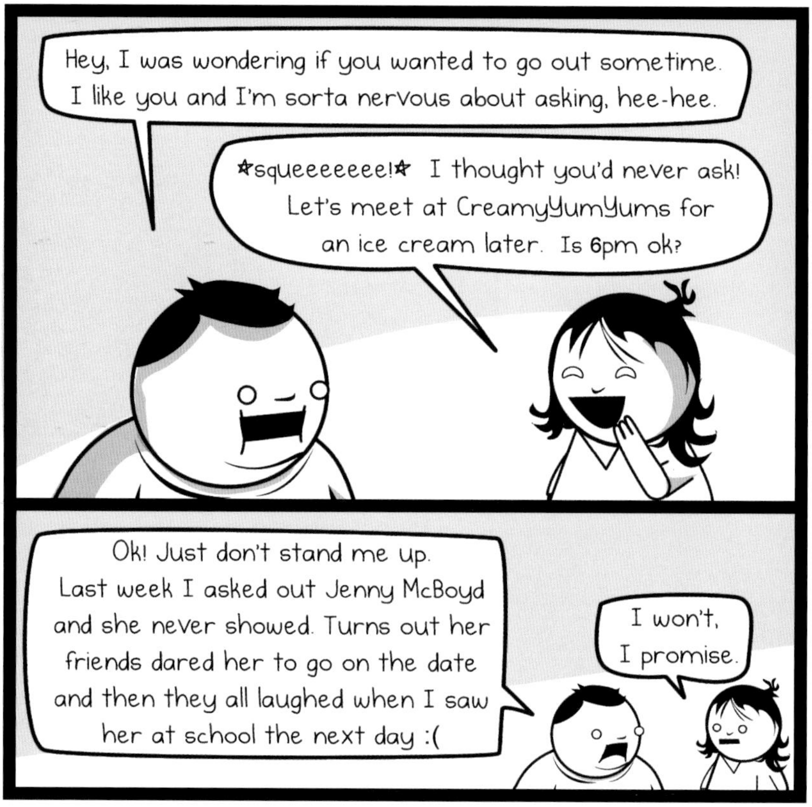

Hey, I was wondering if you wanted to go out sometime. I like you and I'm sorta nervous about asking, hee-hee.
☆squeeeeeeee!☆ I thought you'd never ask! Let's meet at CreamyYumYums for an ice cream later. Is 6pm ok?
Ok! Just don't stand me up. Last week I asked out Jenny McBoyd and she never showed. Turns out her friends dared her to go on the date and then they all laughed when I saw her at school the next day :(
I won't, I promise.

WITH a mobile phone

WITHOUT a mobile phone

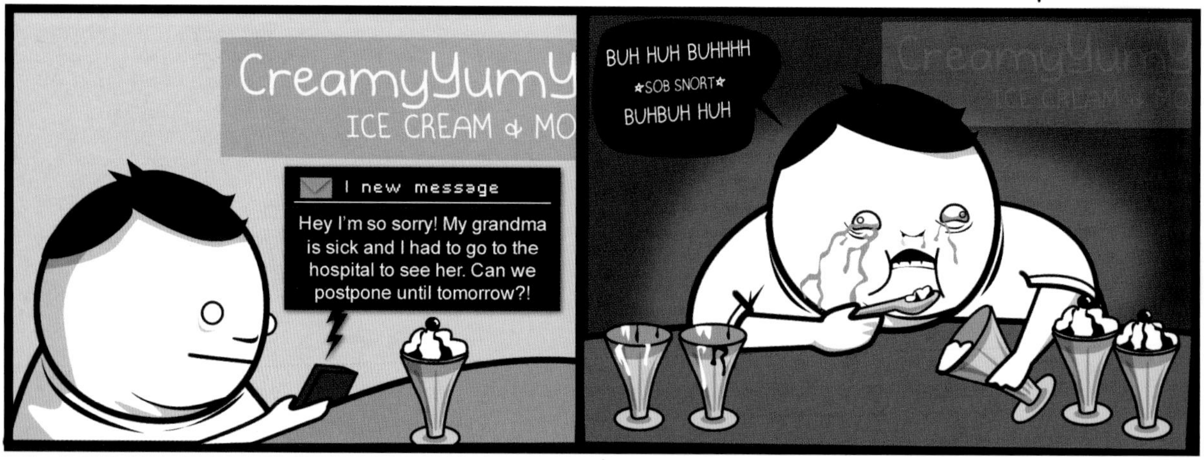

CreamyYumY
ICE CREAM & MO
1 new message
Hey I'm so sorry! My grandma is sick and I had to go to the hospital to see her. Can we postpone until tomorrow?!
BUH HUH BUHHHH
☆SOB SNORT☆
BUHBUH HUH

I absolutely *hate* telling people what kind of phone I have.

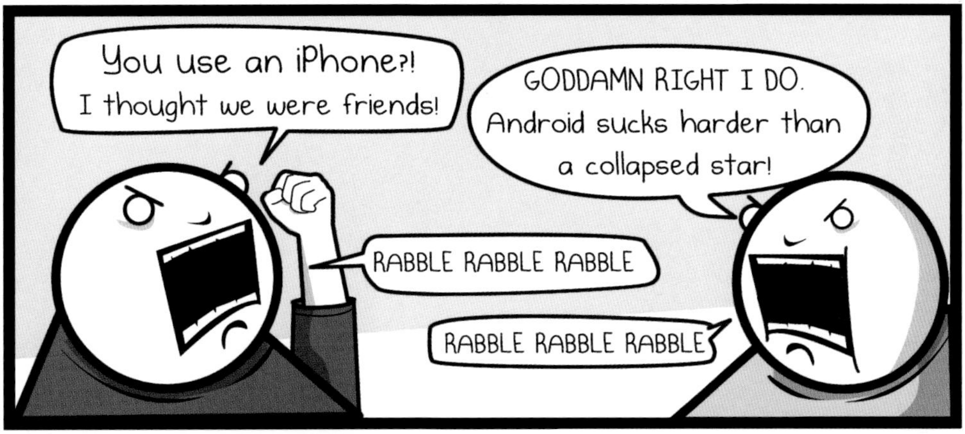

You use an iPhone?! I thought we were friends!
GODDAMN RIGHT I DO. Android sucks harder than a collapsed star!
RABBLE RABBLE RABBLE
RABBLE RABBLE RABBLE

You bring up war, poverty, or famine in conversation and you'll find a barren vacuum of opinions. You announce what kind of phone you have and you'll spend the next hour enduring an obnoxious holy war.

And I hate listening to people complain about their phones.

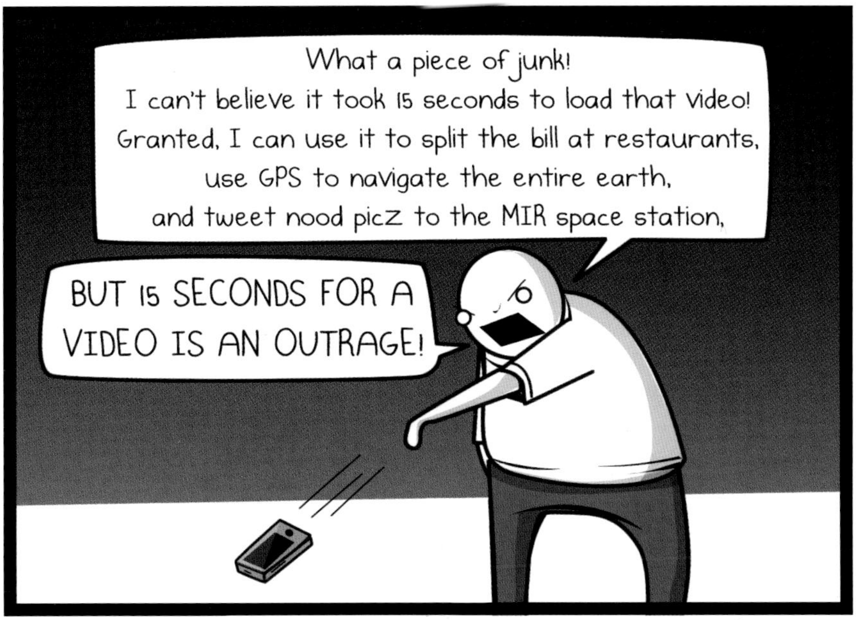

What a piece of junk! I can't believe it took 15 seconds to load that video! Granted, I can use it to split the bill at restaurants, use GPS to navigate the entire earth, and tweet nood picZ to the MIR space station,
BUT 15 SECONDS FOR A VIDEO IS AN OUTRAGE!

Instead of complaining, I simply try to appreciate the fifty bazillion things my phone lets me do that I couldn't do before.

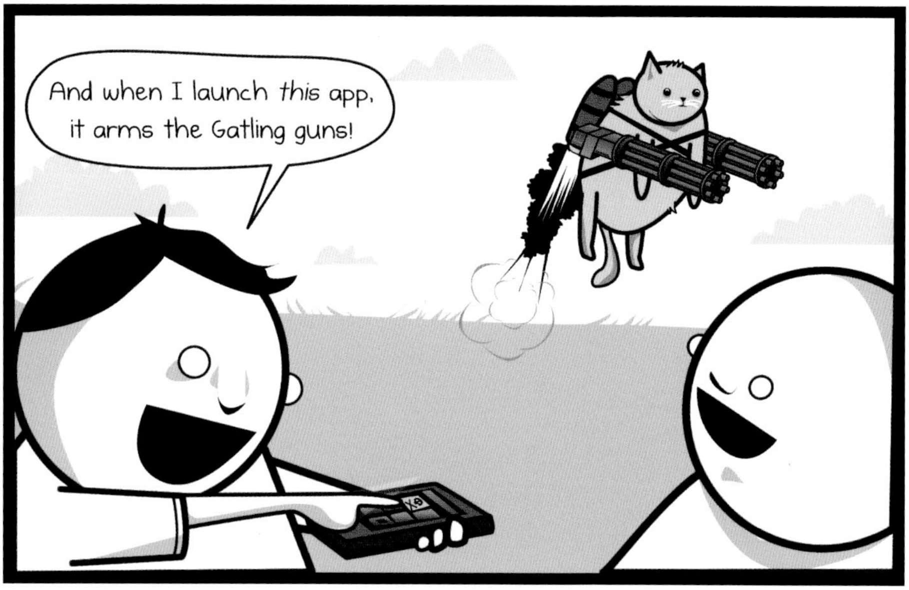
And when I launch *this* app, it arms the Gatling guns!

Meanwhile filling my pink squishy brain with awesome facts.

(All 100% of it)

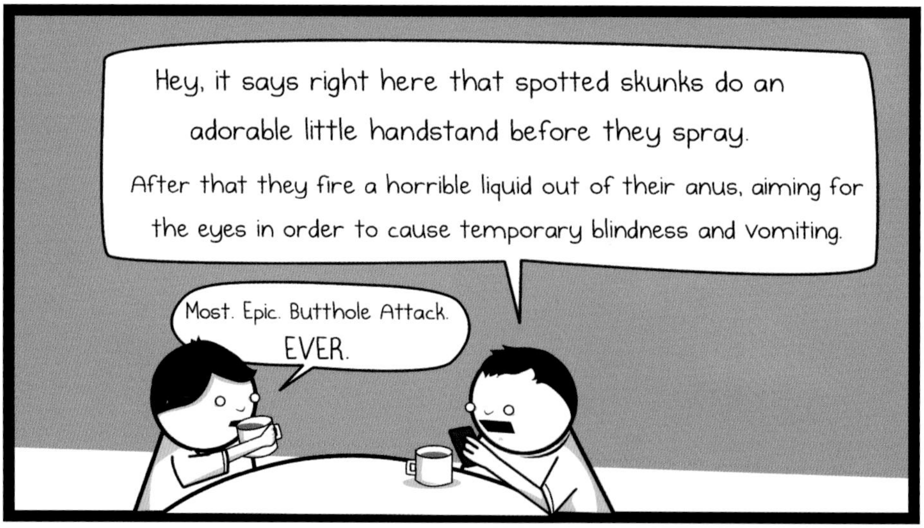
Hey, it says right here that spotted skunks do an adorable little handstand before they spray.
After that they fire a horrible liquid out of their anus, aiming for the eyes in order to cause temporary blindness and vomiting.
Most. Epic. Butthole Attack. EVER.

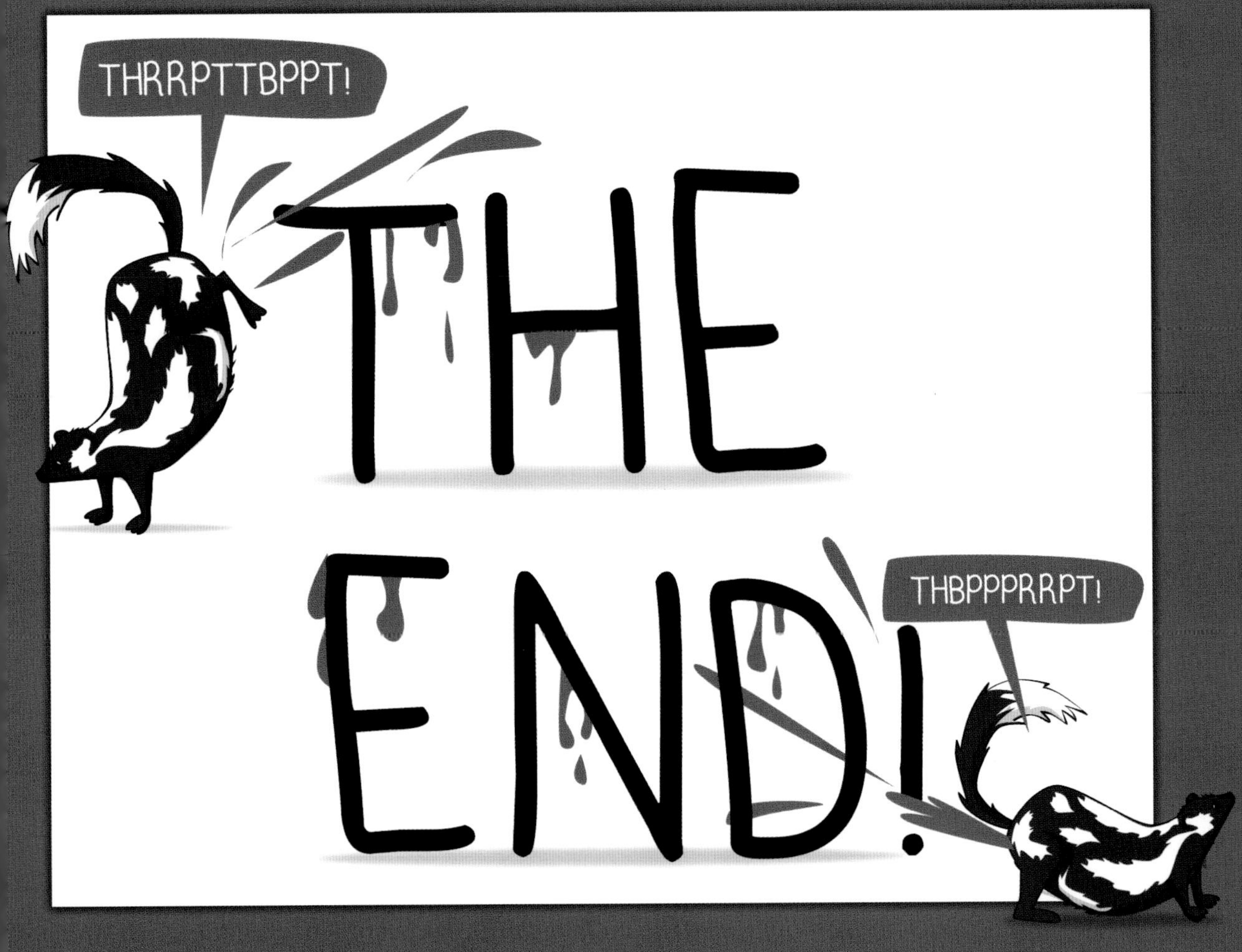
THRRPTTBPPT!
THE END!
THBPPPRRPT!

The pros and cons of a man sitting down to pee

Pros:

- +1 point ► Lets you hunch over and relax
- +1 point ► Who doesn't like a nice sit-down after a long day?
- +1 point ► Can read email, news, etc., on your smartphone
- +1 point ► Penis is 100% safe from zipper
- +1 point ► Can go "hands free" and tinkle without ever touching your manparts
  No need to wash hands after and use up expensive soap - THINK OF THE SAVINGS!
- +1 point ► Can easily change your mind and go two-sies (#2) without changing position
- +1 point ► No aiming required!

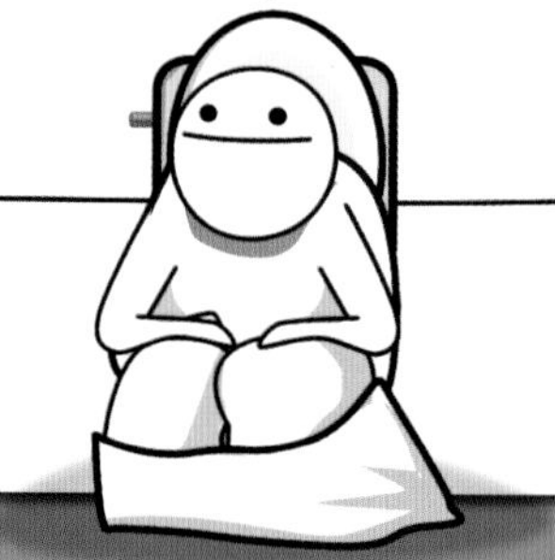

Total: 7 points

Cons:

- -1 point ► Takes more time
- -500 points ► Pretty much makes you a sissy little bitch

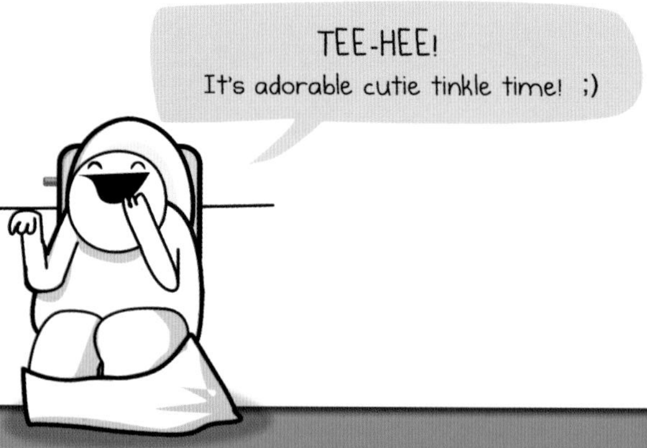
TEE-HEE!
It's adorable cutie tinkle time! ;)

Total: -494 points

Time spent using Tupperware

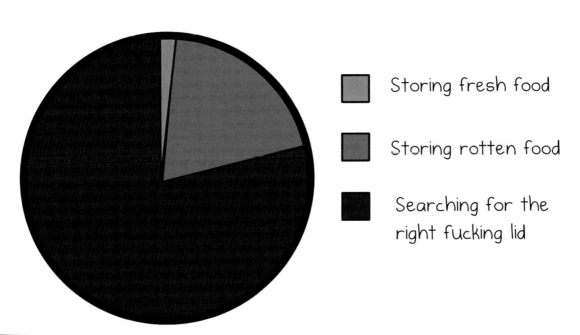

Storing fresh food

Storing rotten food

Searching for the right fucking lid

If you do this in an email, I hate you.

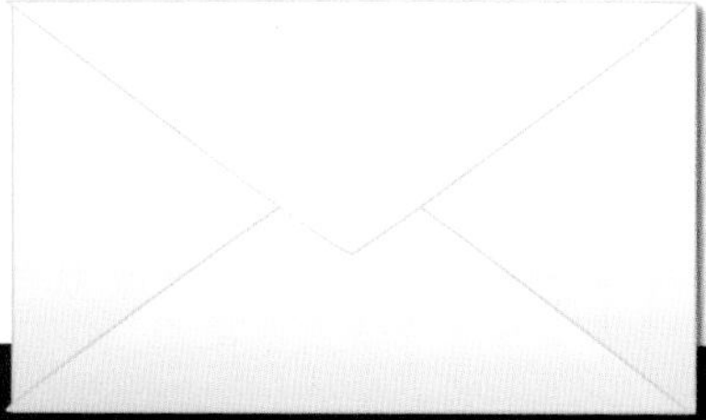

This is bad.

From: Bob
To: Matthew I
CC: Every single human being this person has ever had contact with.
Subject: Fwd: Fwd: Fwd: Fwd: OMG funny pictures of funnyness!

If it's more than a handful of people, use BCC.
If you don't know what BCC is then you shouldn't be using email.

Do not send me funny emails or chain letters.
If you do, I'll assume you were born in the '20s and I'll arrange to have you picked up and put in a nursing home.

This is worse.

From: Christy
To: Bob
CC: Every single human being Bob has ever had contact with.
Subject: Re: Fwd: Fwd: Fwd: Fwd: OMG funny pictures of funnyness!

LOL those ARE funny, Bob! So funny I'm going to hit "reply to all" and serve everyone a second helping of this obnoxious email.

Don't make me sign this stupid thing, just tell me what you're working on.

From: Chad Chadson
To: Matthew I.
Subject: I'm interested in working with you
Attachment: OMG_SecretStuff_NDA.doc

Hey Matt, I'm really interested in working with you. I can't tell you a single detail about the project because it's so amazing that you'd probably steal it and make billions of dollars within the first few days. I can't even tell you that it IS a project - for all you know it's something intangible like love, gravity, or clouds. It's quite amazing, Matt. I told my uncle about it and he LITERALLY pissed his pants. We're talking 9 figure income here and a potential to change anything we've ever known about everything.

Now that you know nothing about the project and I've provided a couple vague data points which are supposed to pique your interest, would you mind downloading, signing, and faxing back the attached 30 page NDA so we can move forward?

-Chad
CEO / Founder of OMG too secret to tell u

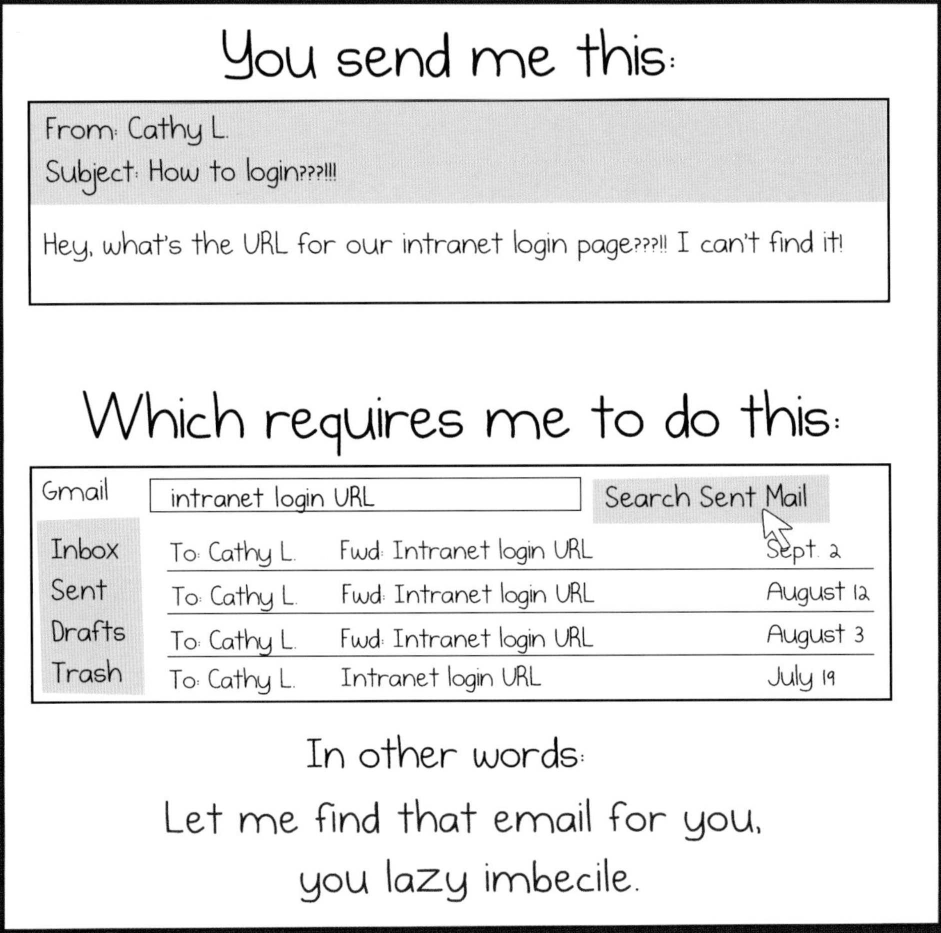

You send me this:

> From: Cathy L.
> Subject: How to login???!!!
>
> Hey, what's the URL for our intranet login page???!! I can't find it!

Which requires me to do this:

Gmail	intranet login URL	Search Sent Mail	
Inbox	To: Cathy L.	Fwd: Intranet login URL	Sept. 2
Sent	To: Cathy L.	Fwd: Intranet login URL	August 12
Drafts	To: Cathy L.	Fwd: Intranet login URL	August 3
Trash	To: Cathy L.	Intranet login URL	July 19

In other words:

Let me find that email for you,
you lazy imbecile.

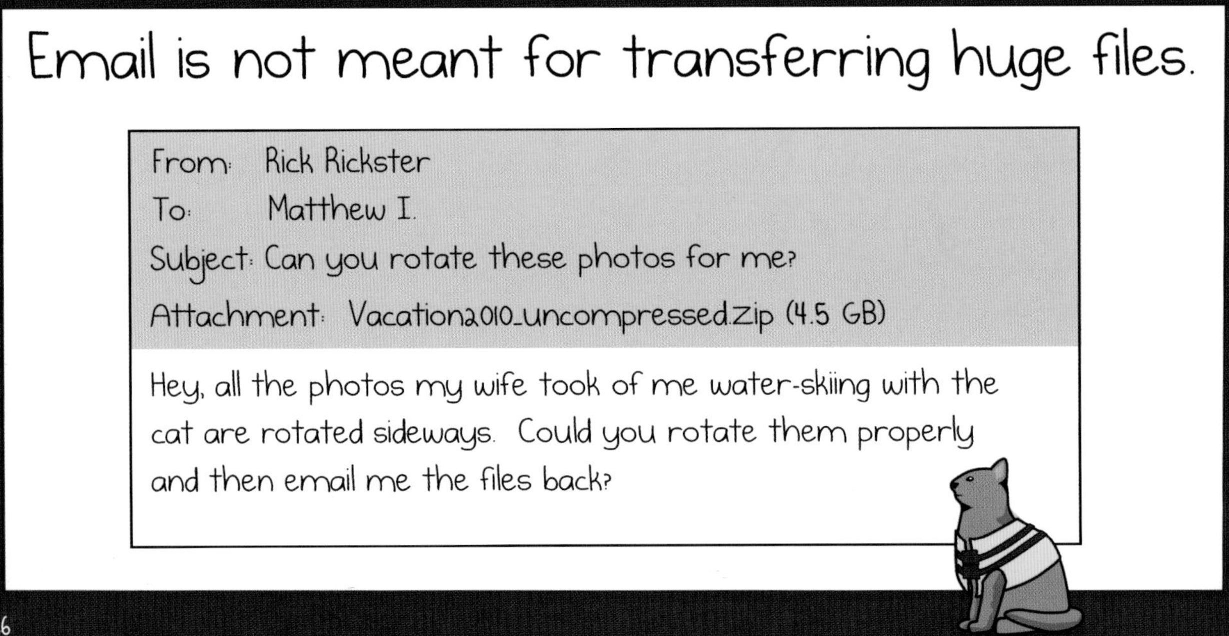

Email is not meant for transferring huge files.

> From: Rick Rickster
> To: Matthew I.
> Subject: Can you rotate these photos for me?
> Attachment: Vacation2010_uncompressed.zip (4.5 GB)
>
> Hey, all the photos my wife took of me water-skiing with the cat are rotated sideways. Could you rotate them properly and then email me the files back?

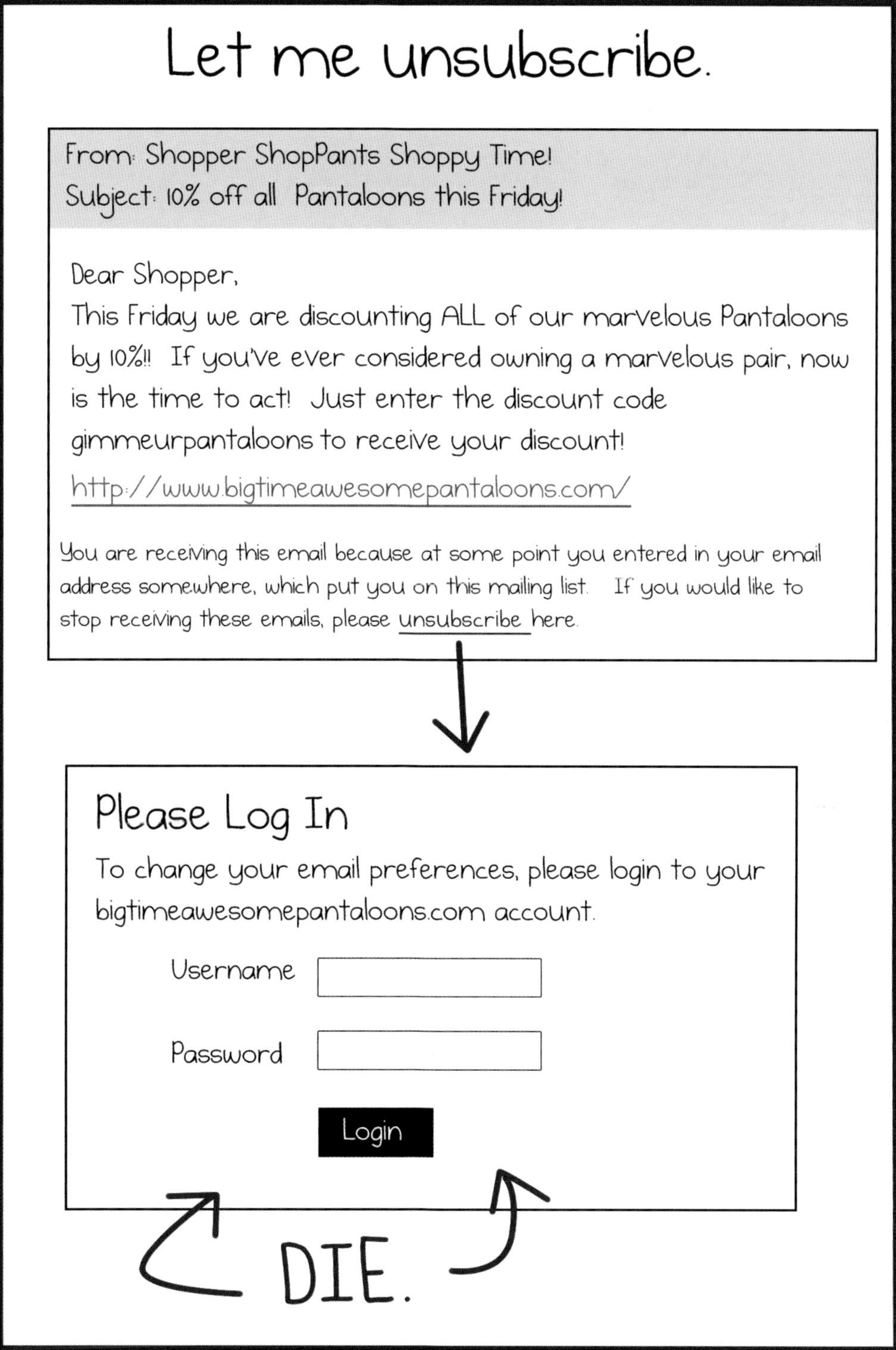
Let me unsubscribe.
From: Shopper ShopPants Shoppy Time!
Subject: 10% off all Pantaloons this Friday!
Dear Shopper,
This Friday we are discounting ALL of our marvelous Pantaloons by 10%!! If you've ever considered owning a marvelous pair, now is the time to act! Just enter the discount code gimmeurpantaloons to receive your discount!
http://www.bigtimeawesomepantaloons.com/
You are receiving this email because at some point you entered in your email address somewhere, which put you on this mailing list. If you would like to stop receiving these emails, please unsubscribe here.
Please Log In
To change your email preferences, please login to your bigtimeawesomepantaloons.com account.
Username
Password
Login
DIE.

I hate your email signature.

From: Deborah Wallace
To: Matthew I.
Subject: you are a computer genius!!!
Attachment: signature.gif   smiley.gif

Hey, just wanted to say thanks for your help yesterday!!!
I had no idea that rebooting would fix my twitters! 😃

Deborah "Debs" Wallace
Social Media LEGEND, Entrepreneur
Founder / CEO of DoucheSpeak Media Group LLC
Engager, Conversation Starter, Communitizer

oucheSpeak
We communitize engagement.

http://www.douchespeak.com

Office: 123 555 5555
Mobile: 123 555 1234
Fax: 123 555 9023
Beeper number: 203 555 9024
Pet gerbil's phone number: 204 555 9002
twitter: @douchespeak   www.facebook.com/douchespeak
linkedin.com/douchespeak

DoucheSpeak Media
5555 Douchey Lane
Seattle, Wa 98121 USA

"Live life passionately and love everyone like they are family, because Jesus is always with you. Jesus loves you seriously bigtime. He'd hug you until your eyeballs exploded out of your skull if he ever met you. He'd windsurf across oceans of dead Nazis which he personally slaughtered just to tell you that your new haircut is the bee's knees. Jesus is a like the monster truck of love and you are an old Geo Metro which he will roar his massive engine over and crush your pathetic fiberglass frame into a crumpled heap. Praise Jesus, especially when it's sunny outside because Jesus would totally be cool with you praising while you get a nice tan."

-Ecclesiastes XII. 7.

DISCLOSURE: The information in this email is confidential. If its contents are disclosed our lawyers will swoop down from helicopters and smash through the skylight nearest you and drag you away with a black bag over your head. They will then take you to our super secret headquarters and make you fight to the death with other people who shared this email. We will then watch said death match and place bets on the winner. You will be given a large buck knife and an unlimited supply of methamphetamines. If the fight becomes boring or there is a stalemate, rabid dogs will be released into the arena to liven things up a bit. If the dogs become docile, we will squirt them with water bottles until they become tempermental. Copyright 2010 DoucheSpeak Media.

Don't make me print stuff out,

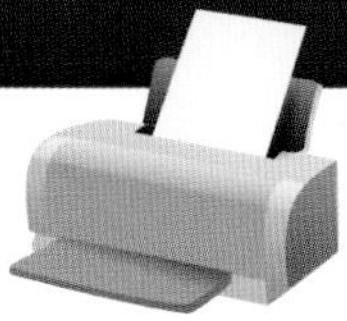

From: Bill Jimmers
Subject: Please return ASAP! Attached: UserAgreement.doc (12 MB)

Hey Matt,
I've attached a 30 page document which I need you to download, print, sign, and fax back to me ASAP.
Thanks! -Bill

because it defeats the purpose of email.

From: Lord Jimmers, Duke of Internet
Subject: Please return ASAP! Attached: UserAgreement.doc (12 MB)

Hey Matt,
Would you mind sailing the Mayflower back to Spain and signing this parchment with a quill? We don't have web forms in the ancient land where I come from, and every nobleman must complete the obnoxious task of riding a majestic steed across the lands to deliver a signed word .doc to prove his valor.
Thanks! - Lord Jimmers

And lastly, email is NOT a place to decorate.

From: Christee Fizzers
To: Matthew I.
Subject: what r u doin Attachment: Various horrific animated GIFs from the 1990s

HI i really like ur face. it's like a mashed potato of cuteness and it makes me gurgle with tee-hees every time i see it.

we should totes go get a soda sometime!!!

TEE-HEE *BURP GURGLE* TEE-HEE!!!

see i did it again!!!! mega burpies cuz I like you!!
-Christee

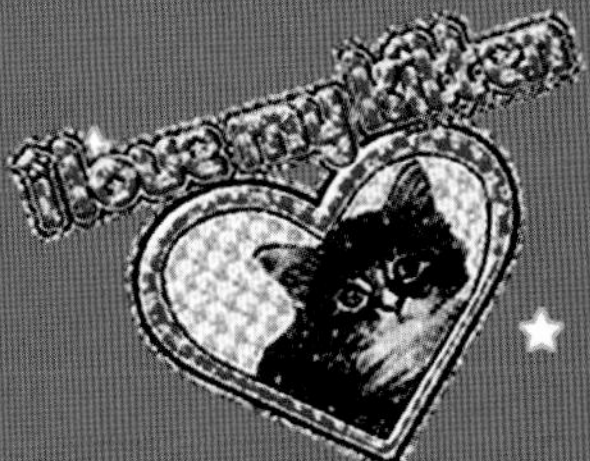

Bee in the house

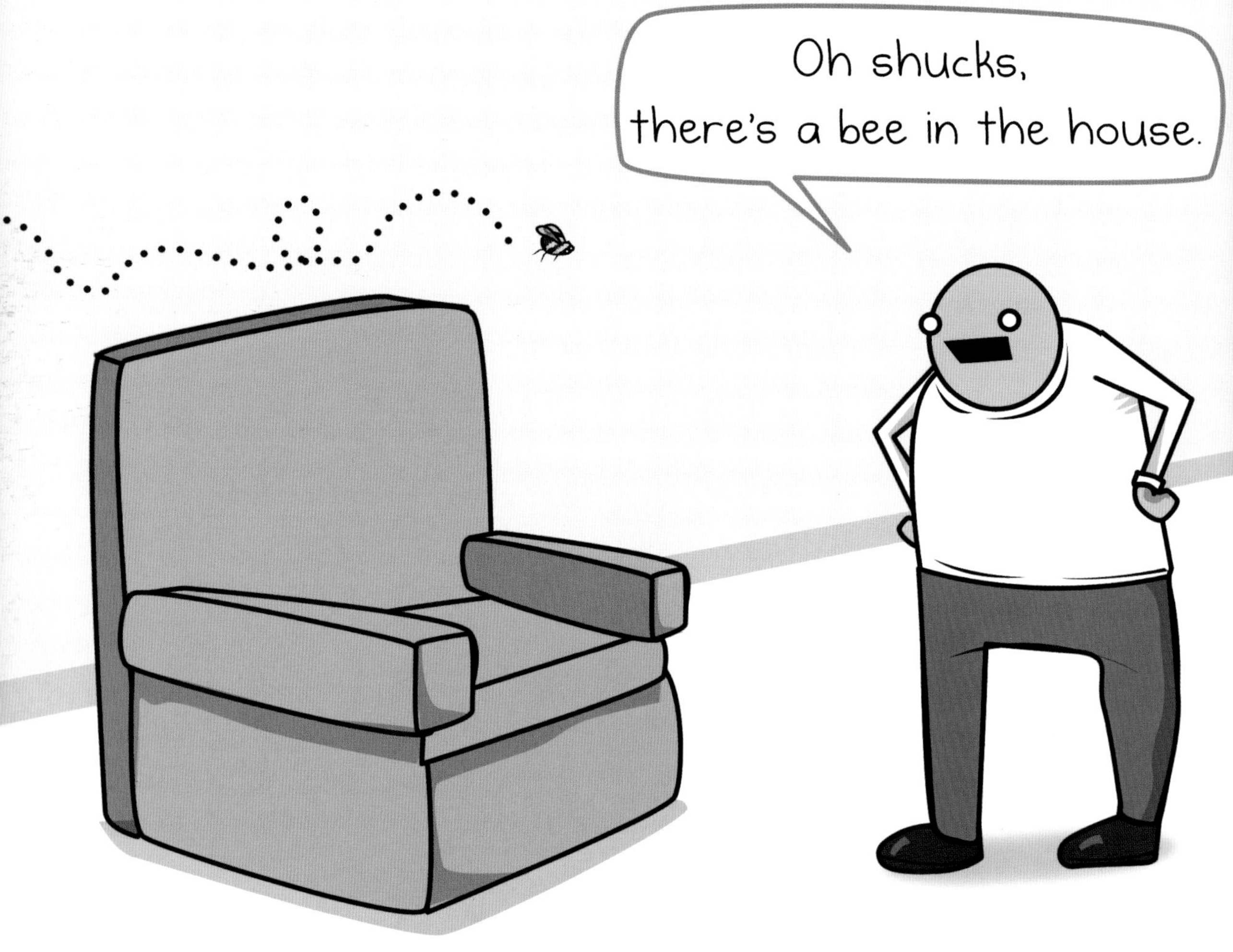
Oh shucks,
there's a bee in the house.

Bee in the car

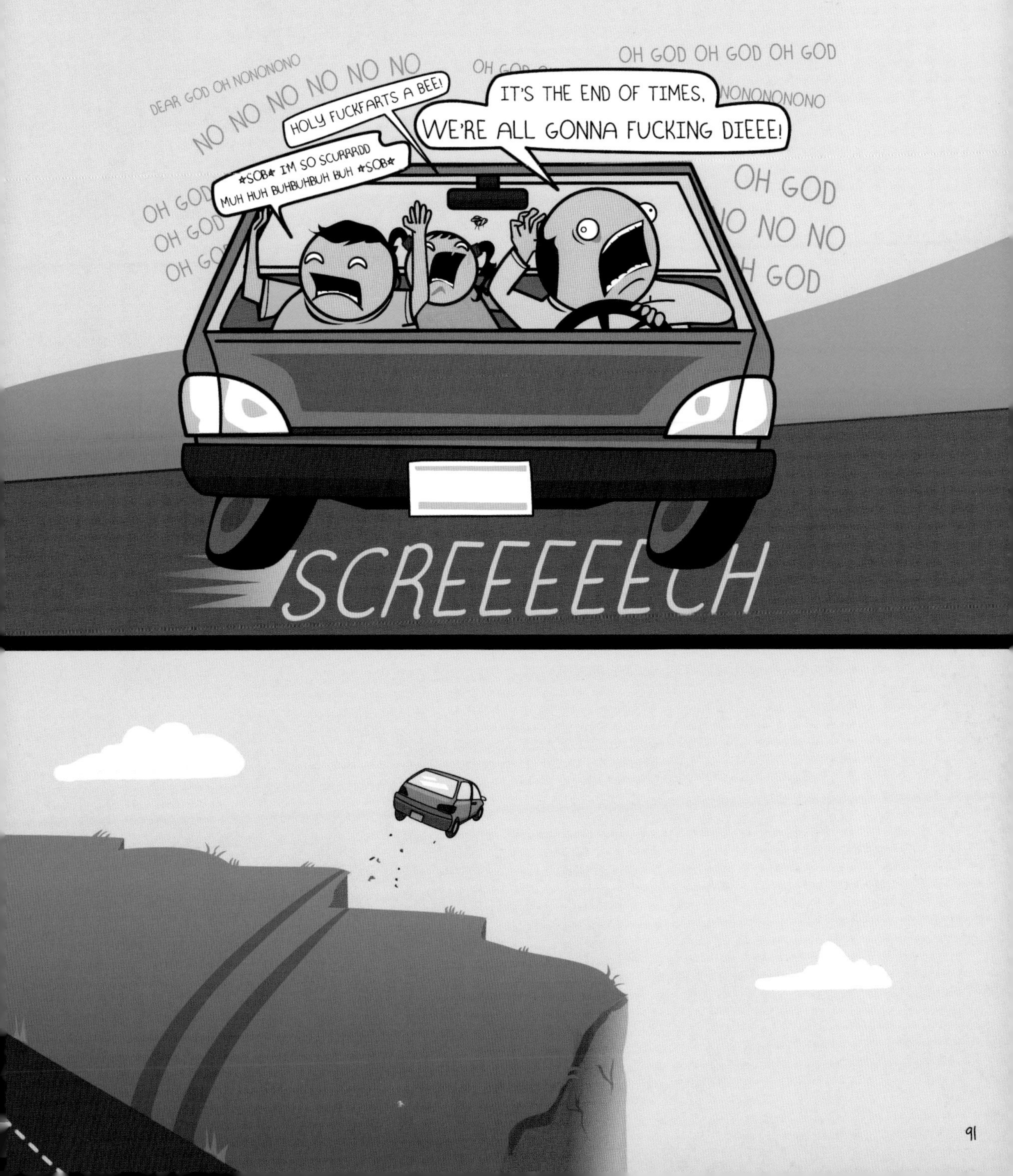
DEAR GOD OH NONONONO
NO NO NO NO NO NO
HOLY FUCKFARTS A BEE!
OH GOD OH GOD OH GOD
IT'S THE END OF TIMES, WE'RE ALL GONNA FUCKING DIEEE!
NONONONONO
SOB I'M SO SCURRRDD MUH HUH BUHBUHBUH BUH *SOB*
OH GOD
OH GOD
SCREEEEEECH

This is how I feel about buying Apps

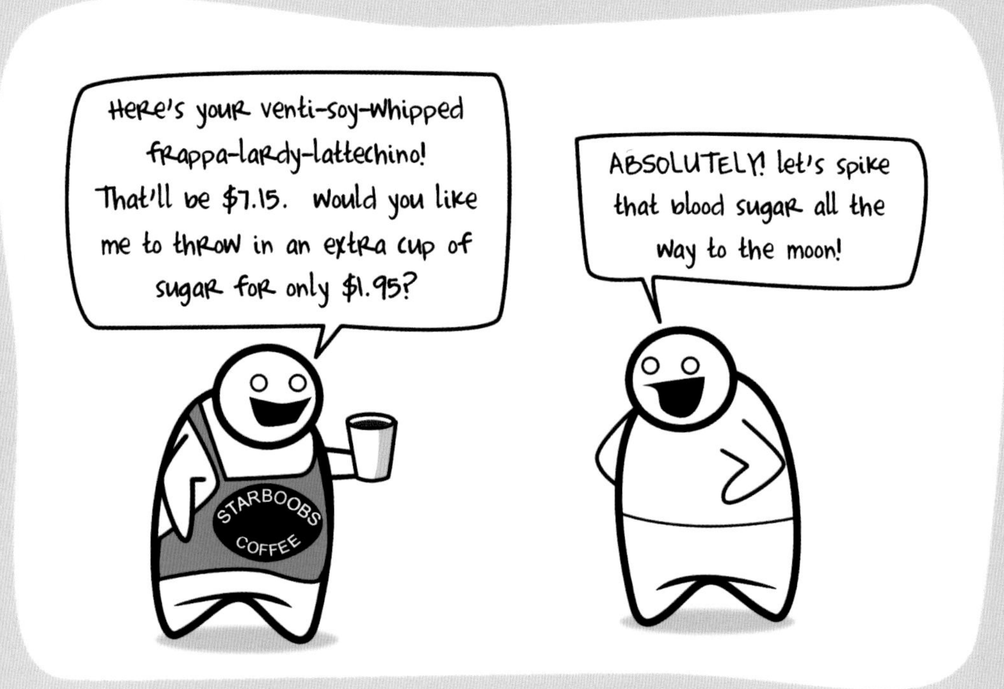
Here's your venti-soy-whipped frappa-lardy-lattechino! That'll be $7.15. Would you like me to throw in an extra cup of sugar for only $1.95?
ABSOLUTELY! let's spike that blood sugar all the way to the moon!
STARBOOBS COFFEE

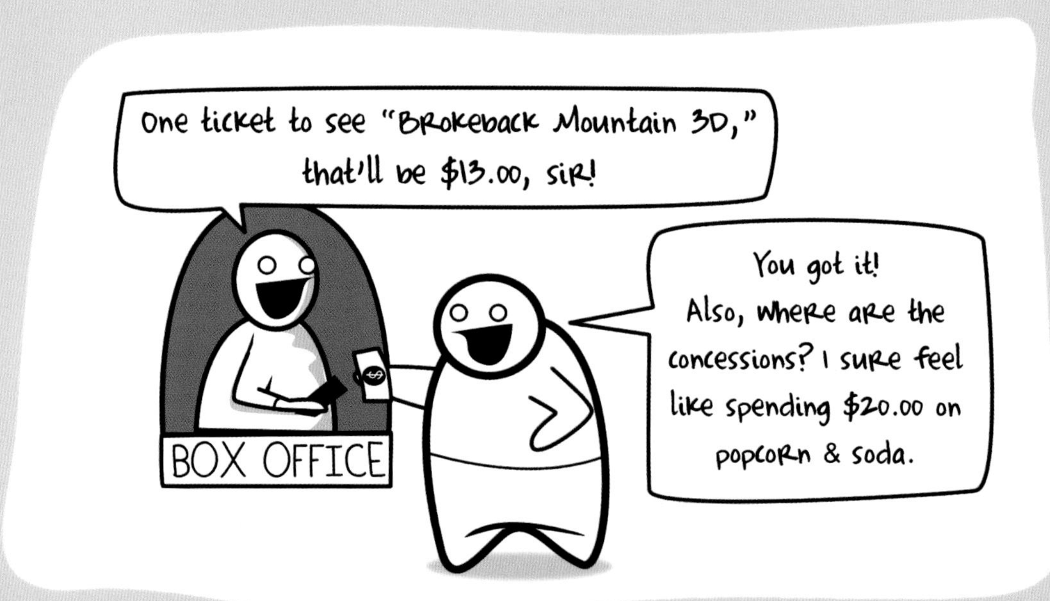
One ticket to see "Brokeback Mountain 3D," that'll be $13.00, sir!
You got it! Also, where are the concessions? I sure feel like spending $20.00 on popcorn & soda.
BOX OFFICE

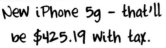

New iPhone 5g - that'll be $425.19 with tax.

Only $425?! That's 1/10 the cost of getting my wife's backhair removed! Charge it, fine sir! Charge like there's no tomorrow!

iPad 4GS with a protective case - that'll be $875.24

$875? That's all?! Hah! I'll take two: one for me and one for my furry friend here!

Downloading App: HorseHunter Extreme!

Click OK to confirm that you want to buy this app for 99 cents.
OK

Whoa whoa whoa! 99 cents?! Gosh, I dunno... that's a lot of money! I should call my accountant first, or at least sleep on it before making a decision.

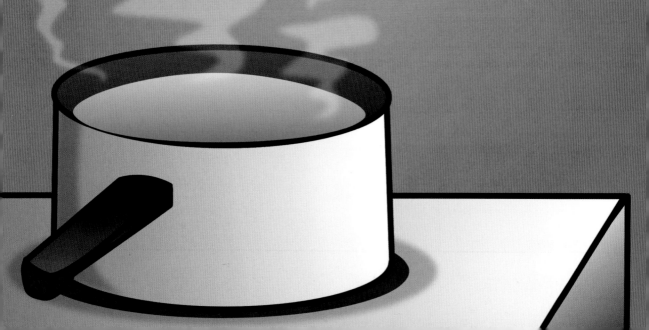
Why I don't cook at home

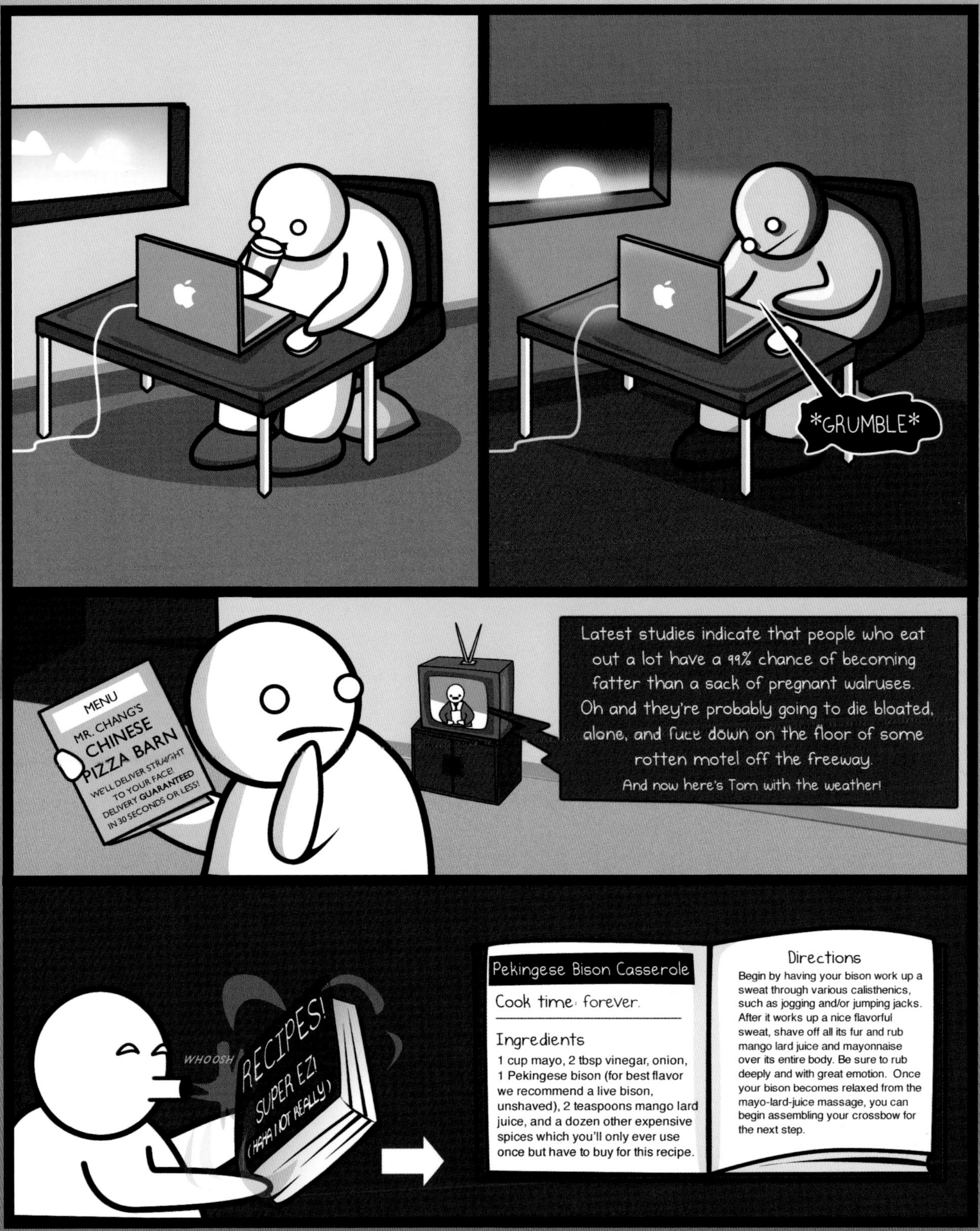
GRUMBLE
MENU
MR. CHANG'S CHINESE PIZZA BARN
WE'LL DELIVER STRAIGHT TO YOUR FACE!
DELIVERY GUARANTEED IN 30 SECONDS OR LESS!
Latest studies indicate that people who eat out a lot have a 99% chance of becoming fatter than a sack of pregnant walruses. Oh and they're probably going to die bloated, alone, and face down on the floor of some rotten motel off the freeway.
And now here's Tom with the weather!
WHOOSH
RECIPES! SUPER EZ! (HAHA! NOT REALLY)
Pekingese Bison Casserole
Cook time: forever.
Ingredients
1 cup mayo, 2 tbsp vinegar, onion, 1 Pekingese bison (for best flavor we recommend a live bison, unshaved), 2 teaspoons mango lard juice, and a dozen other expensive spices which you'll only ever use once but have to buy for this recipe.
Directions
Begin by having your bison work up a sweat through various calisthenics, such as jogging and/or jumping jacks. After it works up a nice flavorful sweat, shave off all its fur and rub mango lard juice and mayonnaise over its entire body. Be sure to rub deeply and with great emotion. Once your bison becomes relaxed from the mayo-lard-juice massage, you can begin assembling your crossbow for the next step.

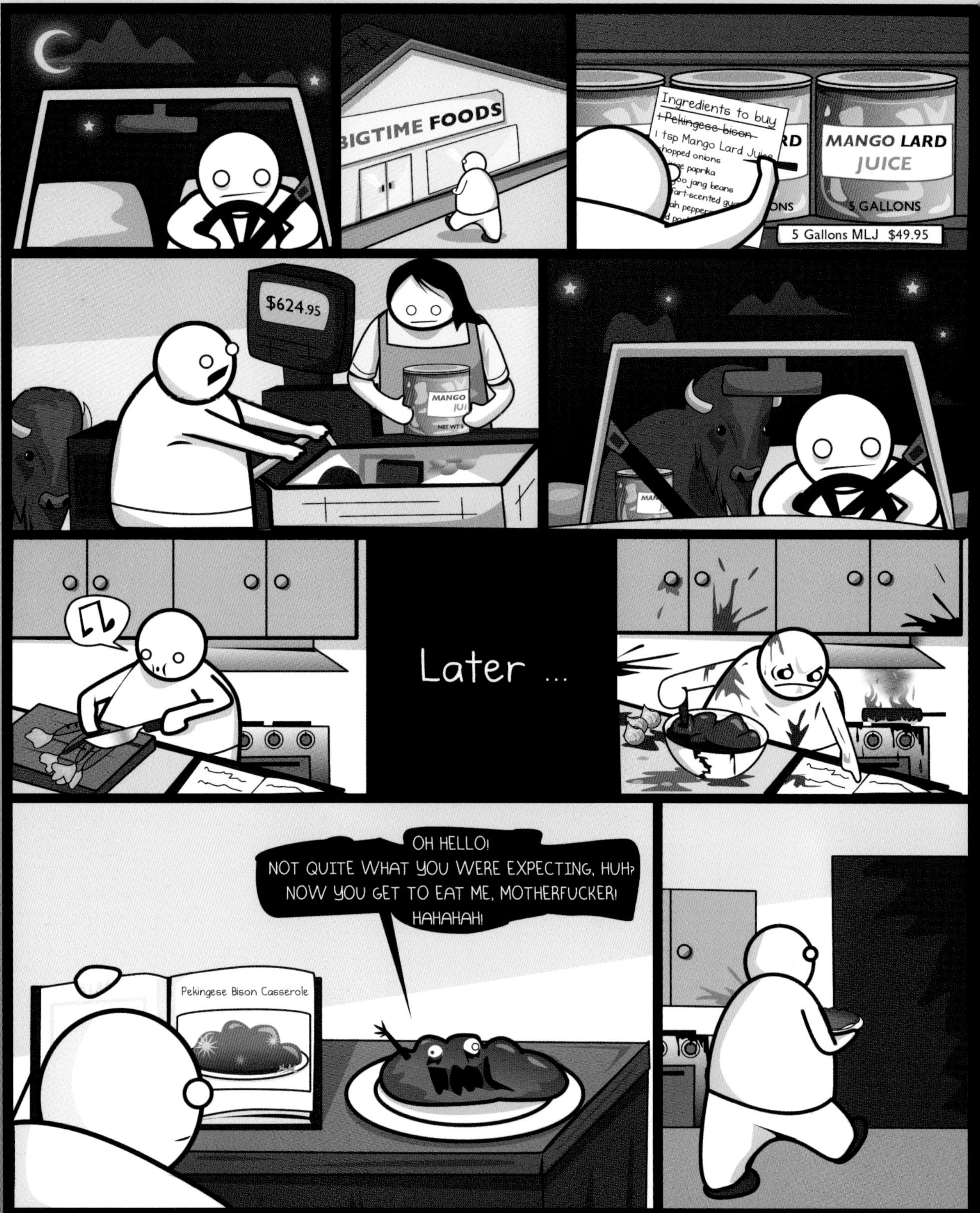
BIGTIME FOODS
Ingredients to buy
Pekingese bison
MANGO LARD JUICE
5 GALLONS
5 Gallons MLJ $49.95
$624.95
Later ...
OH HELLO!
NOT QUITE WHAT YOU WERE EXPECTING, HUH?
NOW YOU GET TO EAT ME, MOTHERFUCKER!
HAHAHAH!
Pekingese Bison Casserole

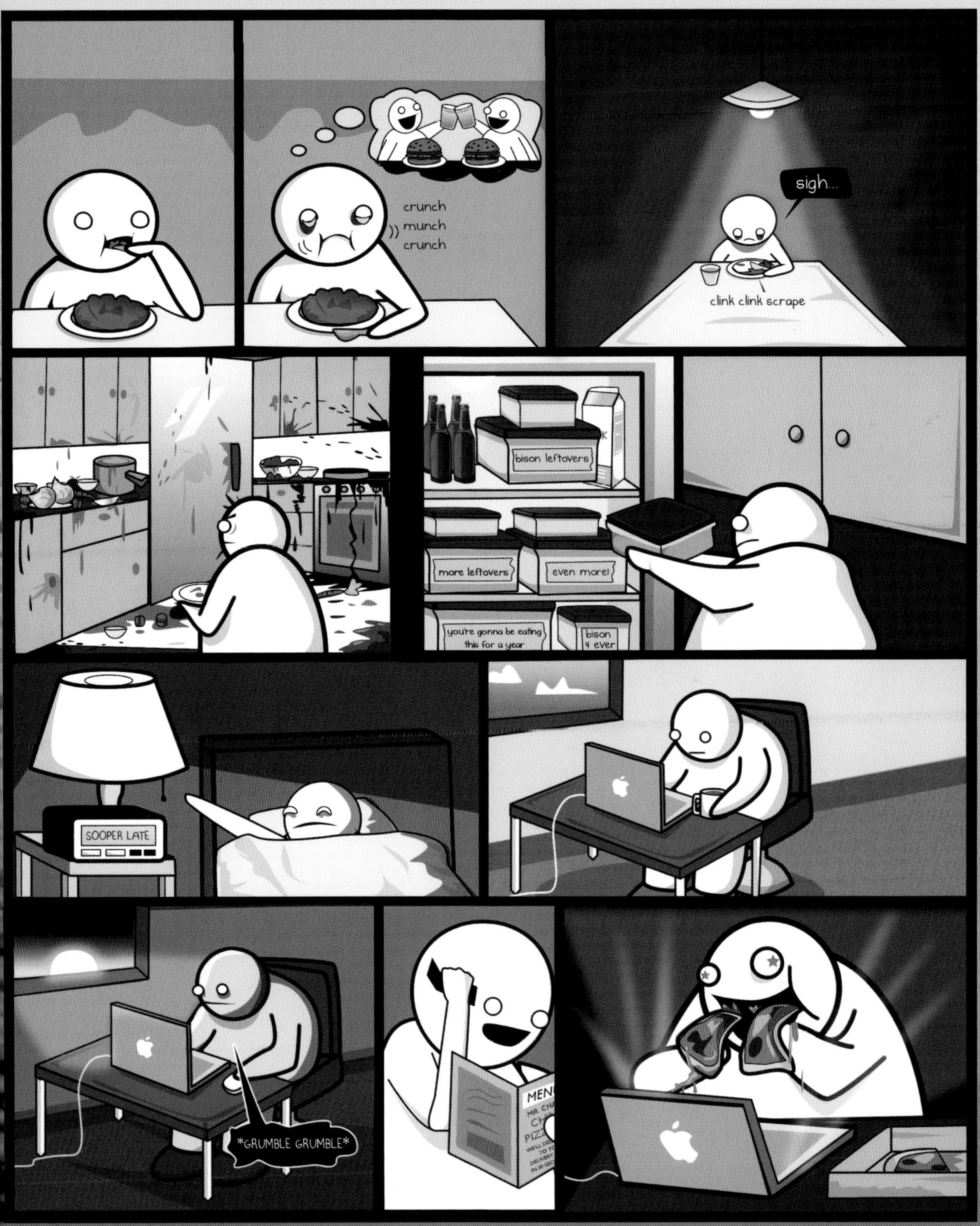
crunch
munch
crunch
sigh...
clink clink scrape
bison leftovers
more leftovers
even more!
you're gonna be eating this for a year
bison 4 ever
SOOPER LATE
GRUMBLE GRUMBLE

What I want from a restaurant website:

- Menu
- Specials and happy hour info
  (Including social promotions such as Foursquare, Groupon, and Twitter specials)
- Address with a link to Google maps
- Online reservation system that actually works
  (instead of one where I make a reservation online, show up, and the hostess gives me a blank, confused stare when I tell her my name)
- Hours of operation, parking and contact info

What I get instead:

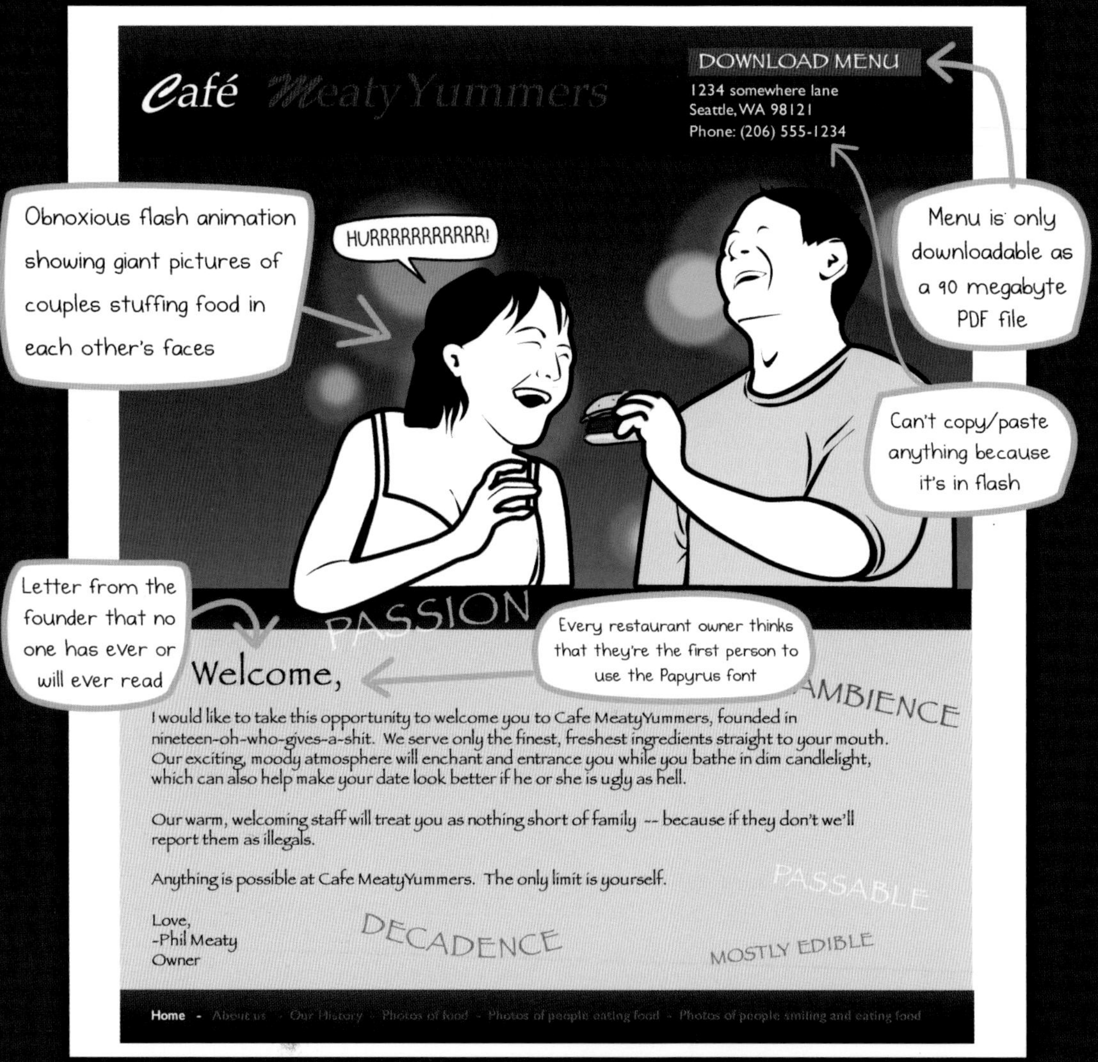

Café MeatyYummers
DOWNLOAD MENU
1234 somewhere lane
Seattle, WA 98121
Phone: (206) 555-1234
Obnoxious flash animation showing giant pictures of couples stuffing food in each other's faces
HURRRRRRRRRRRR!
Menu is only downloadable as a 90 megabyte PDF file
Can't copy/paste anything because it's in flash
Letter from the founder that no one has ever or will ever read
PASSION
Every restaurant owner thinks that they're the first person to use the Papyrus font
AMBIENCE
Welcome,
I would like to take this opportunity to welcome you to Cafe MeatyYummers, founded in nineteen-oh-who-gives-a-shit. We serve only the finest, freshest ingredients straight to your mouth. Our exciting, moody atmosphere will enchant and entrance you while you bathe in dim candlelight, which can also help make your date look better if he or she is ugly as hell.
Our warm, welcoming staff will treat you as nothing short of family -- because if they don't we'll report them as illegals.
Anything is possible at Cafe MeatyYummers. The only limit is yourself.
PASSABLE
Love,
-Phil Meaty
Owner
DECADENCE
MOSTLY EDIBLE
Home - About us - Our History - Photos of food - Photos of people eating food - Photos of people smiling and eating food

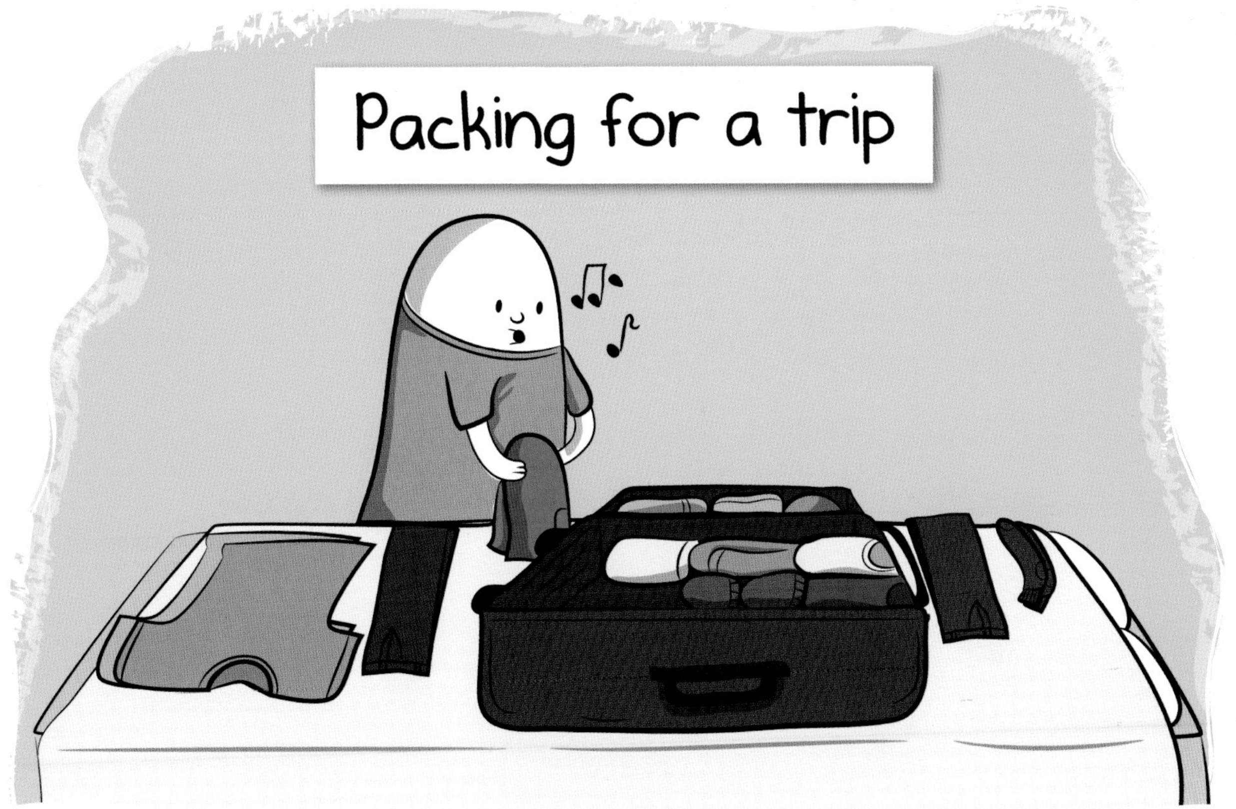
Packing for a trip

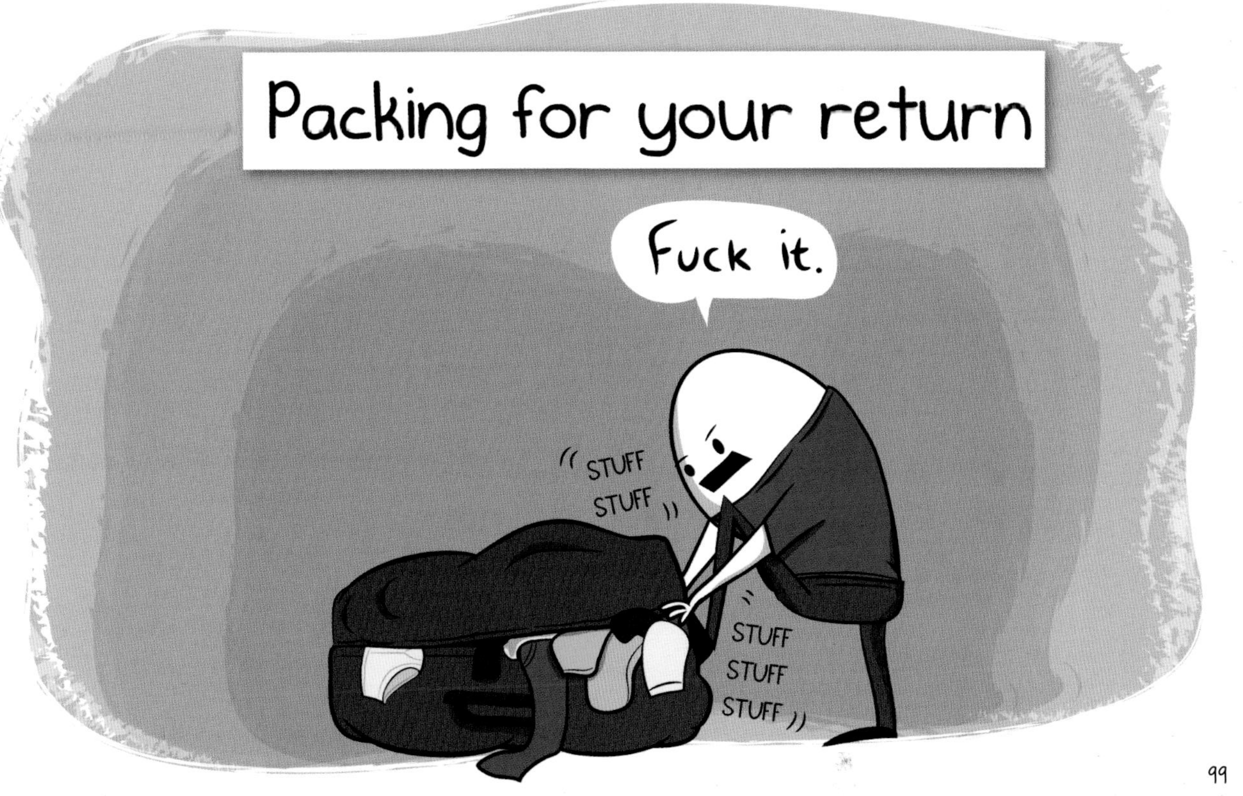
Packing for your return
Fuck it.
STUFF
STUFF
STUFF
STUFF
STUFF

Dear Sriracha,

a.k.a. Rooster Sauce

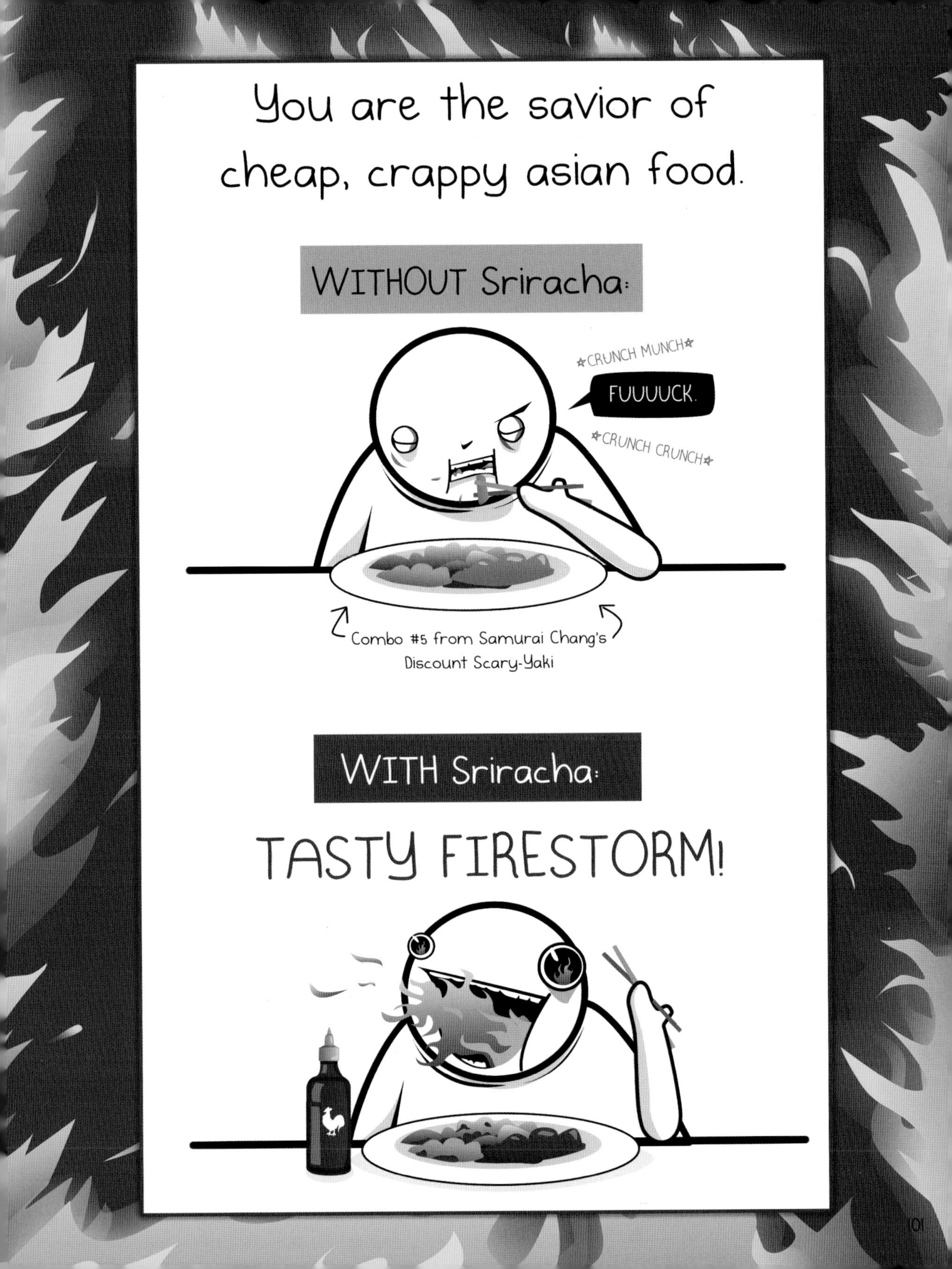

You are the savior of cheap, crappy asian food.
WITHOUT Sriracha:
✰CRUNCH MUNCH✰
FUUUUCK.
✰CRUNCH CRUNCH✰
Combo #5 from Samurai Chang's Discount Scary-Yaki
WITH Sriracha:
TASTY FIRESTORM!

You're good on pizza, sushi, and pretty much any animal who has passed through death and fire and wound up in my mouth.

And you're especially helpful when someone who doesn't like spicy food tries to eat from my plate.

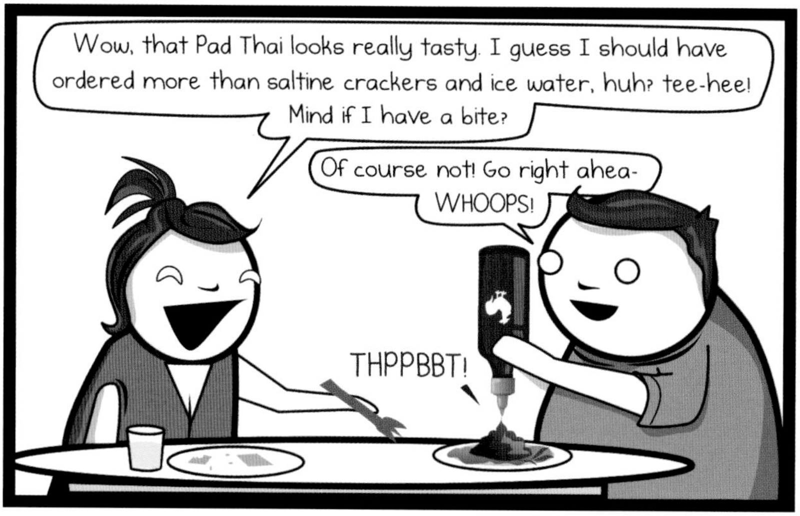
Wow, that Pad Thai looks really tasty. I guess I should have ordered more than saltine crackers and ice water, huh? tee-hee! Mind if I have a bite?
Of course not! Go right ahea- WHOOPS!
THPPBBT!

(I call this practice "Napalming the Jungle.")

And if I accidentally apply too much Sriracha, I simply power through the pain and build my tolerance.

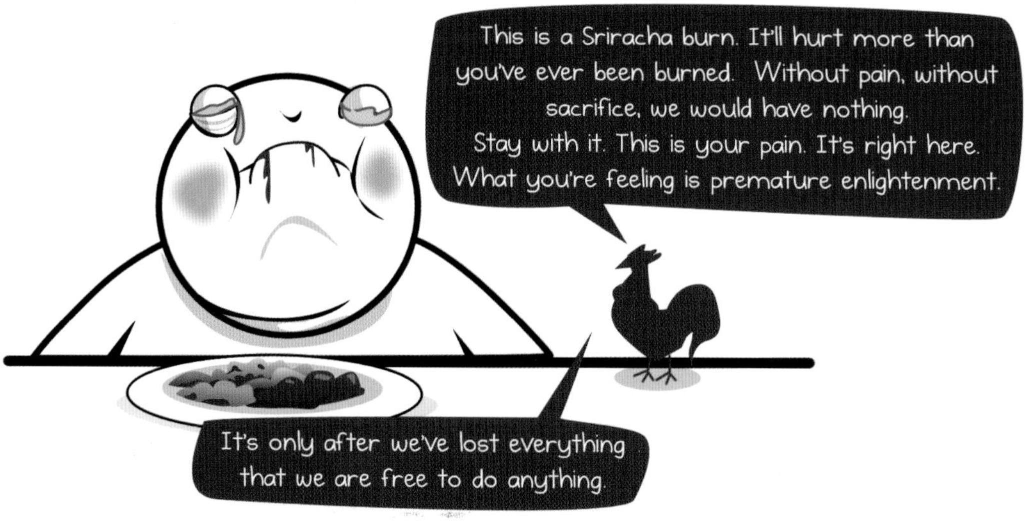
This is a Sriracha burn. It'll hurt more than you've ever been burned. Without pain, without sacrifice, we would have nothing. Stay with it. This is your pain. It's right here. What you're feeling is premature enlightenment.
It's only after we've lost everything that we are free to do anything.

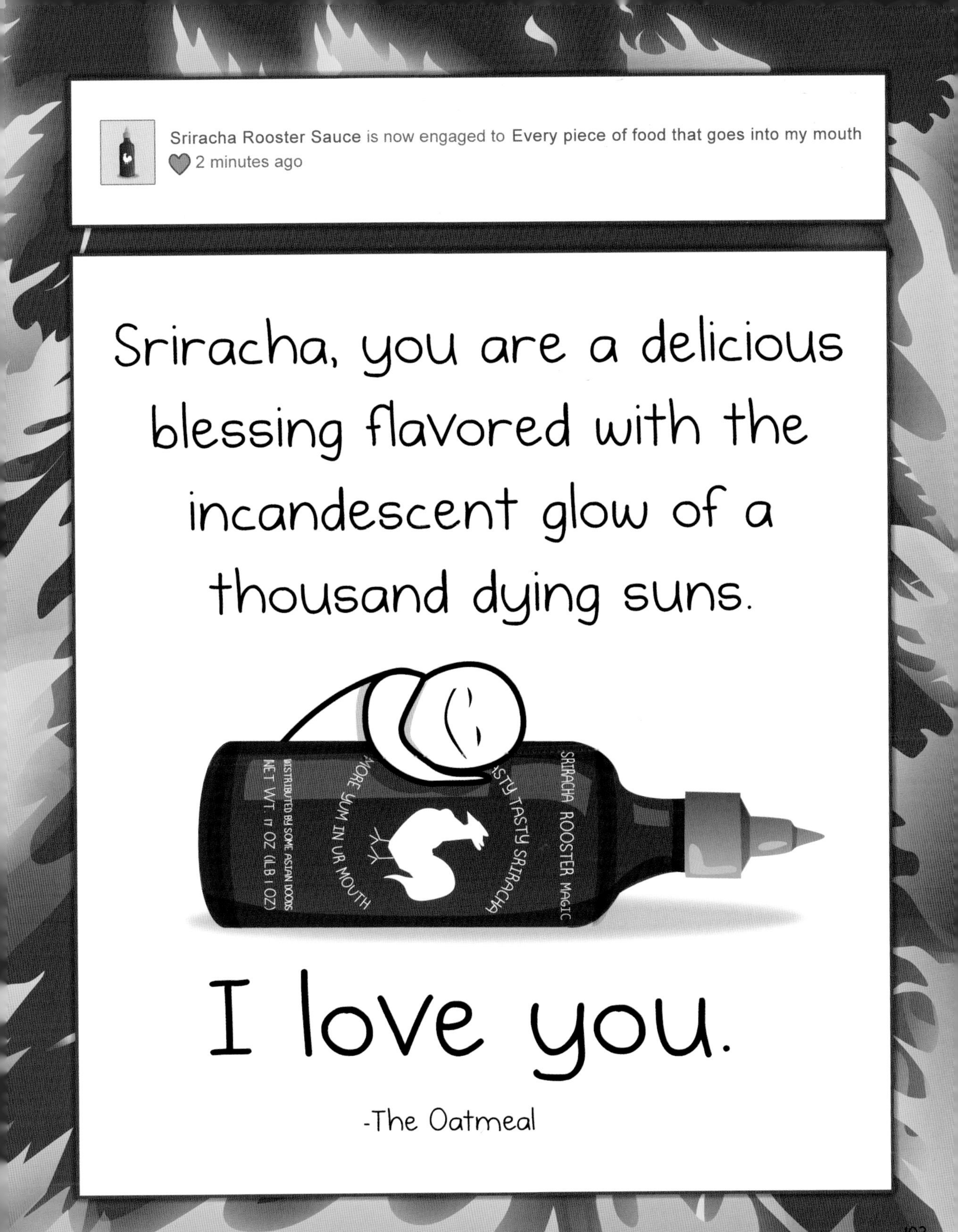
Sriracha Rooster Sauce is now engaged to Every piece of food that goes into my mouth
2 minutes ago
Sriracha, you are a delicious blessing flavored with the incandescent glow of a thousand dying suns.
SRIRACHA ROOSTER MAGIC
TASTY TASTY SRIRACHA
MORE YUM IN UR MOUTH
DISTRIBUTED BY SOME ASIAN DOODS
NET WT. 17 OZ (1LB 1 OZ)
I love you.
-The Oatmeal

A woman wearing nothing but a t-shirt:

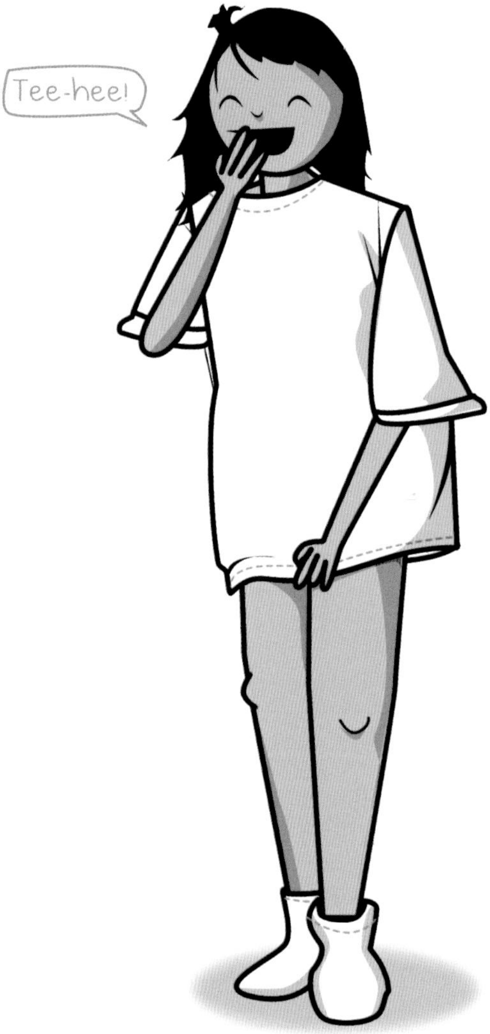
Tee-hee!

✓ Sexy

✓ Playful

✓ Cute

A man wearing nothing but a t-shirt:

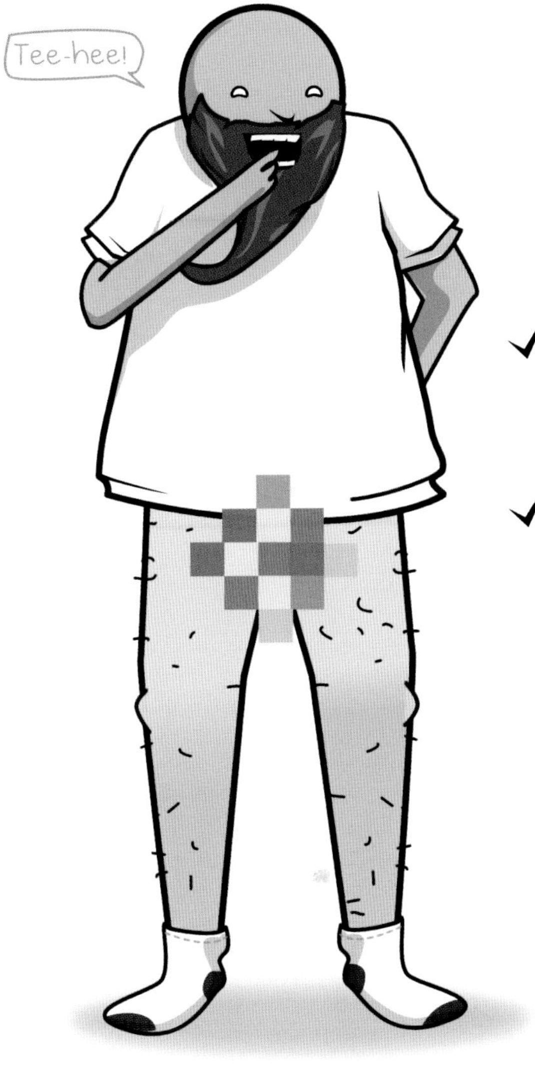
Tee-hee!

✓ Penis looks like a sea cucumber poking out of a wizard's robe

✓ Pretty much the most awful looking thing in the history of awful looking things

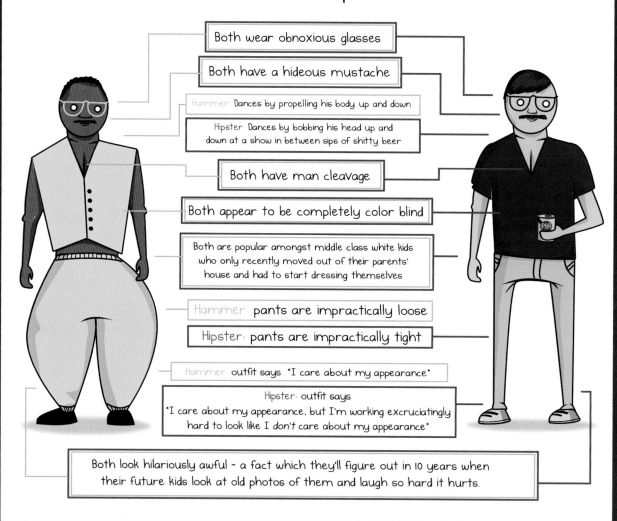

Hammer Pants VS Hipsters

A visual comparison

Both wear obnoxious glasses

Both have a hideous mustache

Hammer: Dances by propelling his body up and down

Hipster: Dances by bobbing his head up and down at a show in between sips of shitty beer

Both have man cleavage

Both appear to be completely color blind

Both are popular amongst middle class white kids who only recently moved out of their parents' house and had to start dressing themselves

Hammer: pants are impractically loose

Hipster: pants are impractically tight

Hammer: outfit says "I care about my appearance"

Hipster: outfit says "I care about my appearance, but I'm working excruciatingly hard to look like I don't care about my appearance"

Both look hilariously awful — a fact which they'll figure out in 10 years when their future kids look at old photos of them and laugh so hard it hurts.

 # How I interpret my beverage options on an airplane

Option A:
Ginger Ale

Benefits:

✓ Good for an upset stomach

✓ Airplanes always have it

✓ I never order it anywhere except at 30k feet. It's magic skyjuice.

✓ So tasty I often suspect it's made from bald eagle tears

Option B:
A bunch of other bullshit drinks

Benefits:

✓ Who gives a fuck it's not ginger ale

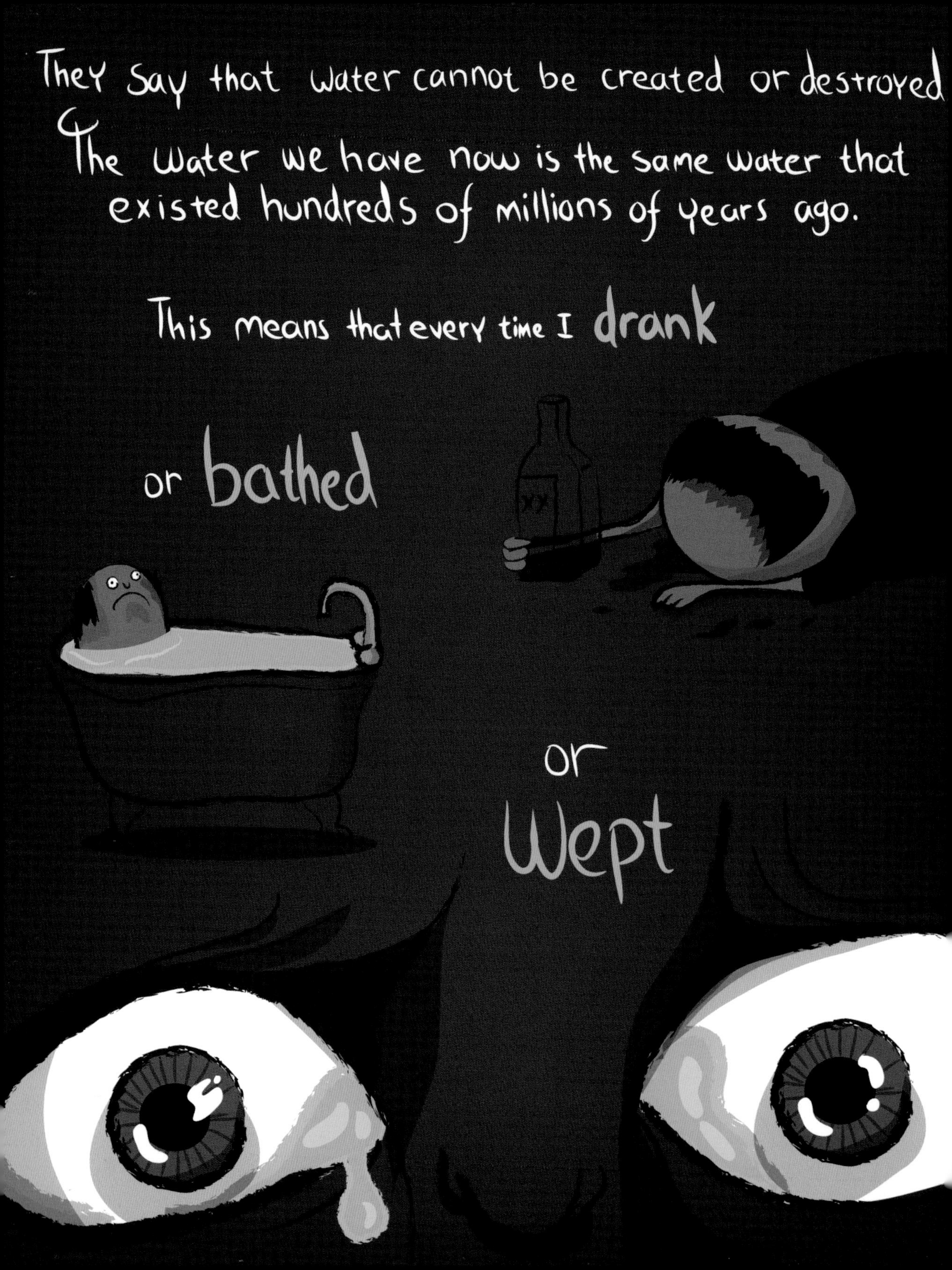
They say that water cannot be created or destroyed
& The water we have now is the same water that existed hundreds of millions of years ago.
This means that every time I drank
or bathed
or Wept

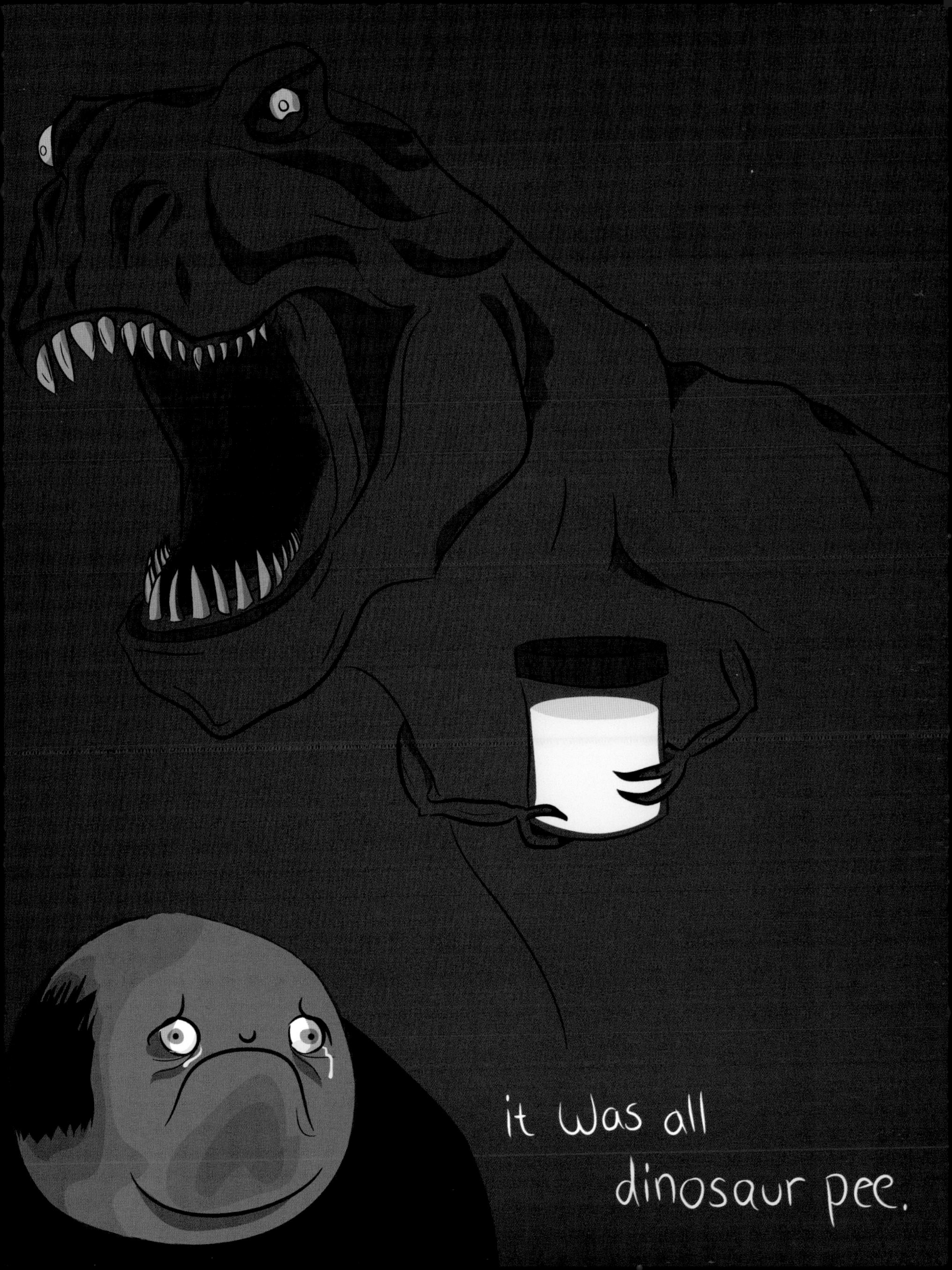
it was all
dinosaur pee.

Hamster Atonement

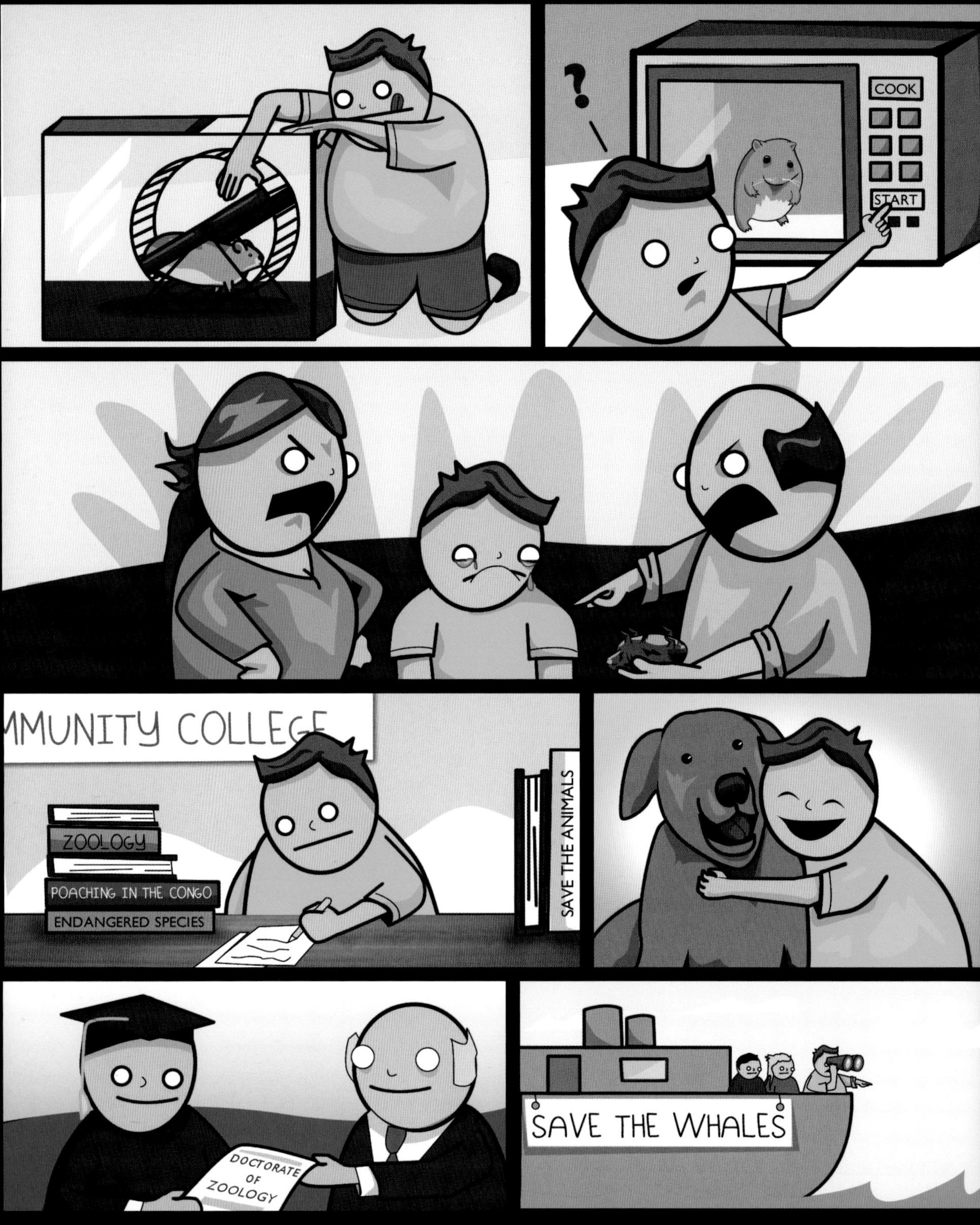
COOK
START
?
MMUNITY COLLEGE
ZOOLOGY
POACHING IN THE CONGO
ENDANGERED SPECIES
SAVE THE ANIMALS
DOCTORATE OF ZOOLOGY
SAVE THE WHALES

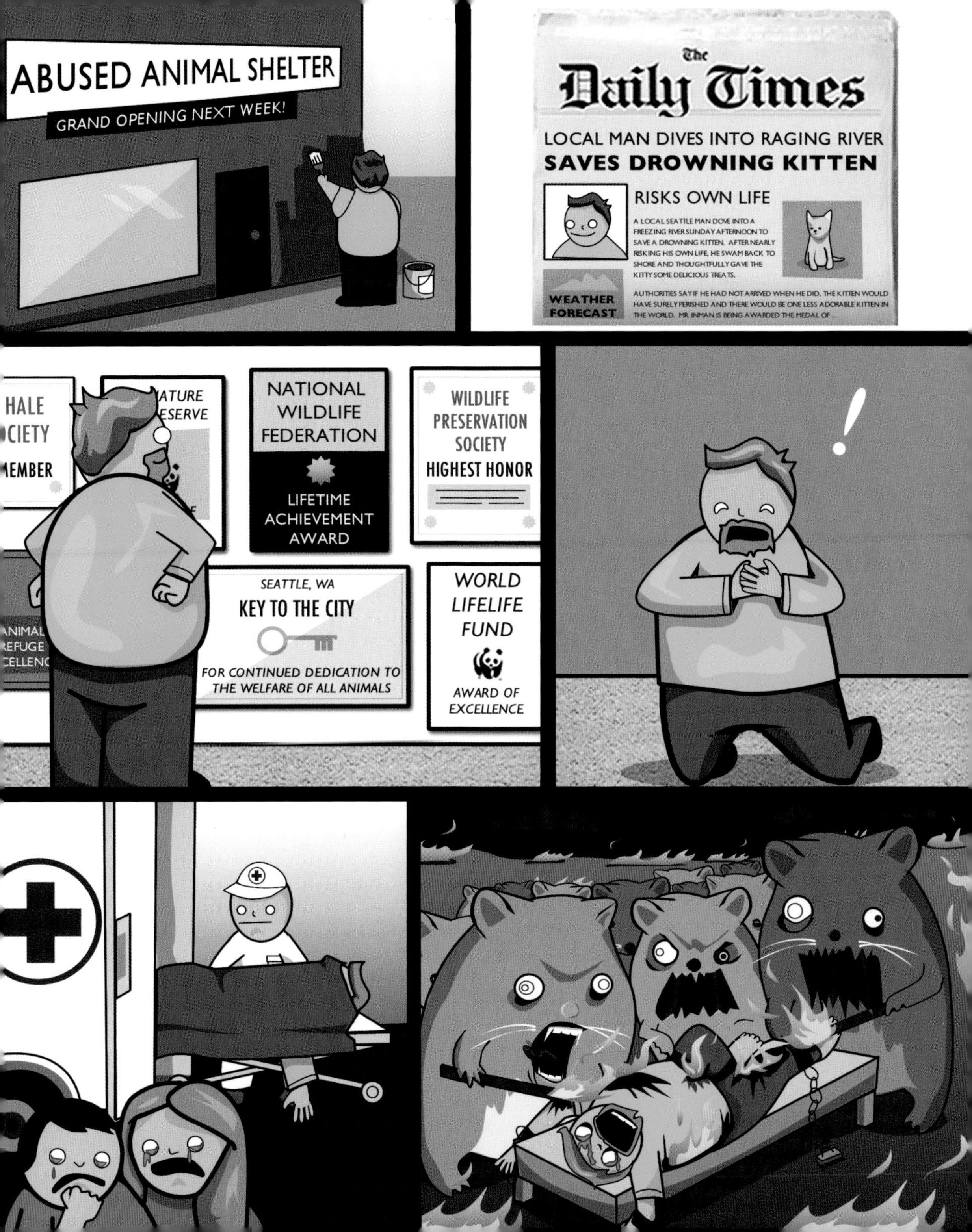
ABUSED ANIMAL SHELTER
GRAND OPENING NEXT WEEK!
The Daily Times
LOCAL MAN DIVES INTO RAGING RIVER
SAVES DROWNING KITTEN
RISKS OWN LIFE
A LOCAL SEATTLE MAN DOVE INTO A FREEZING RIVER SUNDAY AFTERNOON TO SAVE A DROWNING KITTEN. AFTER NEARLY RISKING HIS OWN LIFE, HE SWAM BACK TO SHORE AND THOUGHTFULLY GAVE THE KITTY SOME DELICIOUS TREATS.
AUTHORITIES SAY IF HE HAD NOT ARRIVED WHEN HE DID, THE KITTEN WOULD HAVE SURELY PERISHED AND THERE WOULD BE ONE LESS ADORABLE KITTEN IN THE WORLD. MR. INMAN IS BEING AWARDED THE MEDAL OF ...
WEATHER FORECAST
NATIONAL WILDLIFE FEDERATION
LIFETIME ACHIEVEMENT AWARD
WILDLIFE PRESERVATION SOCIETY
HIGHEST HONOR
SEATTLE, WA
KEY TO THE CITY
FOR CONTINUED DEDICATION TO THE WELFARE OF ALL ANIMALS
WORLD LIFELIFE FUND
AWARD OF EXCELLENCE
!

Why
CAPTAIN HIGGINS
IS MY FAVORITE
PARASITIC FLATWORM

Captain Higgins is a liver fluke (worm) whose real name is

Dicrocoelium dendriticum.

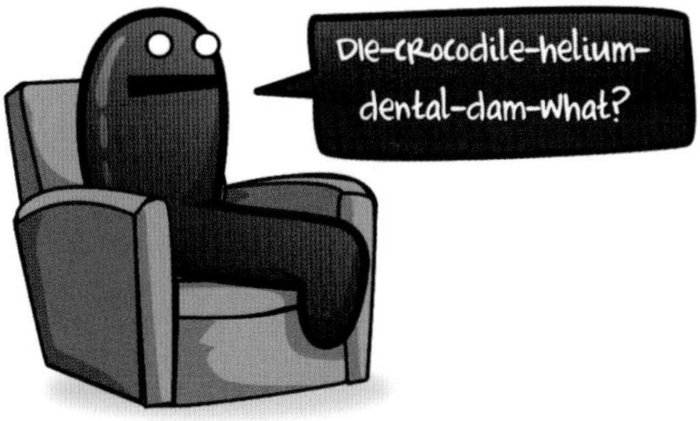
Die-crocodile-helium-dental-dam-what?

That name is impossible to remember, however, and it doesn't give him the respect he deserves.

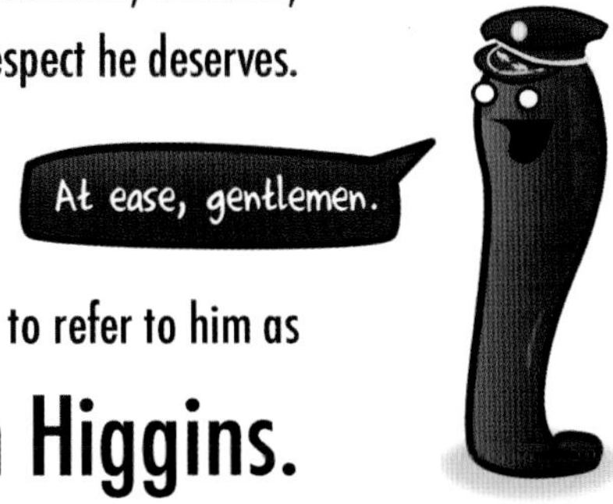
At ease, gentlemen.

Therefore it's just better to refer to him as

Captain Higgins.

Captain Higgins' childhood is spent in a juicy pile of cow dung where he hangs out and waits for a snail to come by for a little poopy snack.

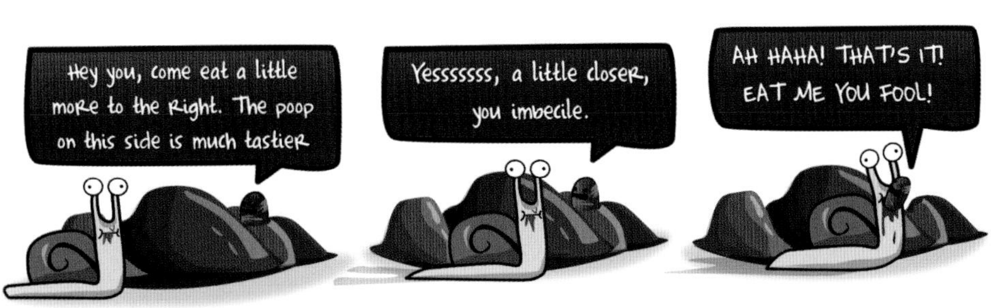
Hey you, come eat a little more to the right. The poop on this side is much tastier
Yesssssss, a little closer, you imbecile.
AH HAHA! THAT'S IT! EAT ME YOU FOOL!

 **Host #1**

Once the snail eats the dung, the Captain winds up inside his gut. From there he drills into the snail's digestive tract where he grows to be a teenager.

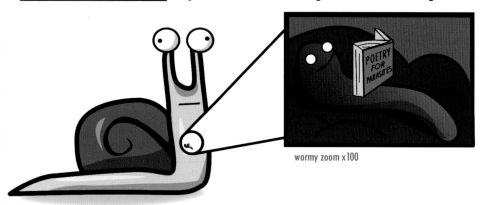

wormy zoom x100

The snail eventually sheds out **slime balls** which the Captain rides off into the world.

Wooooo! Thanks for the free room and board, you slobbering, worthless simpleton.

Ants drink from these slime balls and subsequently become infected by Captain Higgins.

Hey mister thirstypants, DRINK ME. I AM DELICIOUS.

 # Host #2

Once inside the ant's body, the Captain moves to a cluster of nerve cells which control its movements.

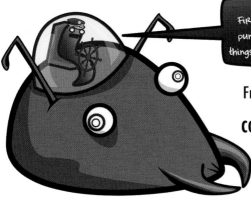

> You're mine now.
> First things first, let's go sucker punch a potato bug. I HATE those things - they give me the mega willies.

From this point on the Captain has **complete control** of the ant's

motor skills.

At first he stays in the colony doing normal ant-like things, but when the sun goes down the Captain drives the infected ant to the top of a blade of grass.

Once on top, he'll clamp the ant's jaws to the grass and stay there until the sun comes up.

When dawn returns, the Captain pilots the ant back down to the colony and he resumes his disguise with the rest of the ants.

> Hey, where'd you wander off to last night?

> Oh, uh ... I went for a walk. I needed to stretch my little anty appendages. I wasn't clutching a blade of grass or anything, if that's what you're implying.

Night after night, Captain Higgins will climb to the top of a blade of grass and wait.

The Captain is smart and knows that if he waits during the day, the heat from the sun will kill both him and the ant.

 **Host #3** Each night he'll wait until he's eventually **eaten** by a **grazing animal**, such as a cow or sheep.

Once eaten, the Captain winds up inside the **liver** of the infected animal and throws a party with all his other flatworm buddies.

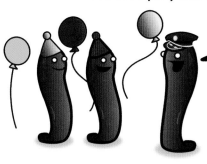

So this one time I had control of an ant and I made him eat his own eyeball while singing 'GREAT BALLS OF FIRE' to the colony. It was hilarious!

The party rages on, and eventually there's a little romance.

Technically we're both hermaphrodites, but that won't stop my love grenades from exploding your heart into little meaty spatters.

OOoh captain! ♥

Shortly thereafter, thousands of little **baby higlets** are born, which end up in the **feces** of the infected host.

Private higlets, for your first mission you'll be deployed by poopy dropship back to earth. GODSPEED, SOLDIER.

The dung lands and the cycle begins all over again.

Psst, hey you ... yeah, you ... the ugly guy. C'mere. The poop on this side tastes like nachos and raspberries.

In short:

Captain Higgins lives in **three** different hosts. He **leeches** from one, turns another into a **zombie slave**, and assaults the bowels of the third in order to perpetuate his own **awesomeness**.

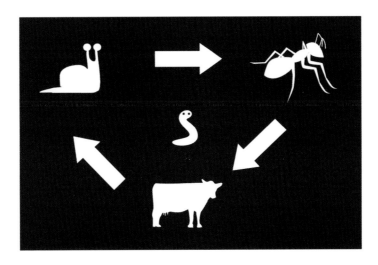

Well played, Captain.

When to use *i.e.* in a sentence

Ever done this?

"When eating a squirrel taco, Bigfoot always adds extra condiments, i.e., ranch dressing."

This is wrong!

Oh drats!
I've been using it wrong
AND I'm out of ranch!

I.e. is an abbreviation of a latin phrase meaning "that is."

It's not used for listing examples; it's used for clarifying a statement.

Think of it as "in essence" or "in other words."

By using it above we're declaring that ranch dressing is the only condiment in existence, which is false.

Sure is!
They forgot alligator dung and yak's blood!

In the previous example we should have used *e.g.*, which means "for example."

So when should I use *i.e.*?

Use *i.e.* when you want to explain what you just said in a different way. A definition, metaphor, or clarification can follow.

For example:

"The best way to take out a unicorn is with a Claymore, i.e., a directional mine which explodes shrapnel into a designated kill zone."

FRONT TOWARD ENEMY

Ideal configuration for blasting a unicorn into unrecognizable bits.

Another example:

"Eating a squirrel taco without any ranch dressing is like playing leapfrog with a unicorn, i.e., a very bad idea."

Here I come, tee-hee!

weeeeee!

An example of *e.g.*

"I love eating meat whose ingredients are a mystery, e.g., bologna, hot dogs, and spam."

In this example we used *e.g.* because it is not a finite list; other mystery meats are out there.

Thank God for that! I couldn't imagine a world without mystery meats!

It'd be like a world without shiny mustaches: sad, cruel, and empty

Another example of *e.g.*

"Women love admiring furry objects (e.g. koalas, armpits, and unkempt back hair)."

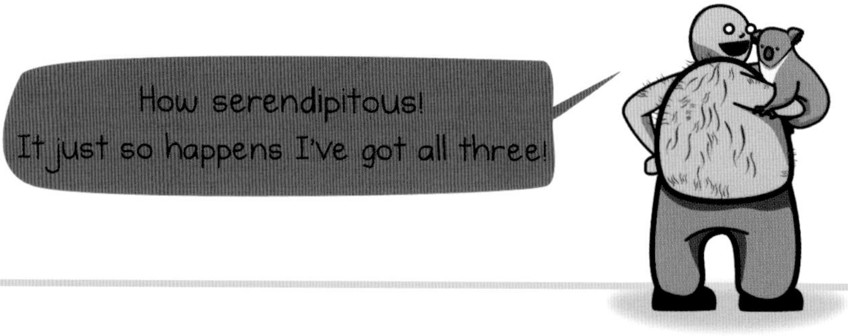

How serendipitous! It just so happens I've got all three!

Should I use parentheses or commas?

(e.g. stuff here)
(i.e. stuff here)

Both are acceptable.

, e.g., stuff here
, i.e., stuff here

Do I need a comma after the *e.g.* or *i.e.*?

Most style guides recommend that you use a comma.

"On Thursdays, I always wear my most expensive pair of pants, i.e., the ones made from rubies and panda bears."

In this example we use *i.e.* because it IS a finite list; the character only has one most expensive pair of pants.

In conclusion

e.g. = examples
(think "egg xamples")

i.e. = clarification
(think "in essence")

The End

Dear public toilets of the world,

these do not work:

Sanitary Sheet
First pull up, then down

All they do is:

➡ Soak up someone else's urine.

Believe it or not, we don't actually enjoy sitting on pee.

➡ Get scrunched up and only end up shielding less than 20% of our precious bums from bubonic ass plague. *

*The Oatmeal is not a doctor but is fairly certain this disease is out there and poses a threat to all citizens of this great country.

➡ Get eaten by the automatic flush,
so you have to put one on the seat and then race to sit down before the artificial intelligence of the toilet robot devours the sheet.

It's like playing nude musical chairs with Skynet.

Fear not, however!
I have a solution.

Disinfectant aerosol spray
(install a wall-mounted dispenser if you're worried about morons stealing the can)

Toilet paper
No additional cost to you!
More money in your pocket!
THIS MEANS SOMEDAY YOU CAN AFFORD A HOT TUB AND FILL IT WITH PROSTITUTES AND GOLD.

1. Spray toilet paper or seat
2. Wipe seat clean
(we use this TP anyway to wipe the seat before putting a sheet on it)

The result?
HAPPY PEOPLE WITH HAPPY ASSES!

How's that marvelous ass of yours, Bill?

Funny you should ask, because it just so happens to feel ASS-tounding!

EXCELLENT! CARRY ON, SOLDIER!

What you **imagine** your life will be like after having kids

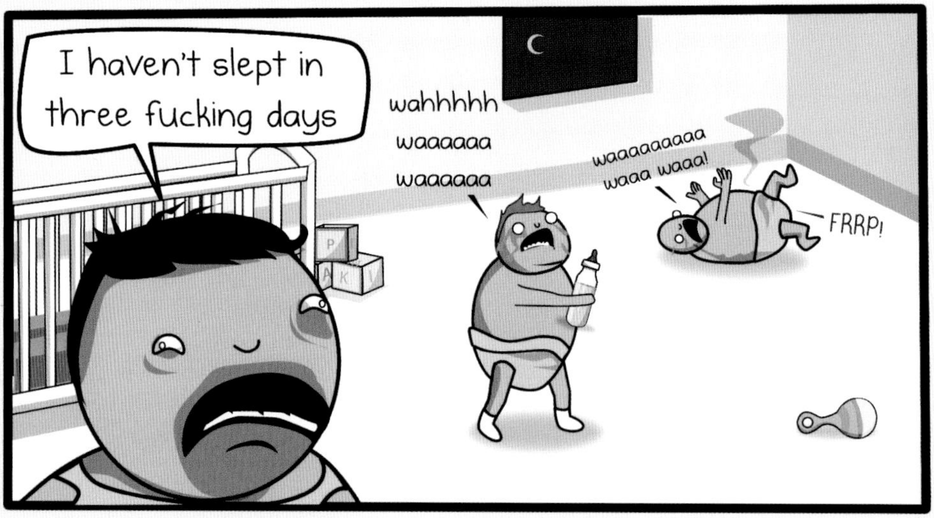
I haven't slept in three fucking days
wahhhhh
waaaaaa
waaaaaa
waaaaaaaaa
waaa waaa!
FRRP!

What your life is **really** like after having kids

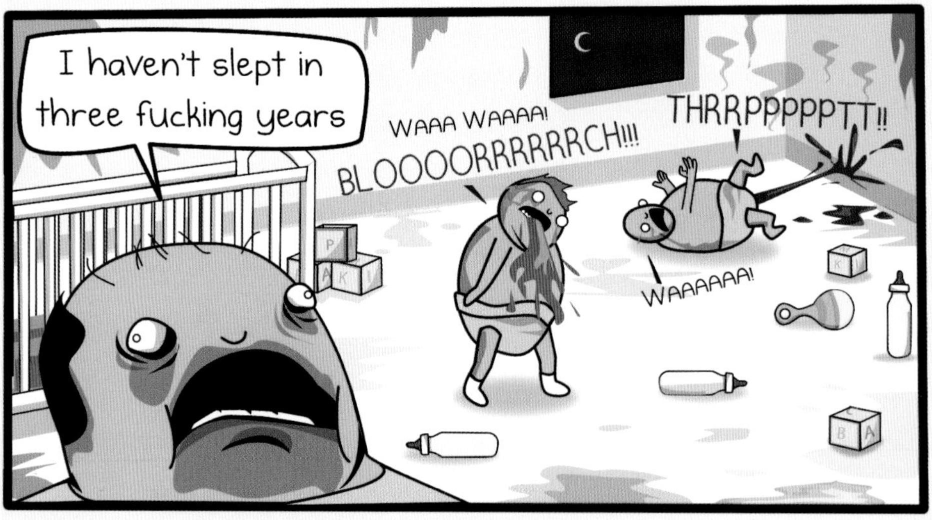
I haven't slept in three fucking years
WAAA WAAAA!
BLOOOORRRRRRCH!!!
THRRPPPPPPTT!!
WAAAAAA!

The primary difference between North and South Korea

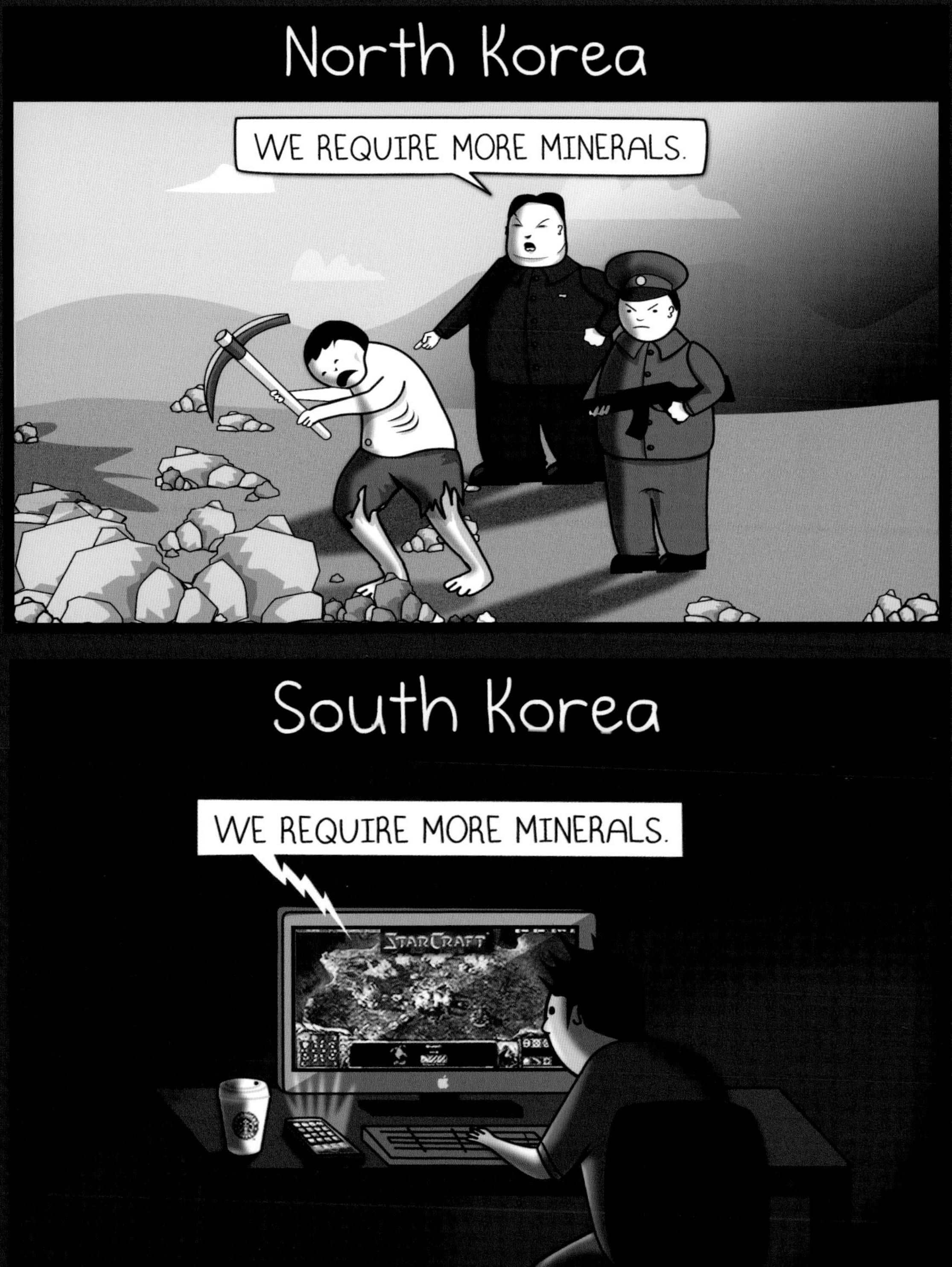
North Korea
WE REQUIRE MORE MINERALS.
South Korea
WE REQUIRE MORE MINERALS.
STARCRAFT

What it's like to play
online games as a grown-up

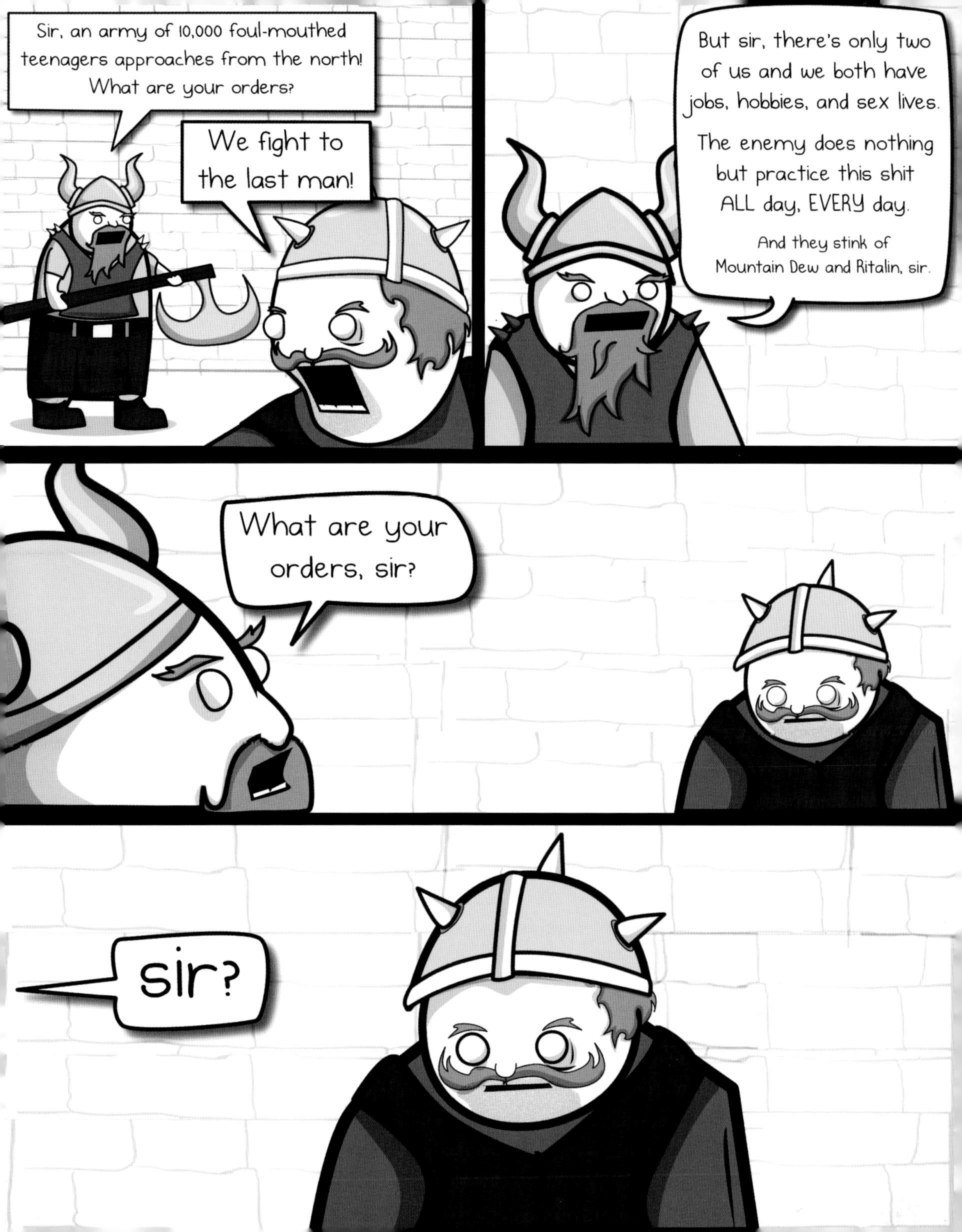

Sir, an army of 10,000 foul-mouthed teenagers approaches from the north! What are your orders?
We fight to the last man!
But sir, there's only two of us and we both have jobs, hobbies, and sex lives.
The enemy does nothing but practice this shit ALL day, EVERY day.
And they stink of Mountain Dew and Ritalin, sir.
What are your orders, sir?
sir?

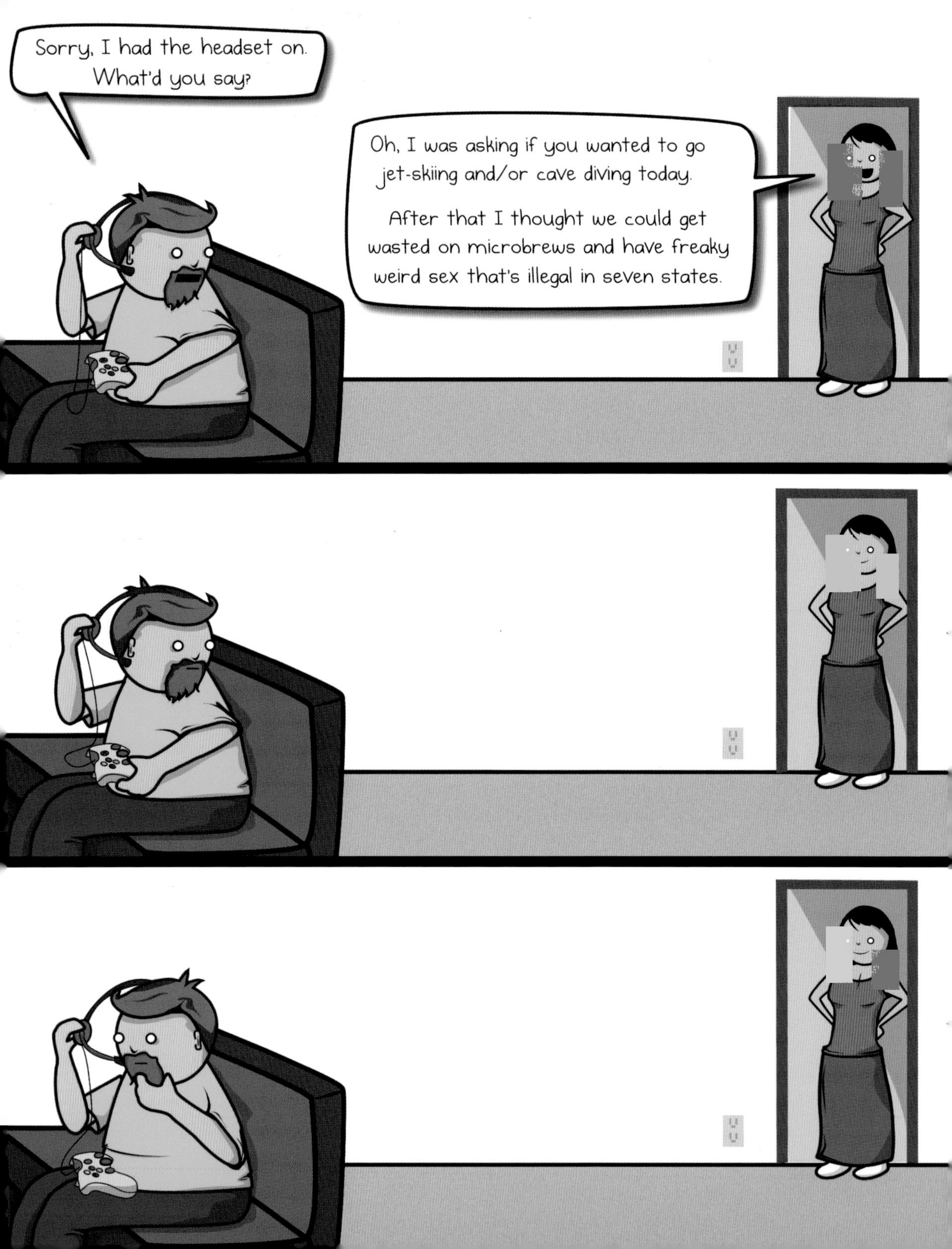
Sorry, I had the headset on. What'd you say?
Oh, I was asking if you wanted to go jet-skiing and/or cave diving today.
After that I thought we could get wasted on microbrews and have freaky weird sex that's illegal in seven states.

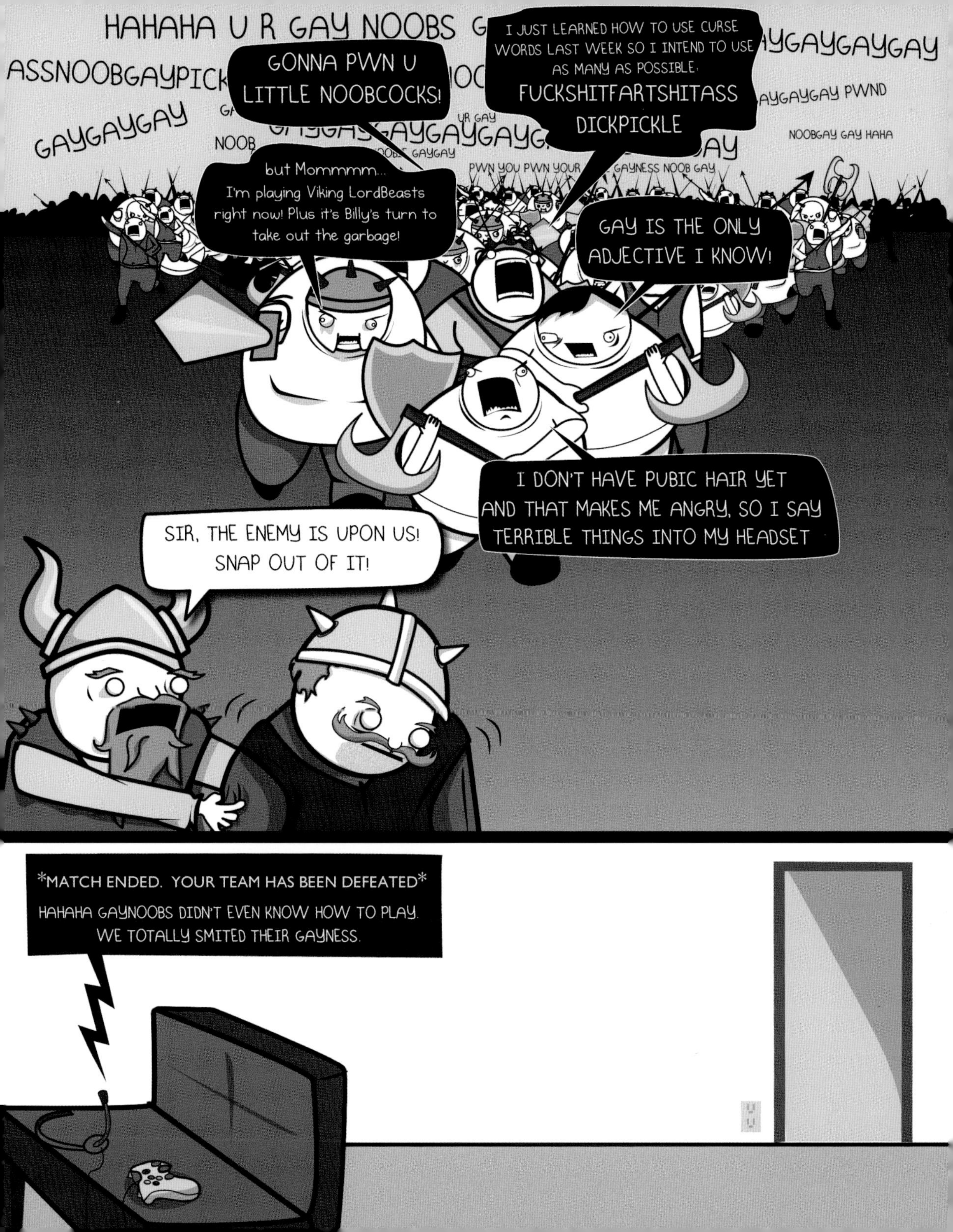
HAHAHA U R GAY NOOBS
GONNA PWN U LITTLE NOOBCOCKS!
I JUST LEARNED HOW TO USE CURSE WORDS LAST WEEK SO I INTEND TO USE AS MANY AS POSSIBLE.
FUCKSHITFARTSHITASS DICKPICKLE
but Mommmm... I'm playing Viking LordBeasts right now! Plus it's Billy's turn to take out the garbage!
GAY IS THE ONLY ADJECTIVE I KNOW!
I DON'T HAVE PUBIC HAIR YET AND THAT MAKES ME ANGRY, SO I SAY TERRIBLE THINGS INTO MY HEADSET
SIR, THE ENEMY IS UPON US! SNAP OUT OF IT!
MATCH ENDED. YOUR TEAM HAS BEEN DEFEATED
HAHAHA GAYNOOBS DIDN'T EVEN KNOW HOW TO PLAY. WE TOTALLY SMITED THEIR GAYNESS.

How my handwriting has changed since Kindergarten

Kindergarten

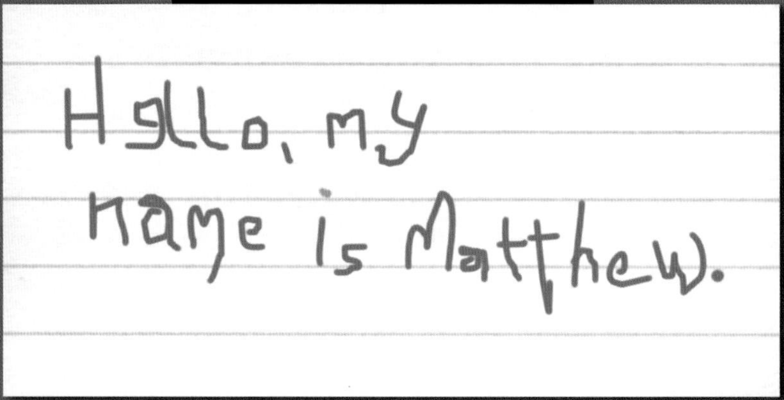
Hello, my
name is Matthew.

Elementary school

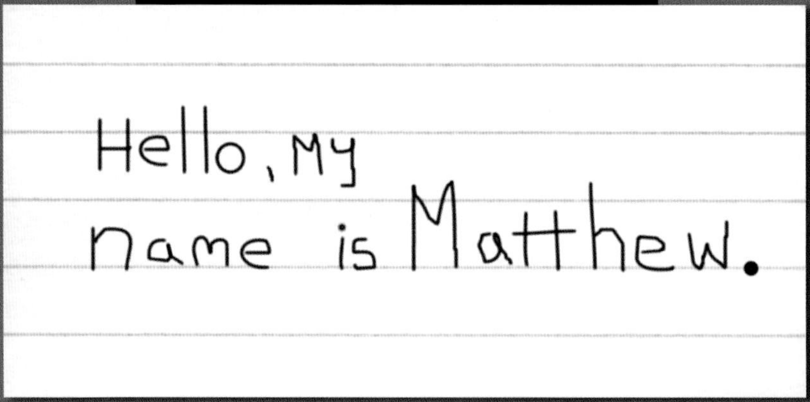
Hello, my
name is Matthew.

Middle / High School

Hello, my name is Matthew.

ENTER THE KEYBOARD!

3 years later

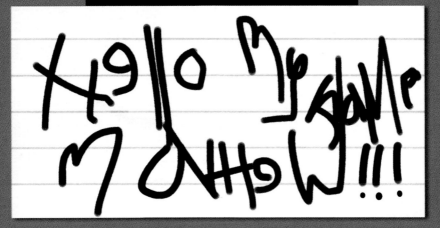

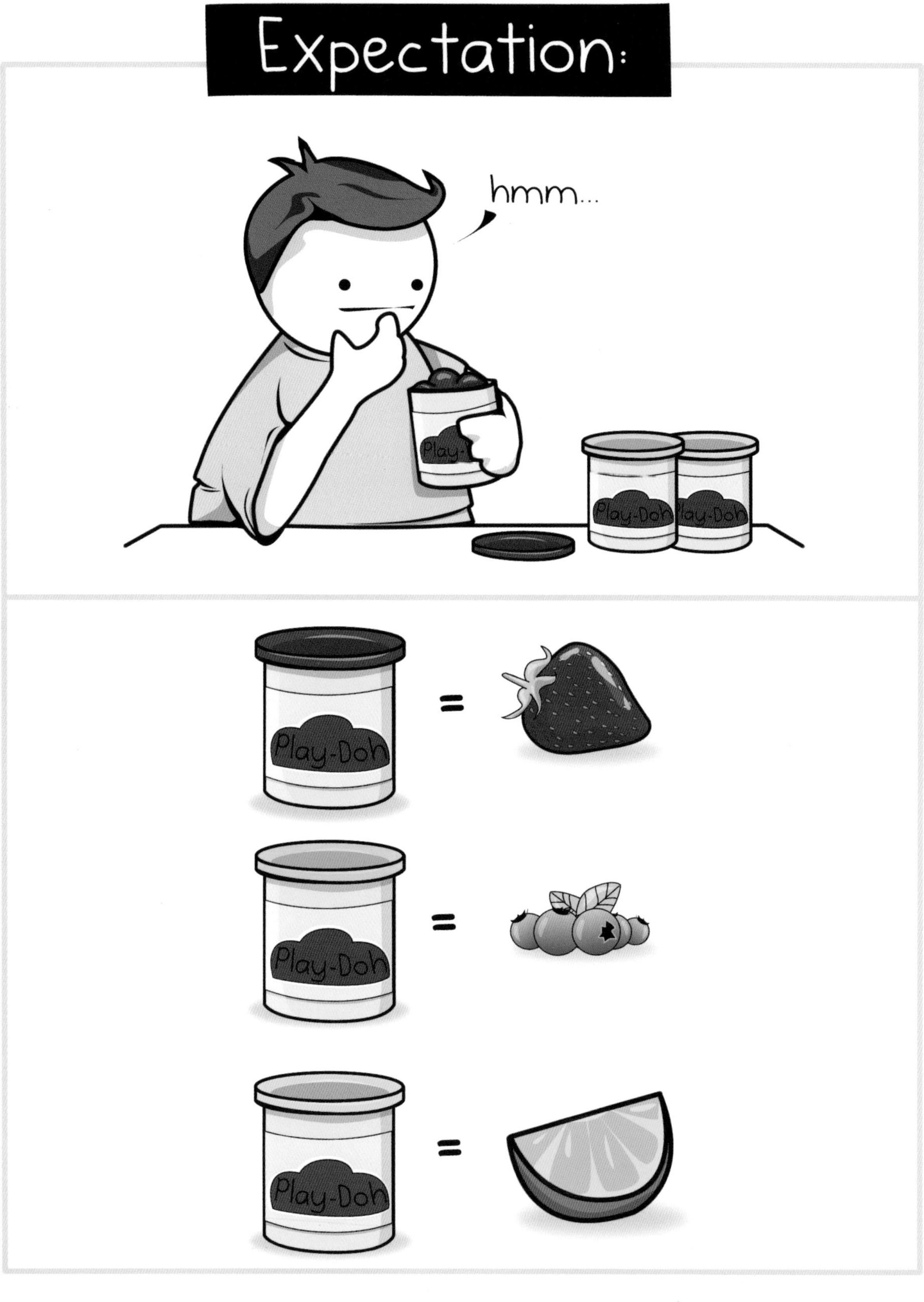
Expectation:
hmm...
Play-Doh
Play-Doh
Play-Doh
Play-Doh
=
Play-Doh
=
Play-Doh
=

Reality:

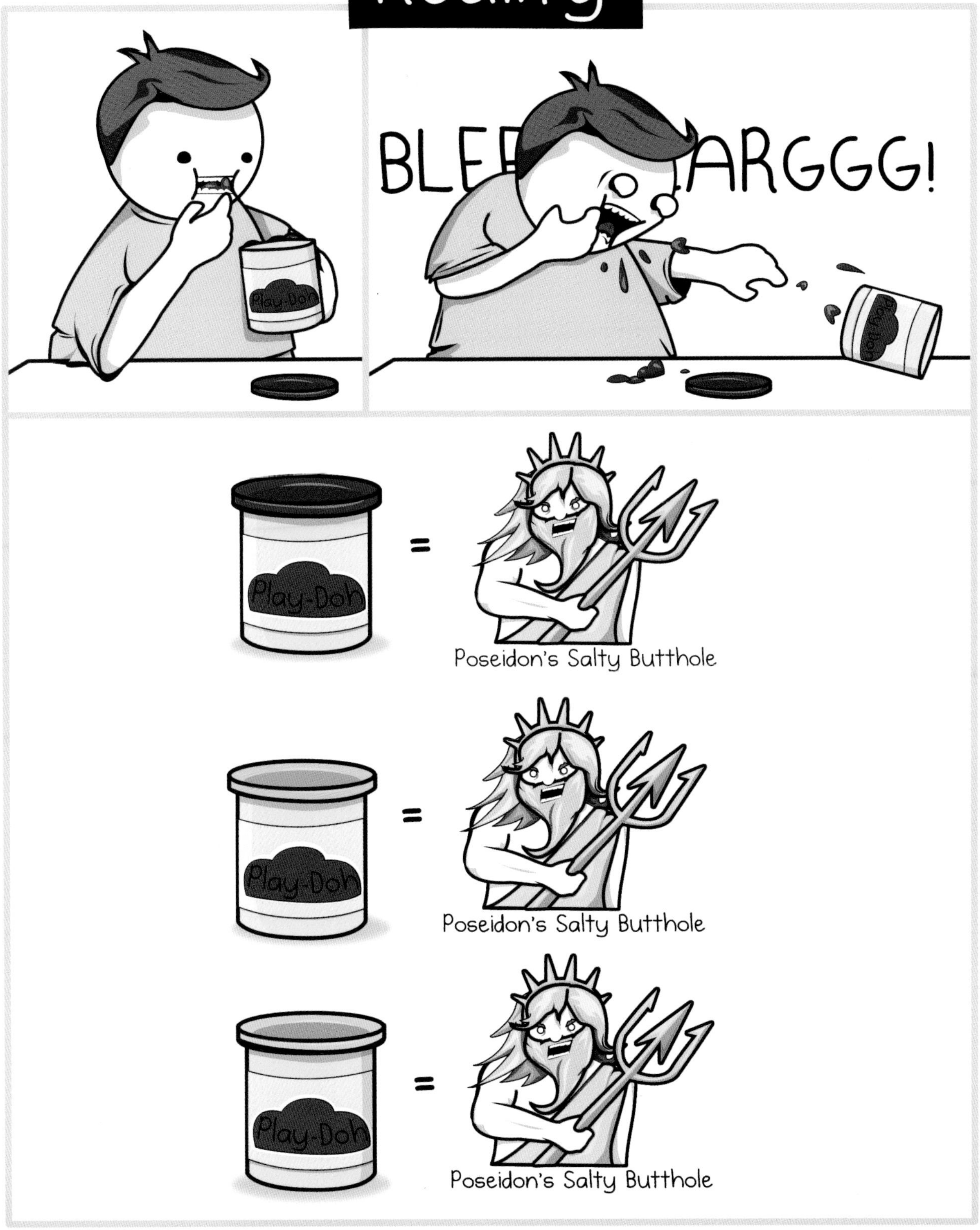
Play-Doh
BLE
ARGGG!
Play-Doh
Play-Doh
=
Poseidon's Salty Butthole
Play-Doh
=
Poseidon's Salty Butthole
Play-Doh
=
Poseidon's Salty Butthole

Seats warmed by robots

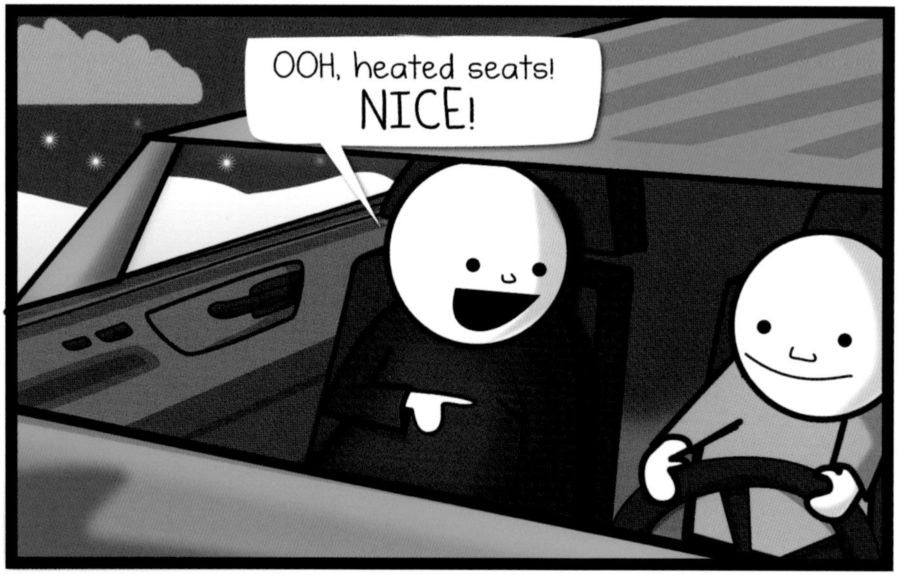
OOH, heated seats!
NICE!

Seats warmed by humans

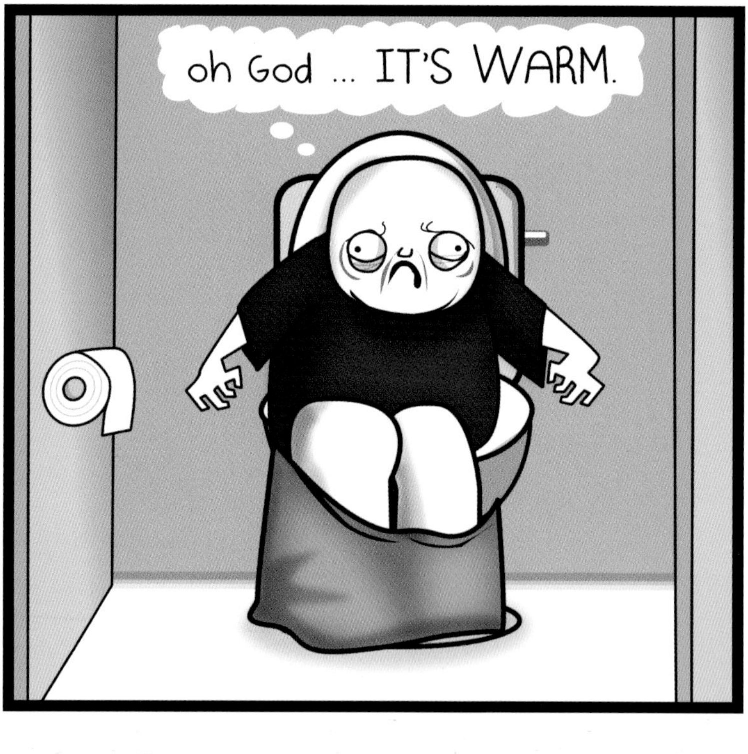
oh God ... IT'S WARM.

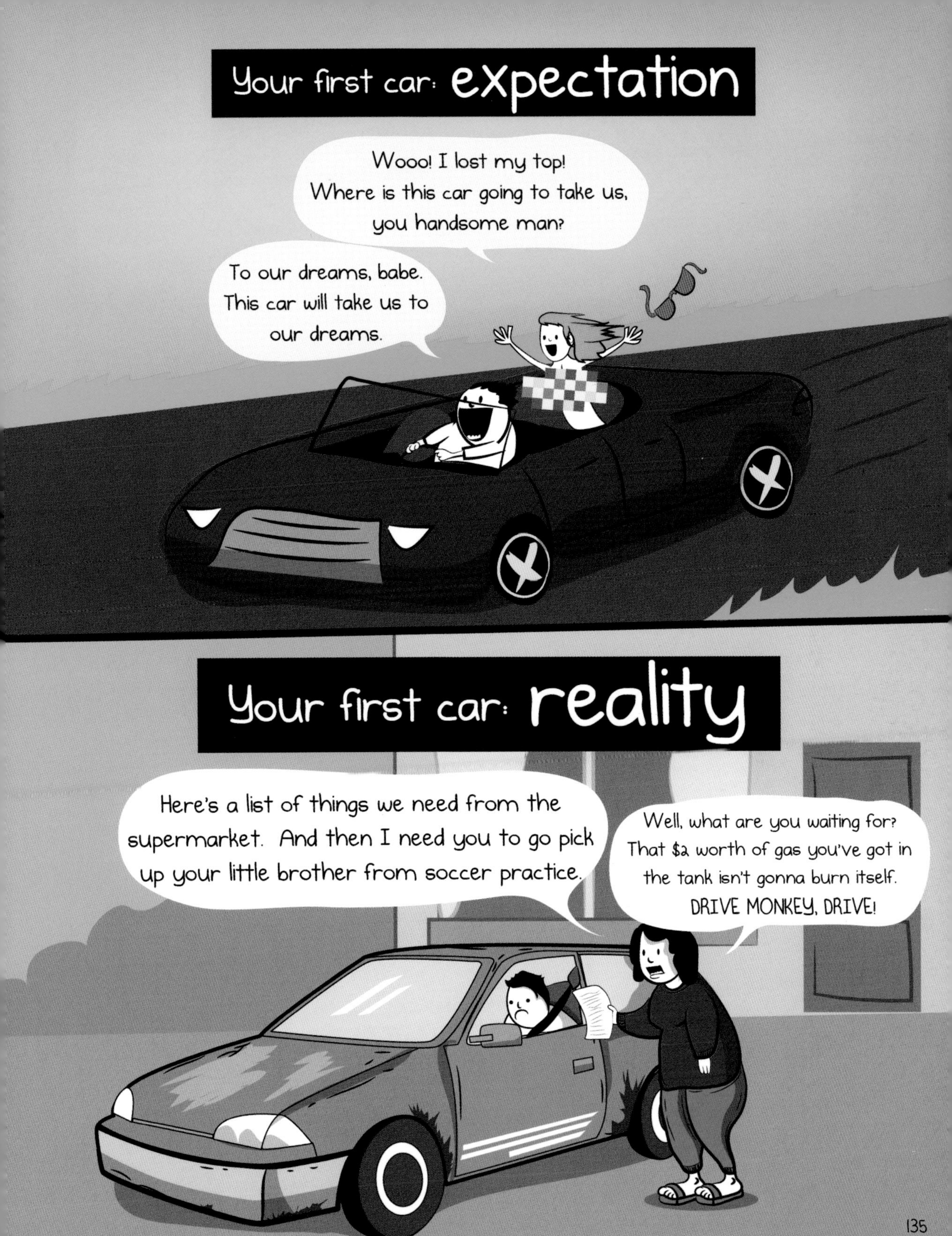
Your first car: expectation
Wooo! I lost my top! Where is this car going to take us, you handsome man?
To our dreams, babe. This car will take us to our dreams.
Your first car: reality
Here's a list of things we need from the supermarket. And then I need you to go pick up your little brother from soccer practice.
Well, what are you waiting for? That $2 worth of gas you've got in the tank isn't gonna burn itself. DRIVE MONKEY, DRIVE!

What we **should** have been taught

in our senior year

of **high school**

English

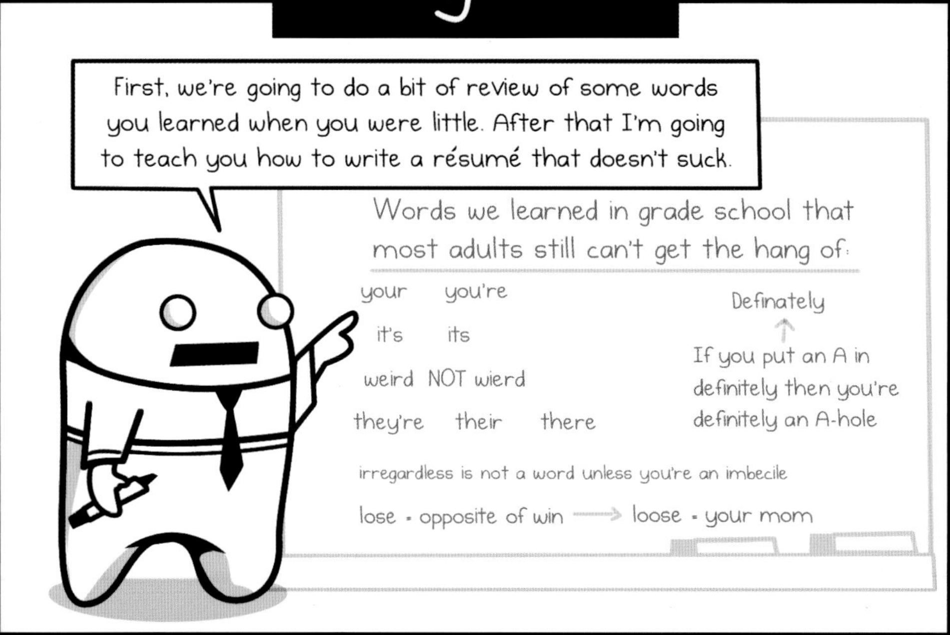
First, we're going to do a bit of review of some words you learned when you were little. After that I'm going to teach you how to write a résumé that doesn't suck.
Words we learned in grade school that most adults still can't get the hang of:
your you're
it's its
weird NOT wierd
they're their there
Definately
If you put an A in definitely then you're definitely an A-hole
irregardless is not a word unless you're an imbecile
lose = opposite of win → loose = your mom

Home Economics

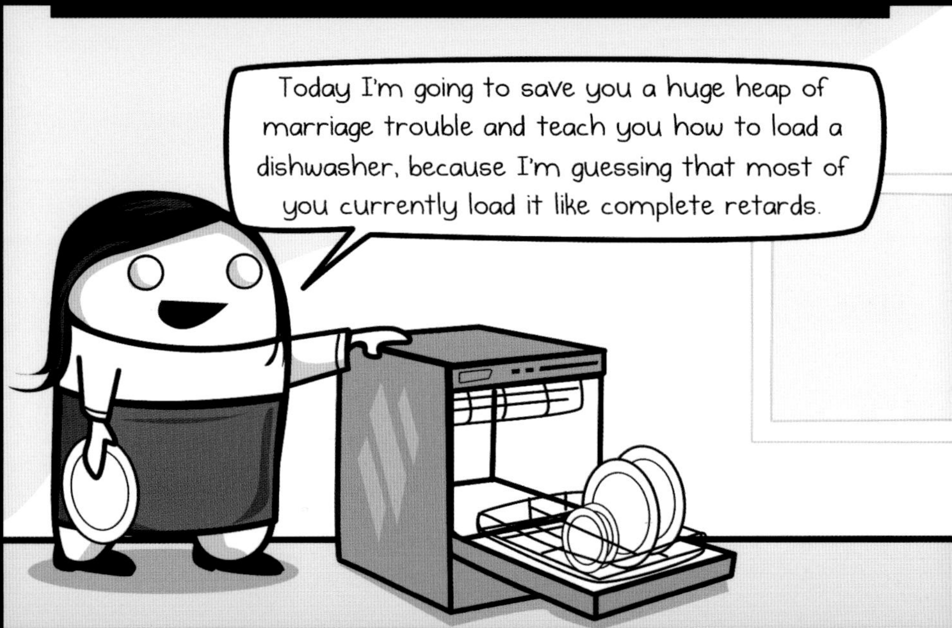
Today I'm going to save you a huge heap of marriage trouble and teach you how to load a dishwasher, because I'm guessing that most of you currently load it like complete retards.

Science

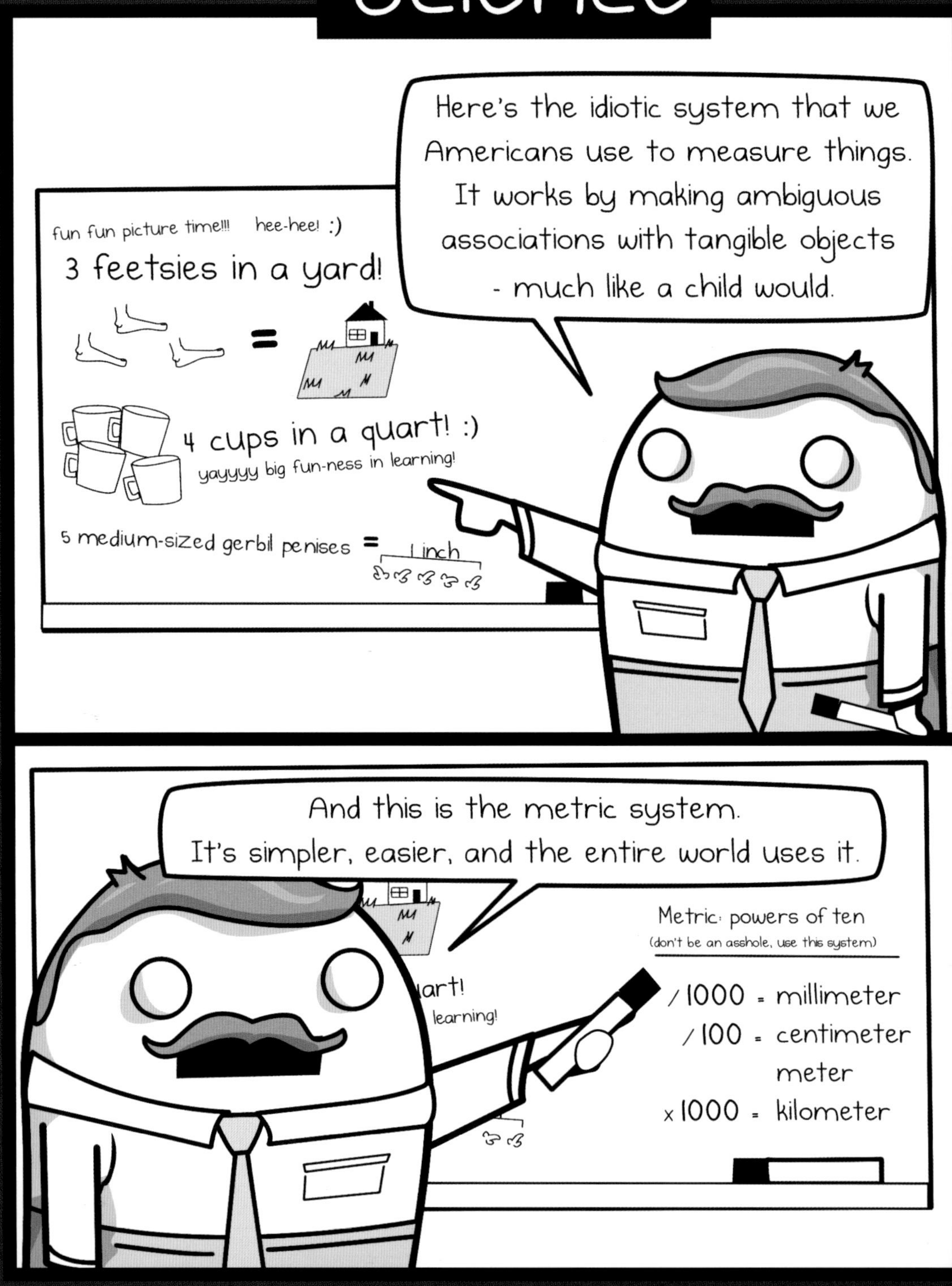
fun fun picture time!!! hee-hee! :)
3 feetsies in a yard!
4 cups in a quart! :)
yayyyy big fun-ness in learning!
5 medium-sized gerbil penises = 1 inch
Here's the idiotic system that we Americans use to measure things. It works by making ambiguous associations with tangible objects - much like a child would.
And this is the metric system. It's simpler, easier, and the entire world uses it.
learning!
Metric: powers of ten
(don't be an asshole, use this system)
/1000 = millimeter
/100 = centimeter
meter
x1000 = kilometer

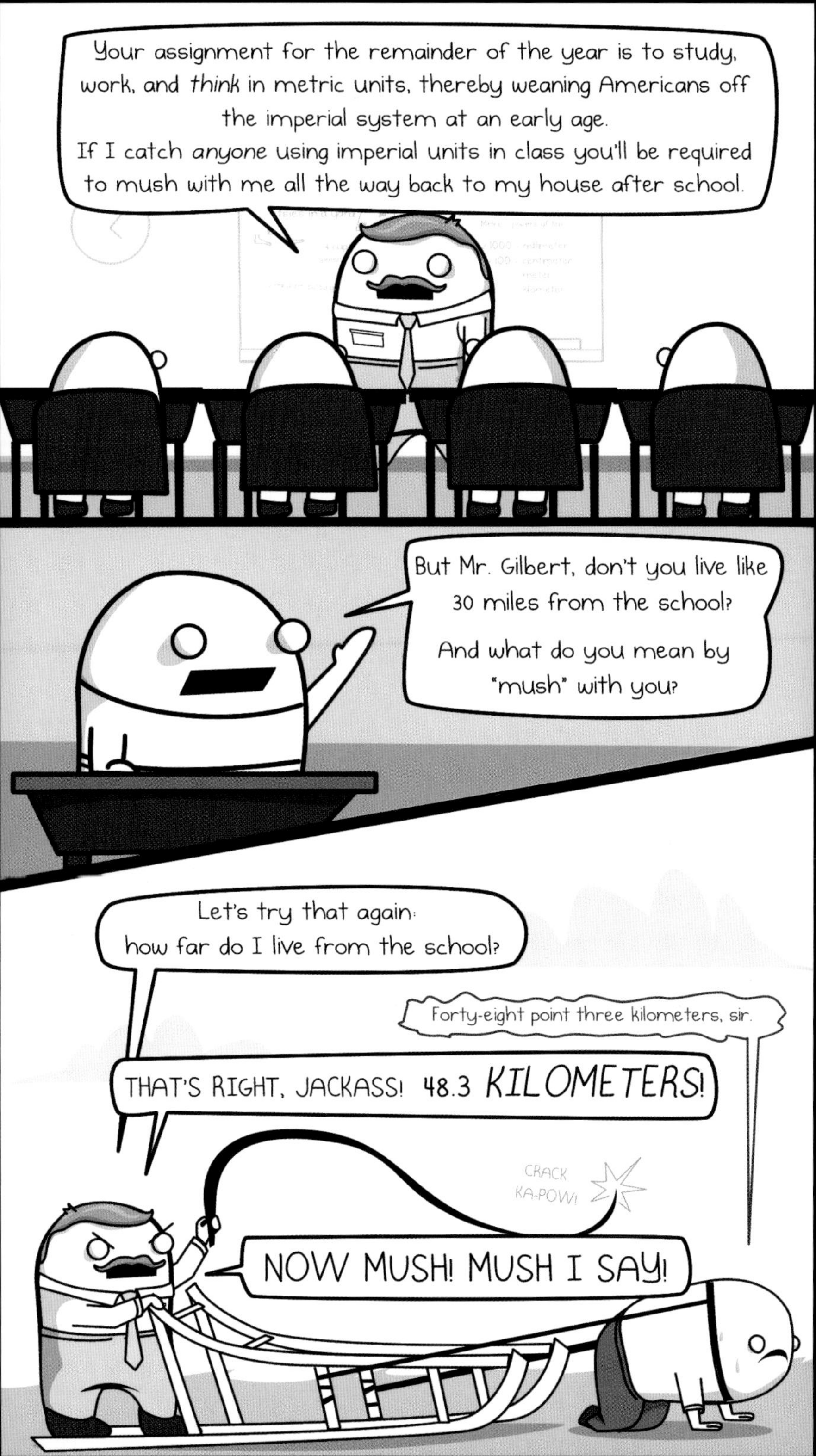

Your assignment for the remainder of the year is to study, work, and *think* in metric units, thereby weaning Americans off the imperial system at an early age.
If I catch *anyone* using imperial units in class you'll be required to mush with me all the way back to my house after school.
But Mr. Gilbert, don't you live like 30 miles from the school?
And what do you mean by "mush" with you?
Let's try that again: how far do I live from the school?
Forty-eight point three kilometers, sir.
THAT'S RIGHT, JACKASS! 48.3 KILOMETERS!
CRACK
KA-POW!
NOW MUSH! MUSH I SAY!

P.E.

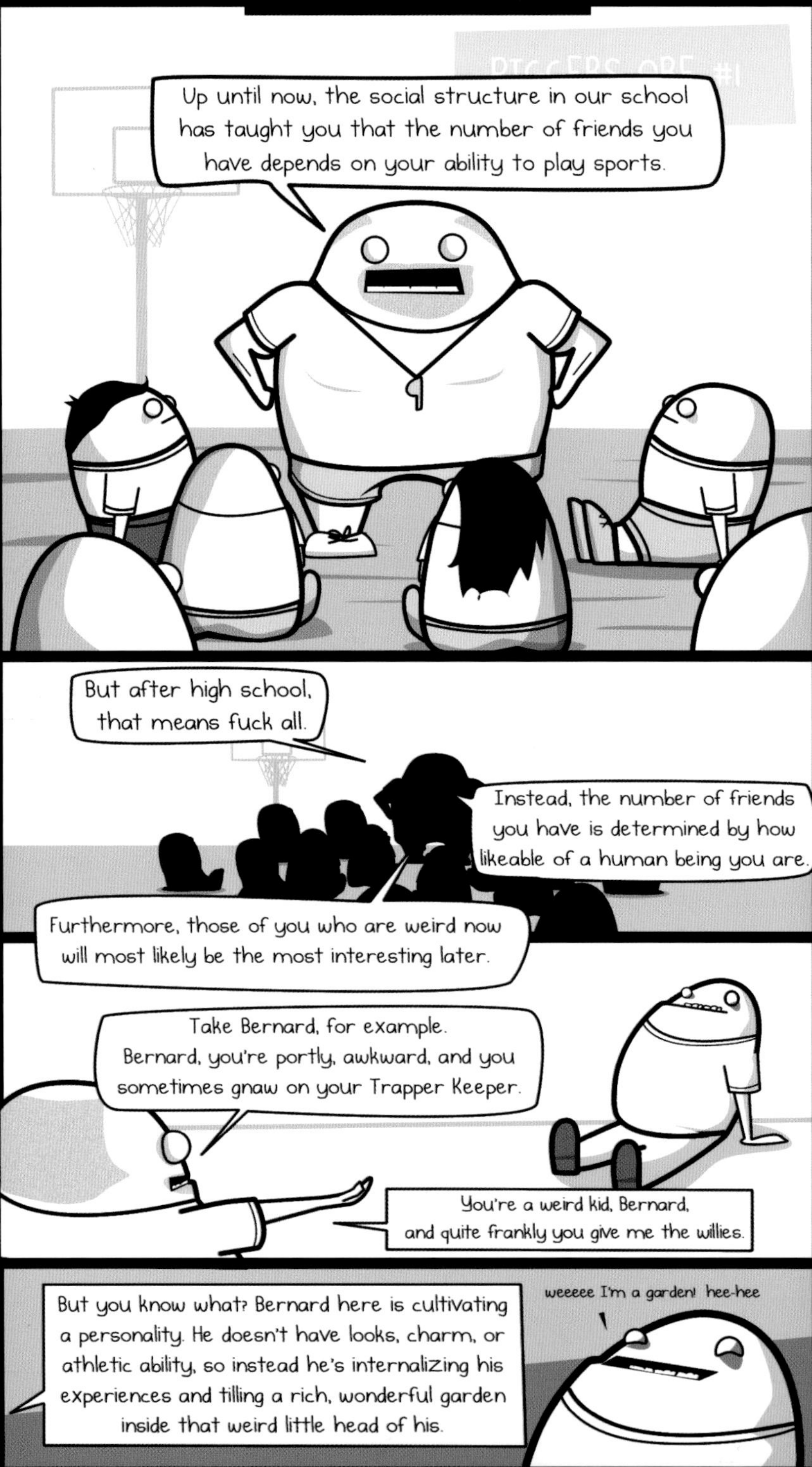
Up until now, the social structure in our school has taught you that the number of friends you have depends on your ability to play sports.
But after high school, that means fuck all.
Instead, the number of friends you have is determined by how likeable of a human being you are.
Furthermore, those of you who are weird now will most likely be the most interesting later.
Take Bernard, for example. Bernard, you're portly, awkward, and you sometimes gnaw on your Trapper Keeper.
You're a weird kid, Bernard, and quite frankly you give me the willies.
But you know what? Bernard here is cultivating a personality. He doesn't have looks, charm, or athletic ability, so instead he's internalizing his experiences and tilling a rich, wonderful garden inside that weird little head of his.
weeeee I'm a garden! hee-hee

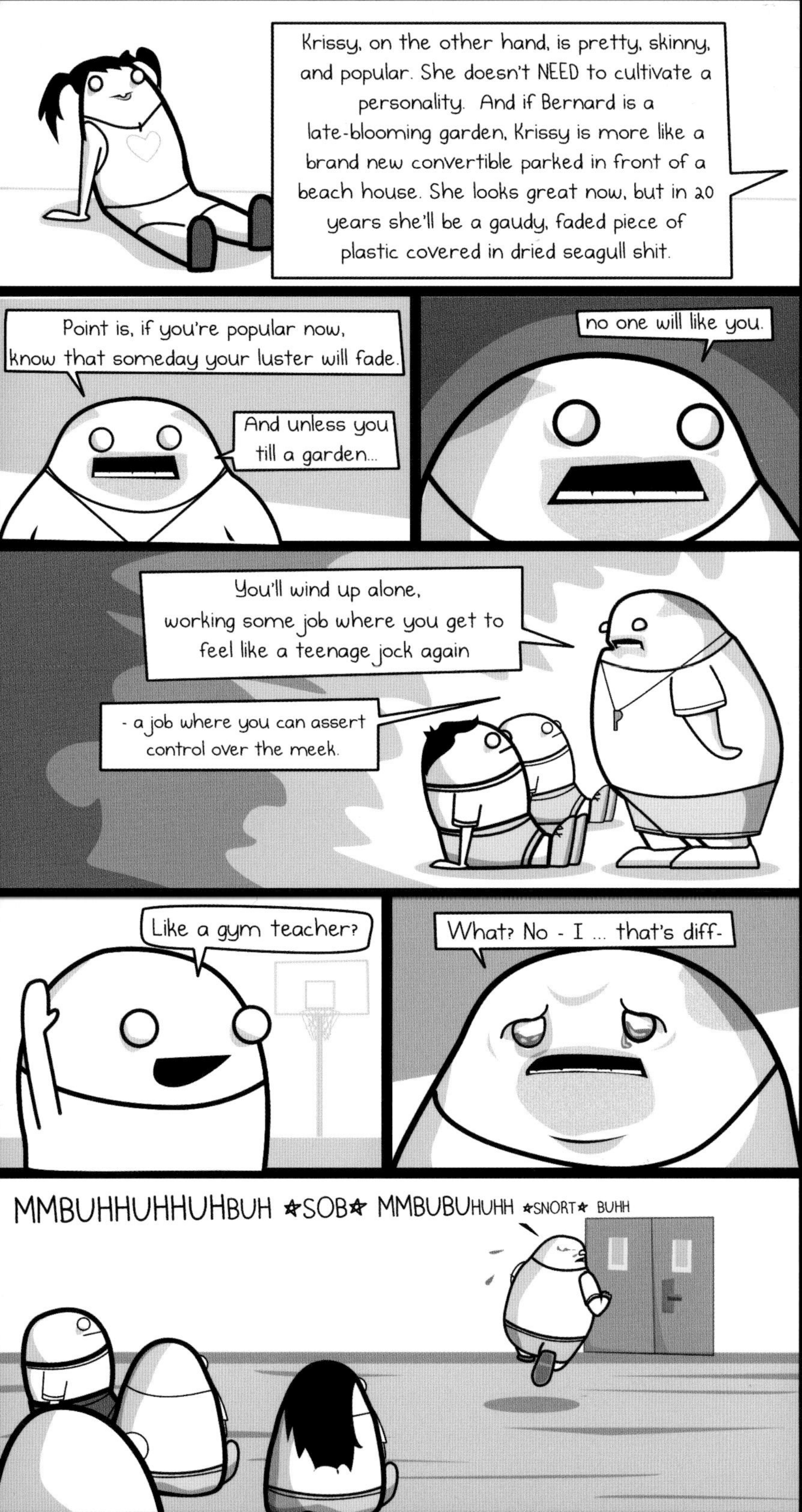

Krissy, on the other hand, is pretty, skinny, and popular. She doesn't NEED to cultivate a personality. And if Bernard is a late-blooming garden, Krissy is more like a brand new convertible parked in front of a beach house. She looks great now, but in 20 years she'll be a gaudy, faded piece of plastic covered in dried seagull shit.
Point is, if you're popular now, know that someday your luster will fade.
And unless you till a garden...
no one will like you.
You'll wind up alone, working some job where you get to feel like a teenage jock again
- a job where you can assert control over the meek.
Like a gym teacher?
What? No - I ... that's diff-
MMBUHHUHHUHBUH *SOB* MMBUBUHUHH *SNORT* BUHH

Math

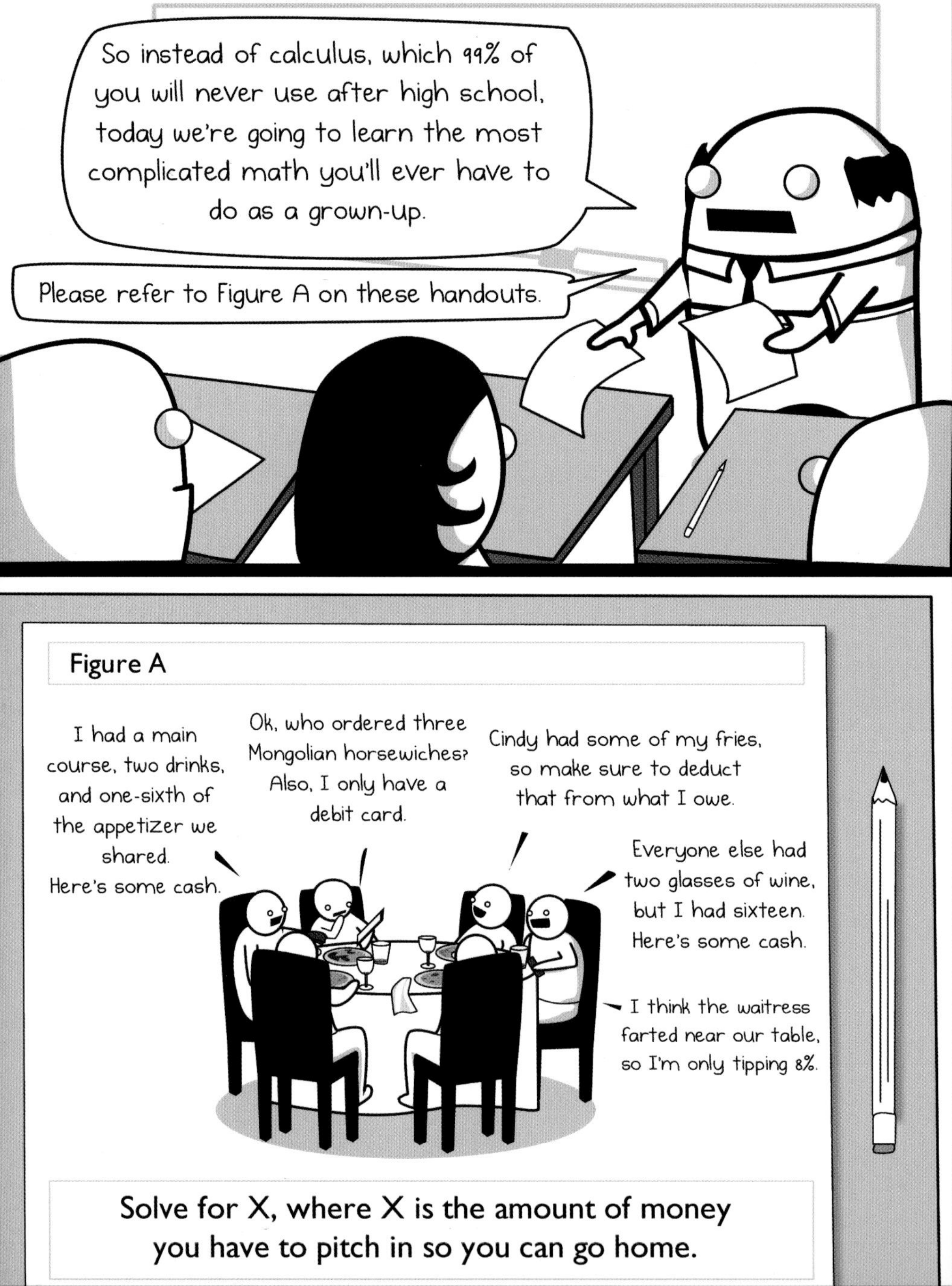
So instead of calculus, which 99% of you will never use after high school, today we're going to learn the most complicated math you'll ever have to do as a grown-up.
Please refer to Figure A on these handouts.
Figure A
I had a main course, two drinks, and one-sixth of the appetizer we shared. Here's some cash.
Ok, who ordered three Mongolian horsewiches? Also, I only have a debit card.
Cindy had some of my fries, so make sure to deduct that from what I owe.
Everyone else had two glasses of wine, but I had sixteen. Here's some cash.
I think the waitress farted near our table, so I'm only tipping 8%.
Solve for X, where X is the amount of money you have to pitch in so you can go home.

Sex Ed

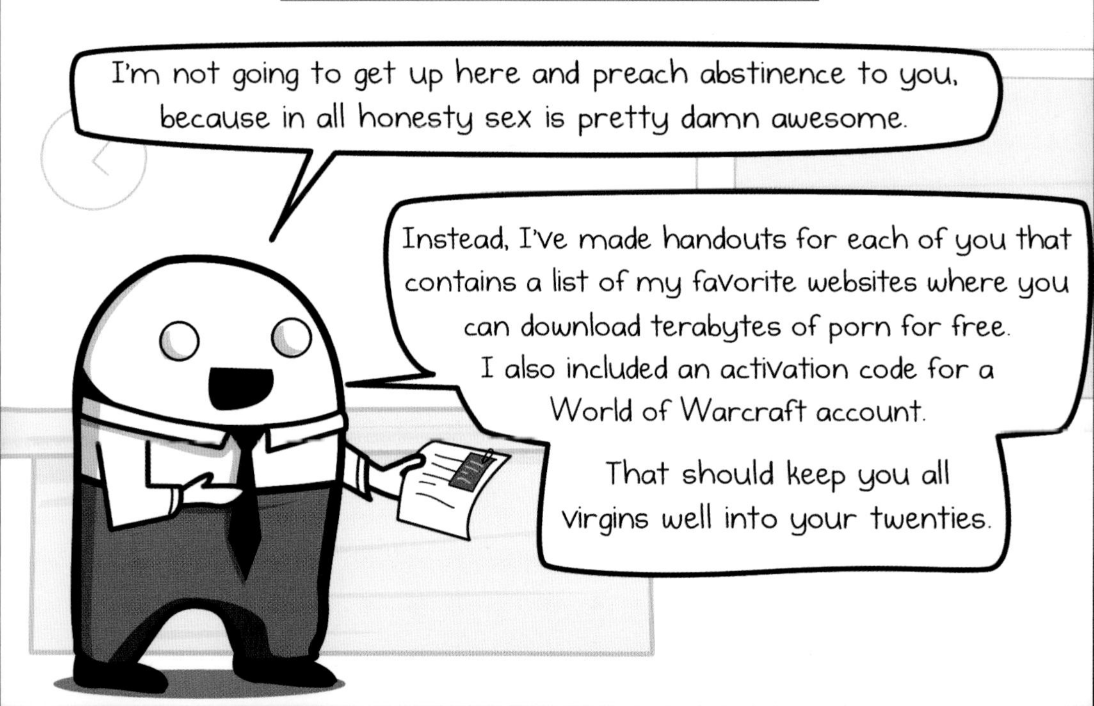
I'm not going to get up here and preach abstinence to you, because in all honesty sex is pretty damn awesome.
Instead, I've made handouts for each of you that contains a list of my favorite websites where you can download terabytes of porn for free. I also included an activation code for a World of Warcraft account.
That should keep you all virgins well into your twenties.

How movie theaters SHOULD be laid out

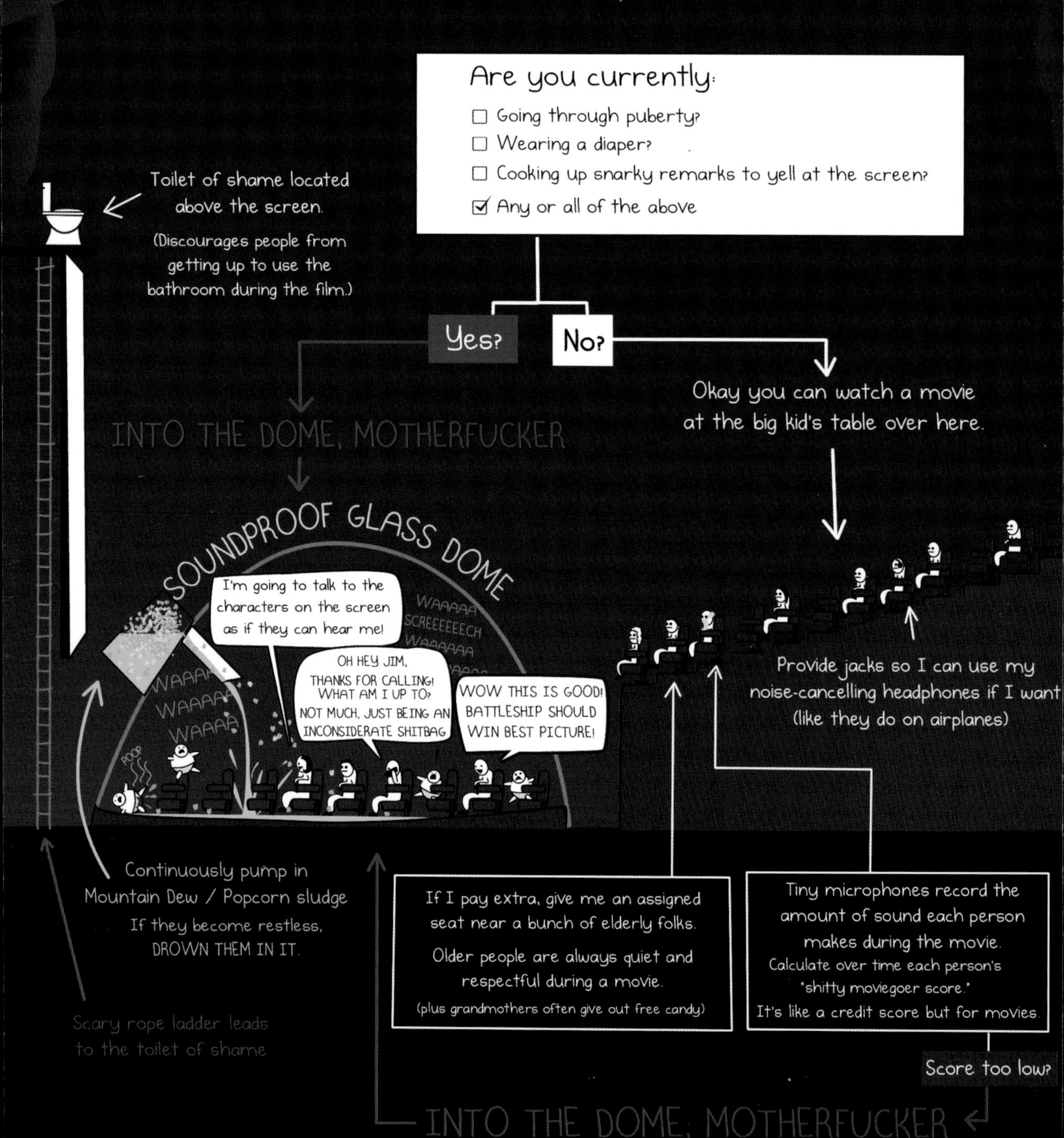

Are you currently:
☐ Going through puberty?
☐ Wearing a diaper?
☐ Cooking up snarky remarks to yell at the screen?
☑ Any or all of the above
Yes?
No?
INTO THE DOME, MOTHERFUCKER
Okay you can watch a movie at the big kid's table over here.
Toilet of shame located above the screen.
(Discourages people from getting up to use the bathroom during the film.)
SOUNDPROOF GLASS DOME
I'm going to talk to the characters on the screen as if they can hear me!
WAAAAA
SCREEEEEECH
WAAAAAA
WAAAH
WAAAAA
WAAAA
POOP
OH HEY JIM, THANKS FOR CALLING! WHAT AM I UP TO? NOT MUCH, JUST BEING AN INCONSIDERATE SHITBAG
WOW THIS IS GOOD! BATTLESHIP SHOULD WIN BEST PICTURE!
Provide jacks so I can use my noise-cancelling headphones if I want (like they do on airplanes)
Continuously pump in Mountain Dew / Popcorn sludge
If they become restless, DROWN THEM IN IT.
Scary rope ladder leads to the toilet of shame
If I pay extra, give me an assigned seat near a bunch of elderly folks.
Older people are always quiet and respectful during a movie.
(plus grandmothers often give out free candy)
Tiny microphones record the amount of sound each person makes during the movie.
Calculate over time each person's "shitty moviegoer score."
It's like a credit score but for movies.
Score too low?
INTO THE DOME, MOTHERFUCKER

Young men
in the locker room

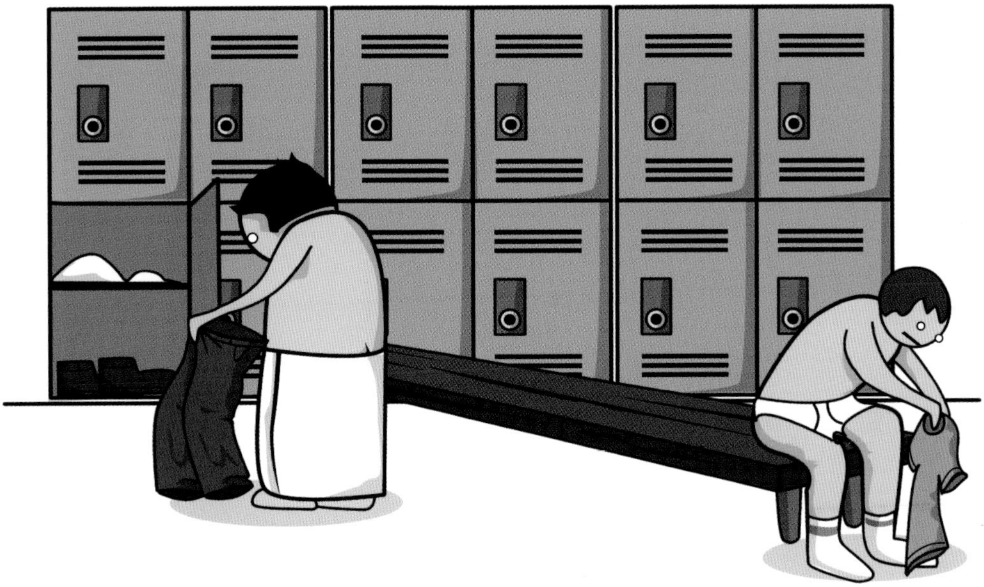

Old men
in the locker room

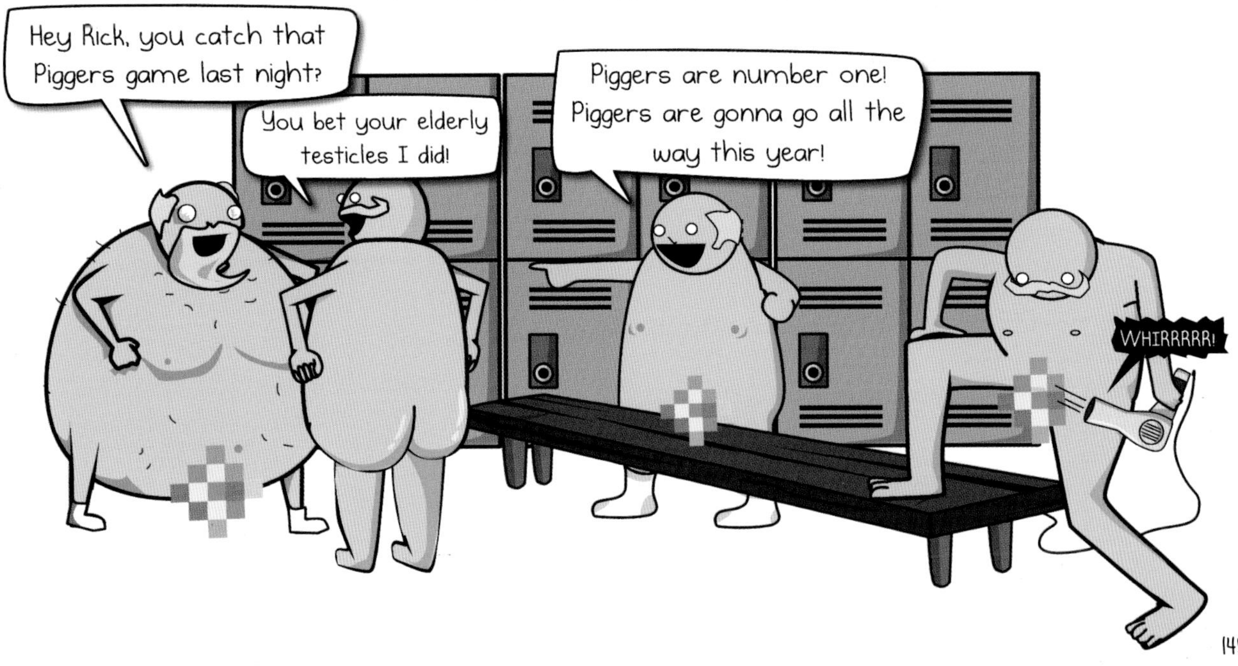
Hey Rick, you catch that Piggers game last night?
You bet your elderly testicles I did!
Piggers are number one! Piggers are gonna go all the way this year!
WHIRRRRR!

The pros and cons of living with your significant other

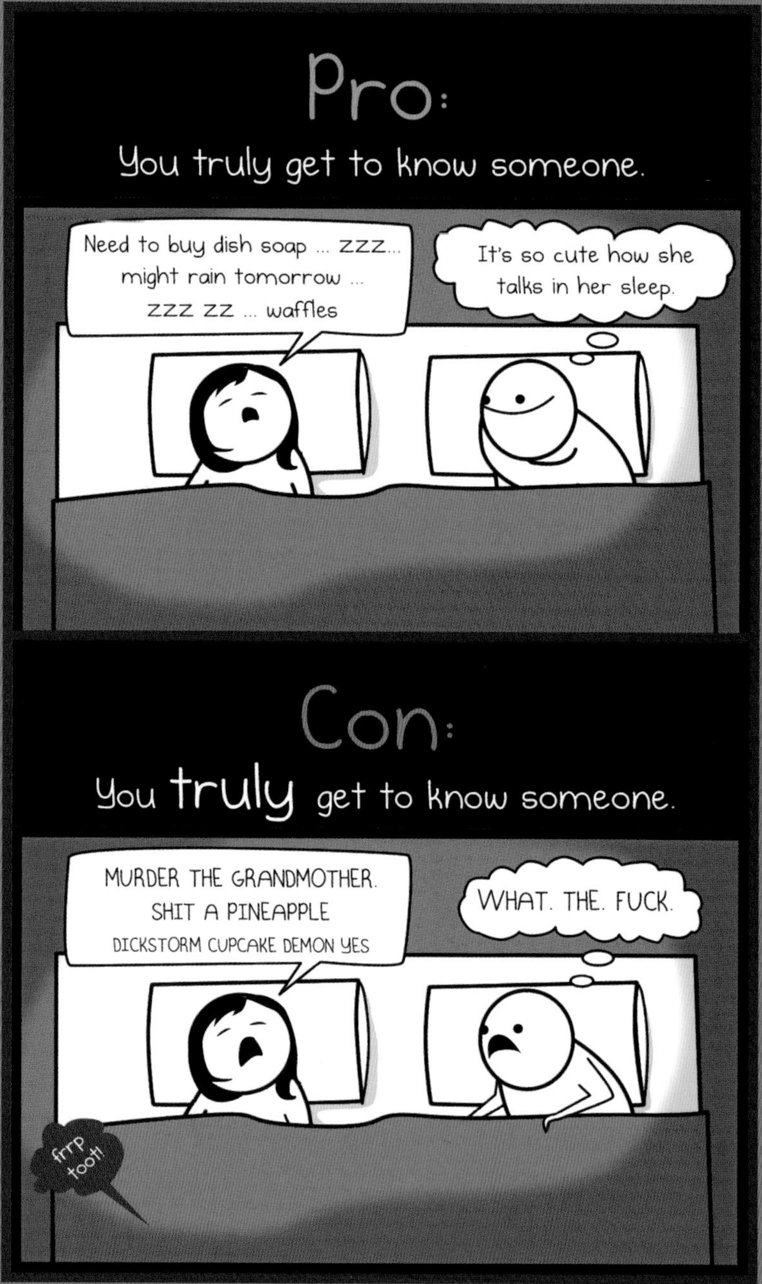
Pro:
You truly get to know someone.
Need to buy dish soap ... ZZZ... might rain tomorrow ... ZZZ ZZ ... waffles
It's so cute how she talks in her sleep.
Con:
You truly get to know someone.
MURDER THE GRANDMOTHER. SHIT A PINEAPPLE DICKSTORM CUPCAKE DEMON YES
WHAT. THE. FUCK.
frrp toot!

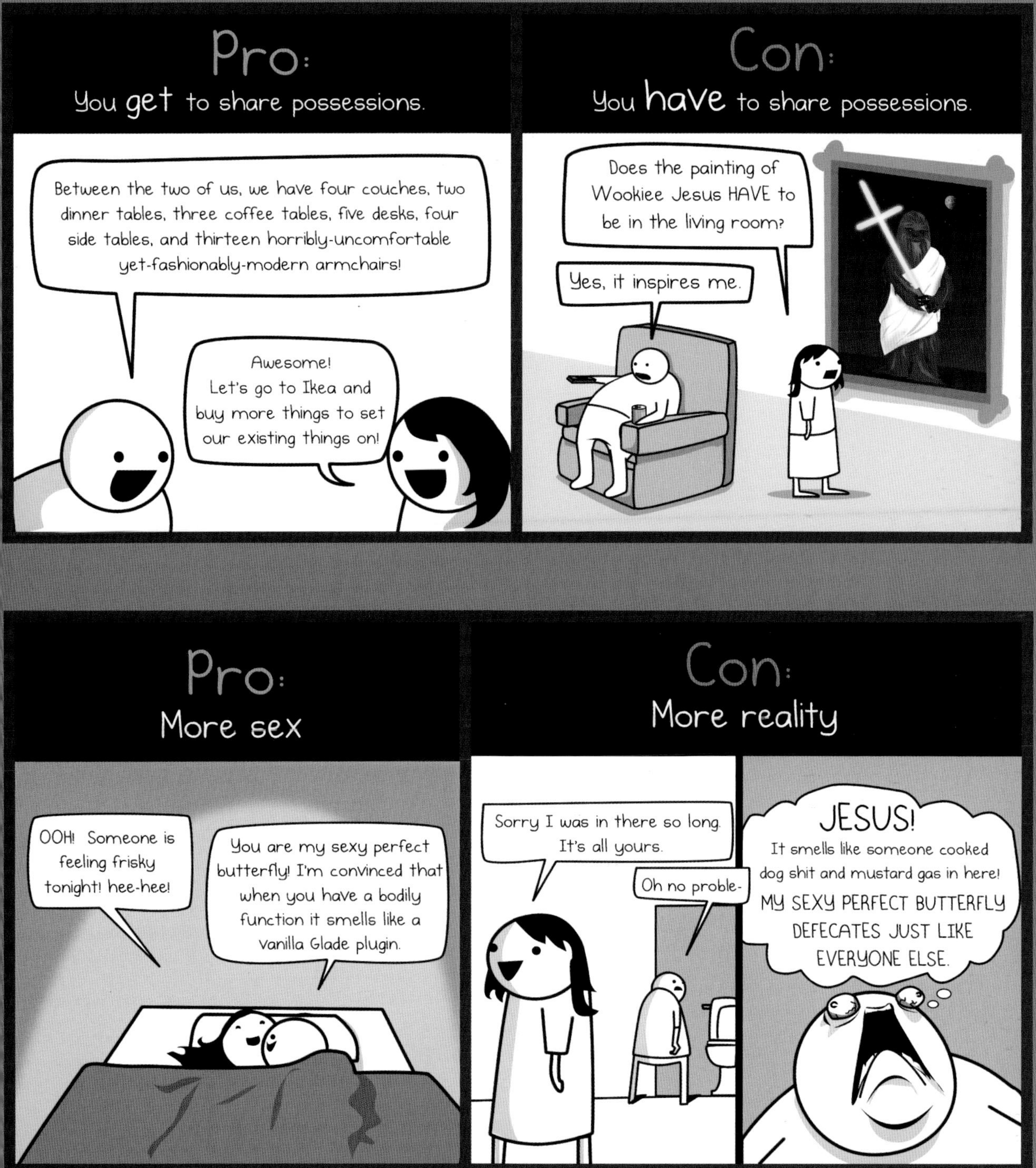

Pro:
You get to share possessions.
Between the two of us, we have four couches, two dinner tables, three coffee tables, five desks, four side tables, and thirteen horribly-uncomfortable yet-fashionably-modern armchairs!
Awesome! Let's go to Ikea and buy more things to set our existing things on!
Con:
You have to share possessions.
Does the painting of Wookiee Jesus HAVE to be in the living room?
Yes, it inspires me.
Pro:
More sex
OOH! Someone is feeling frisky tonight! hee-hee!
You are my sexy perfect butterfly! I'm convinced that when you have a bodily function it smells like a vanilla Glade plugin.
Con:
More reality
Sorry I was in there so long. It's all yours.
Oh no proble-
JESUS! It smells like someone cooked dog shit and mustard gas in here! MY SEXY PERFECT BUTTERFLY DEFECATES JUST LIKE EVERYONE ELSE.

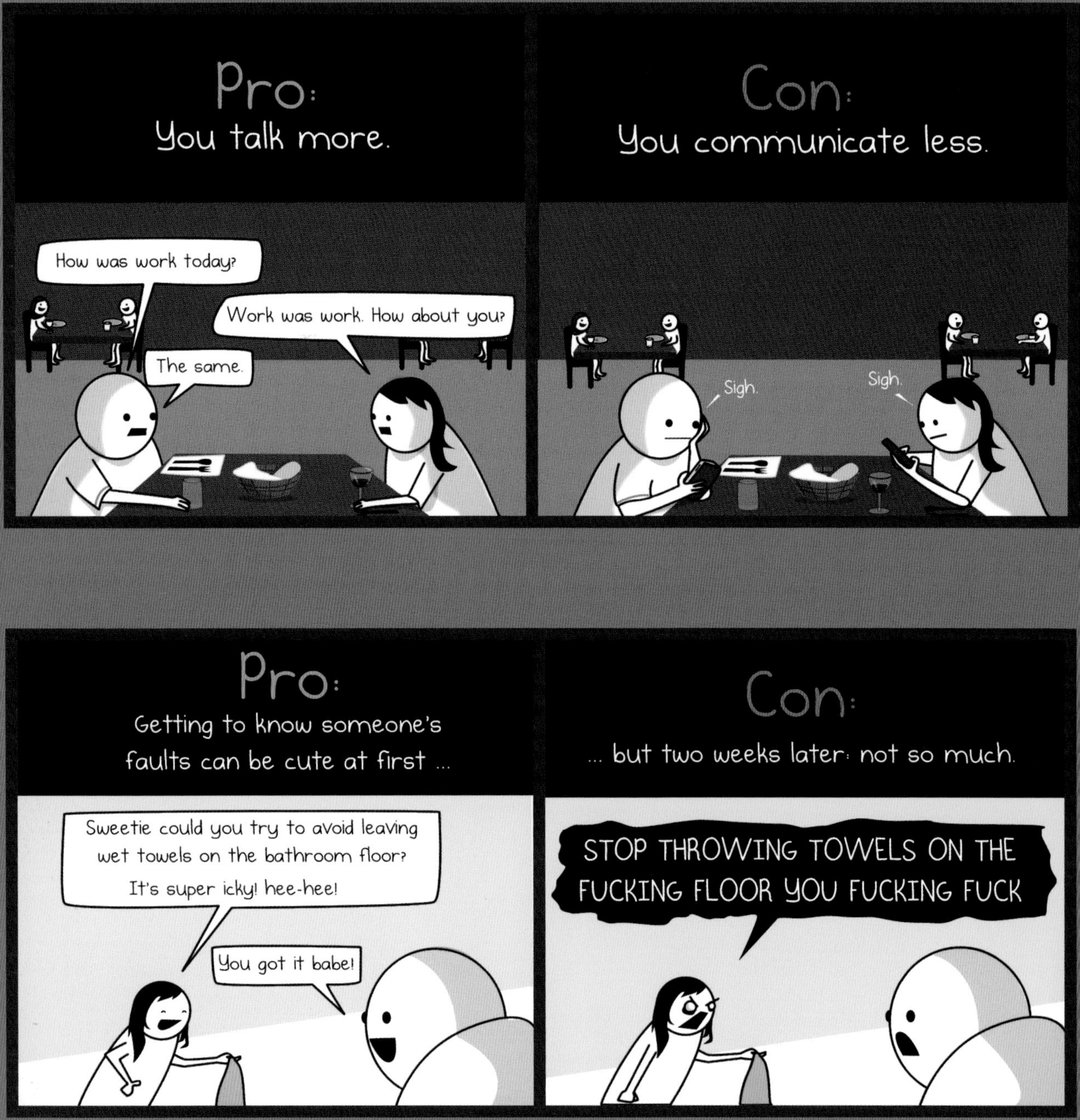
Pro:
You talk more.
How was work today?
Work was work. How about you?
The same.
Con:
You communicate less.
Sigh.
Sigh.
Pro:
Getting to know someone's faults can be cute at first ...
Sweetie could you try to avoid leaving wet towels on the bathroom floor? It's super icky! hee-hee!
You got it babe!
Con:
... but two weeks later: not so much.
STOP THROWING TOWELS ON THE FUCKING FLOOR YOU FUCKING FUCK

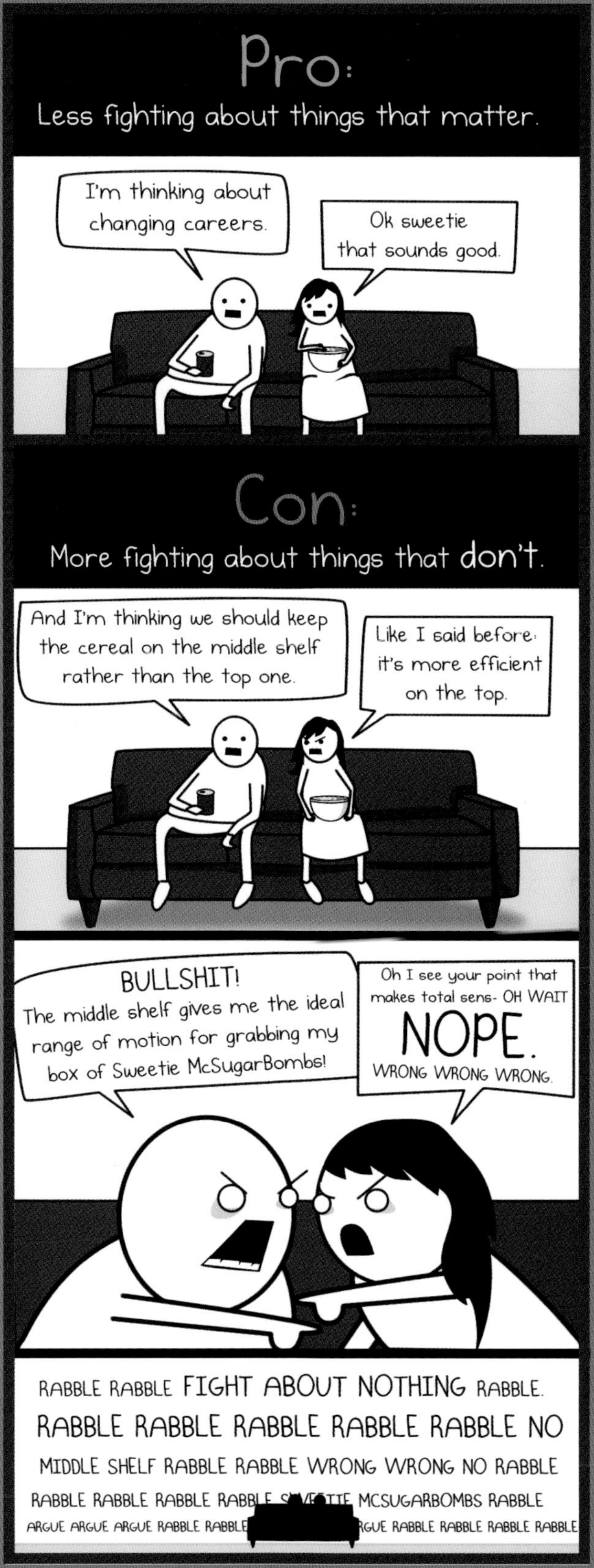

Pro:
Less fighting about things that matter.
I'm thinking about changing careers.
Ok sweetie that sounds good.
Con:
More fighting about things that don't.
And I'm thinking we should keep the cereal on the middle shelf rather than the top one.
Like I said before: it's more efficient on the top.
BULLSHIT! The middle shelf gives me the ideal range of motion for grabbing my box of Sweetie McSugarBombs!
Oh I see your point that makes total sens- OH WAIT
NOPE.
WRONG WRONG WRONG.
RABBLE RABBLE FIGHT ABOUT NOTHING RABBLE.
RABBLE RABBLE RABBLE RABBLE RABBLE NO
MIDDLE SHELF RABBLE RABBLE WRONG WRONG NO RABBLE
RABBLE RABBLE RABBLE
MCSUGARBOMBS RABBLE
ARGUE ARGUE ARGUE RABBLE RABBLE
RABBLE RABBLE RABBLE RABBLE

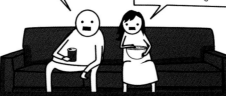

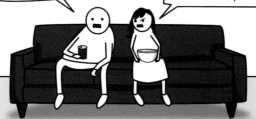

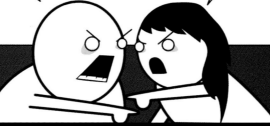

Everyone I know has
dreams...

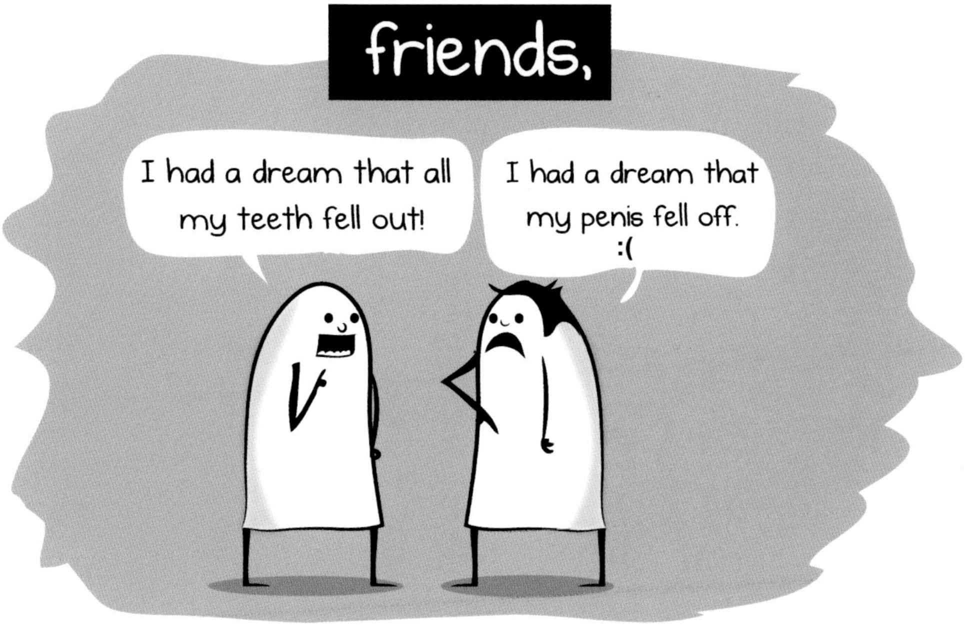
friends,
I had a dream that all my teeth fell out!
I had a dream that my penis fell off. :(

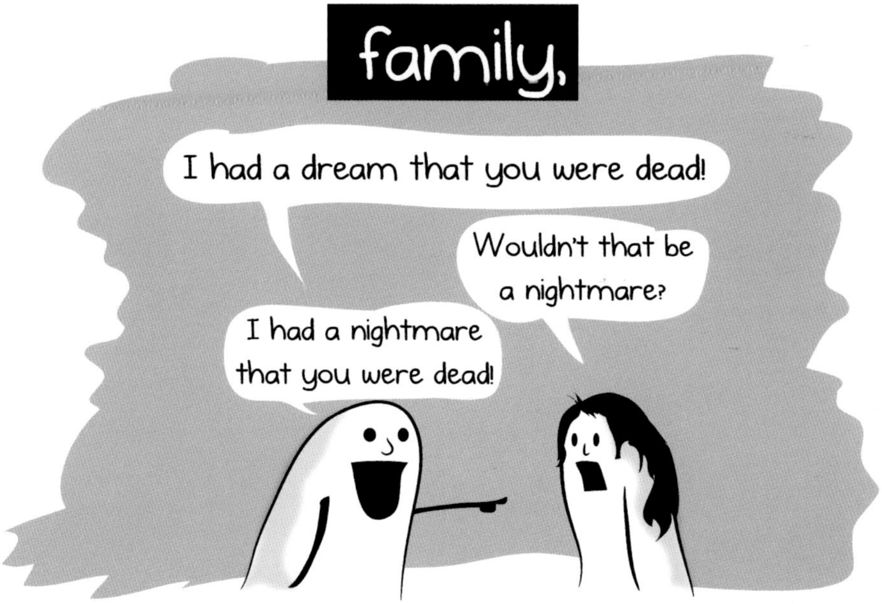
family,
I had a dream that you were dead!
Wouldn't that be a nightmare?
I had a nightmare that you were dead!

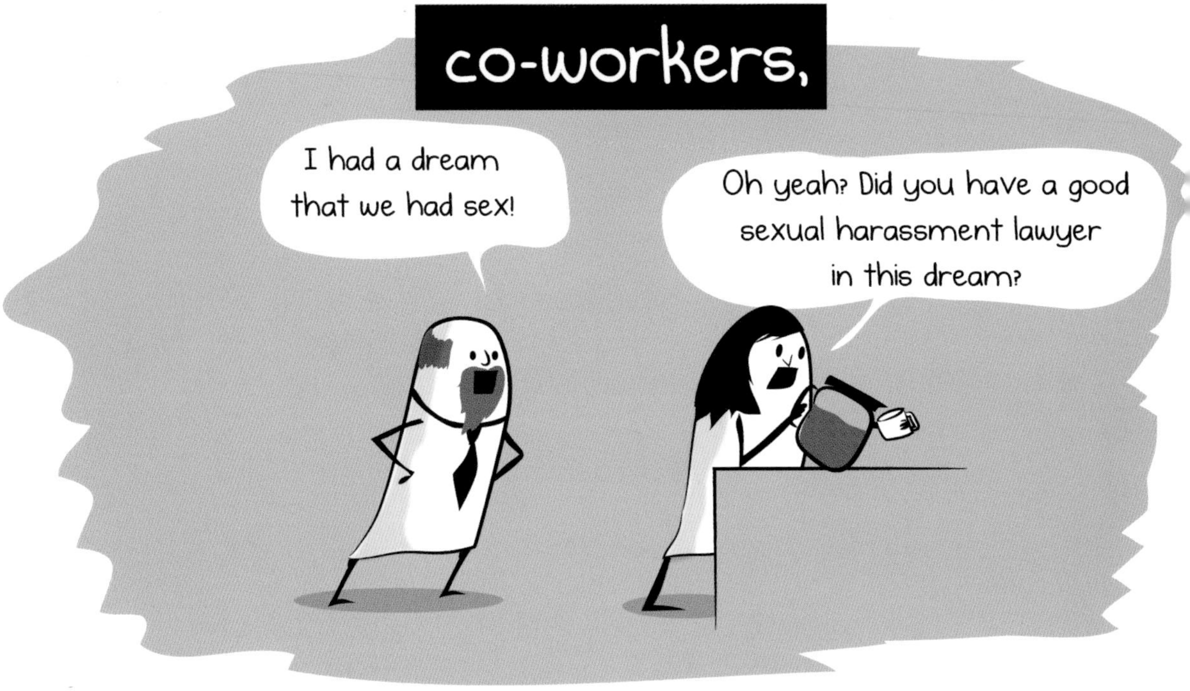
co-workers,
I had a dream that we had sex!
Oh yeah? Did you have a good sexual harassment lawyer in this dream?

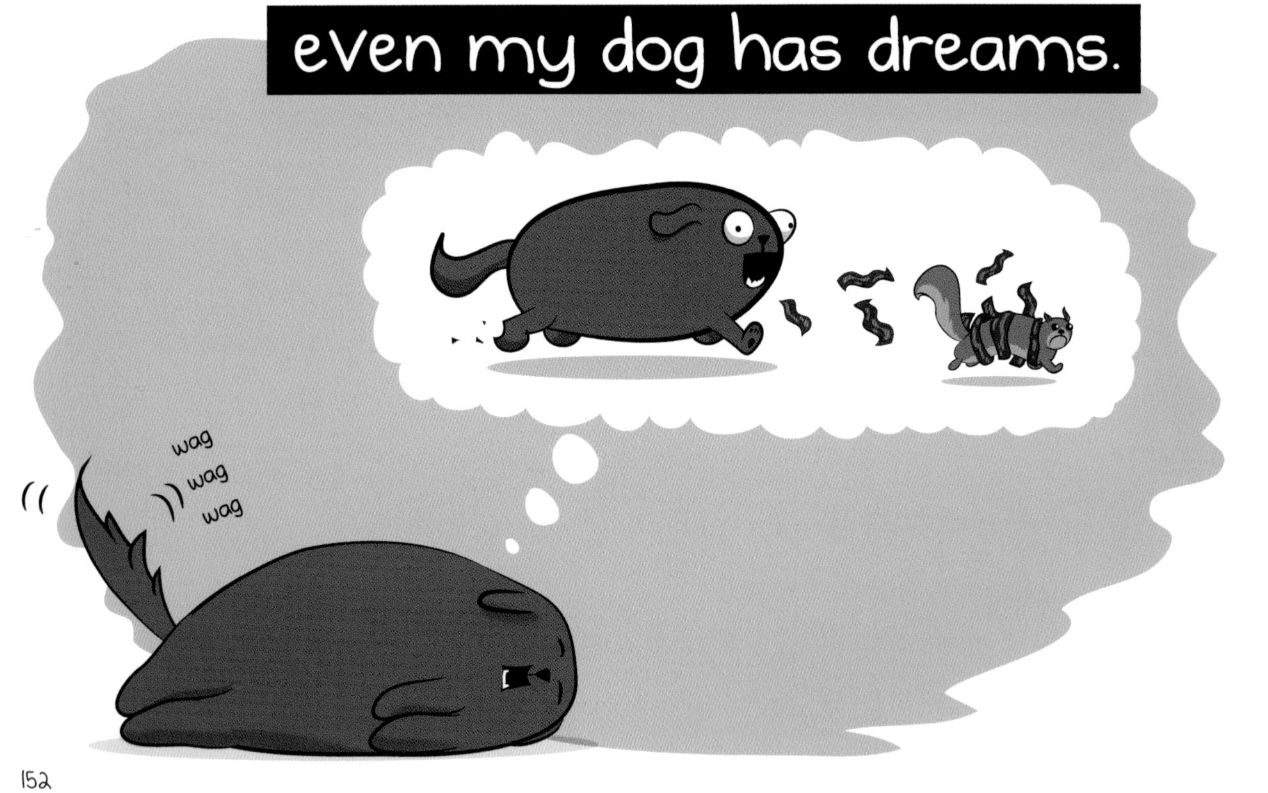
even my dog has dreams.
wag
wag
wag

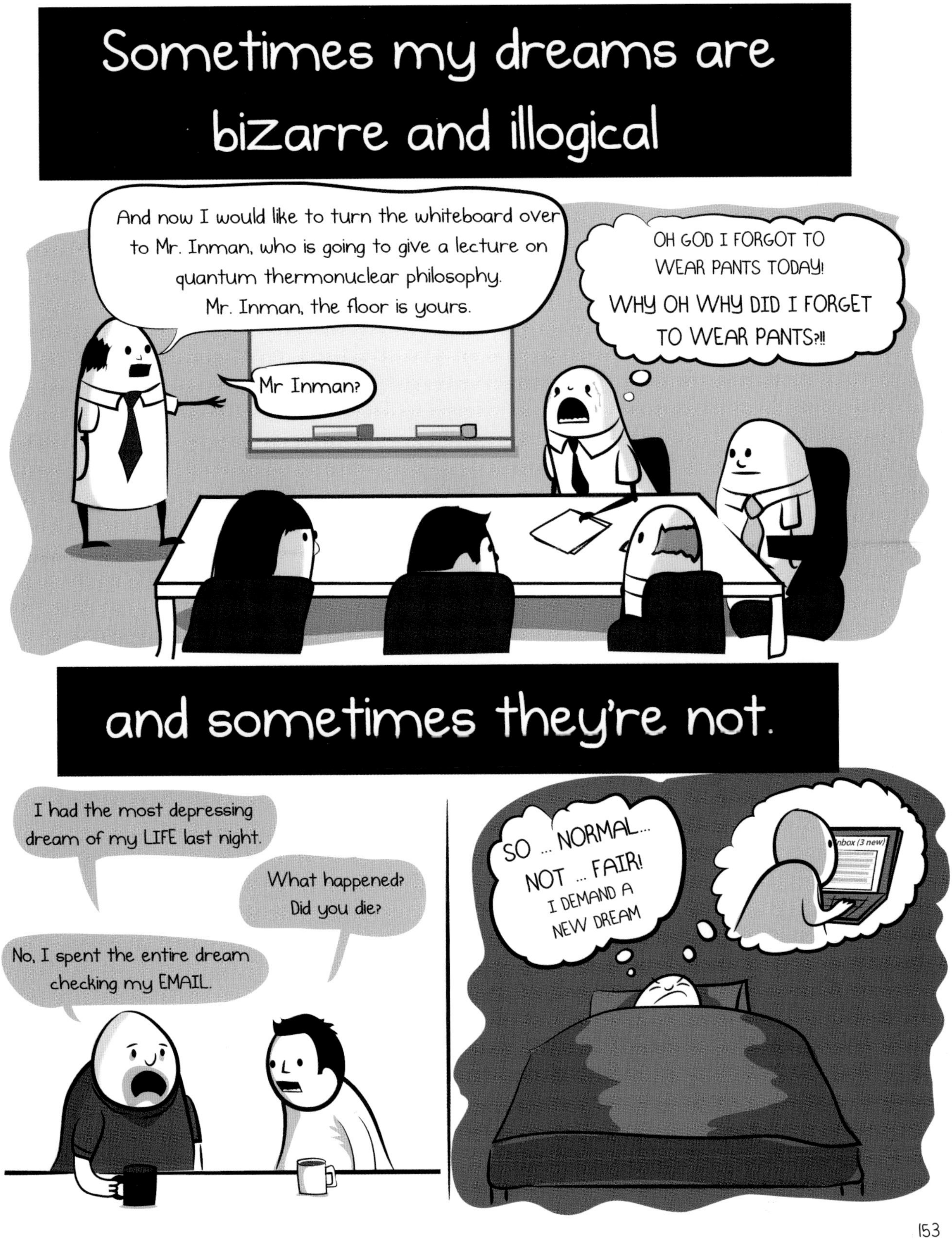
Sometimes my dreams are bizarre and illogical
And now I would like to turn the whiteboard over to Mr. Inman, who is going to give a lecture on quantum thermonuclear philosophy. Mr. Inman, the floor is yours.
Mr Inman?
OH GOD I FORGOT TO WEAR PANTS TODAY! WHY OH WHY DID I FORGET TO WEAR PANTS?!!
and sometimes they're not.
I had the most depressing dream of my LIFE last night.
What happened? Did you die?
No, I spent the entire dream checking my EMAIL.
SO ... NORMAL... NOT ... FAIR! I DEMAND A NEW DREAM
Inbox (3 new)

Sometimes my dreams make me feel good

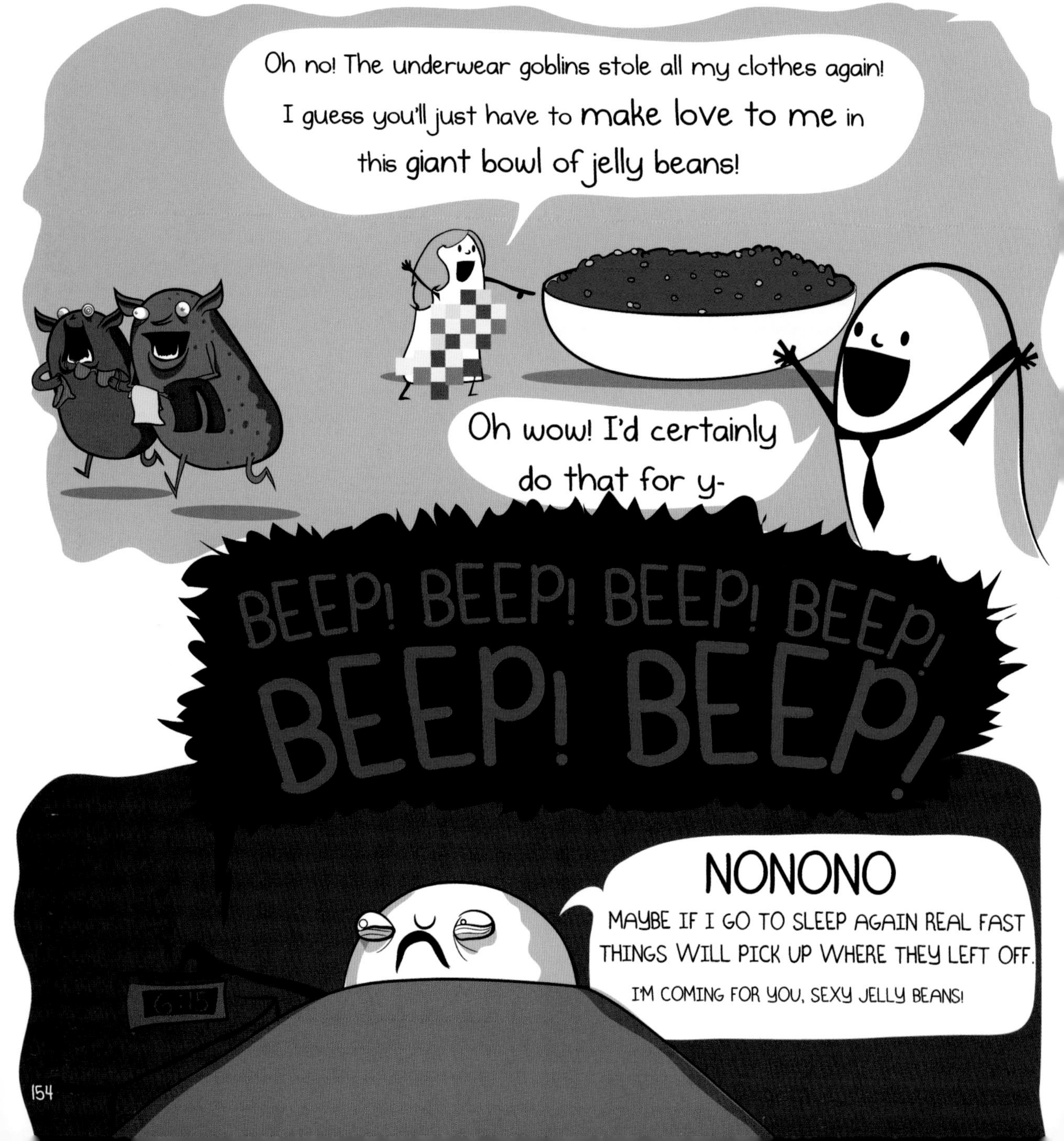
Oh no! The underwear goblins stole all my clothes again! I guess you'll just have to make love to me in this giant bowl of jelly beans!
Oh wow! I'd certainly do that for y-
BEEP! BEEP! BEEP! BEEP! BEEP! BEEP!
NONONO
MAYBE IF I GO TO SLEEP AGAIN REAL FAST THINGS WILL PICK UP WHERE THEY LEFT OFF.
I'M COMING FOR YOU, SEXY JELLY BEANS!
6:15

and sometimes they make me feel very, very bad.

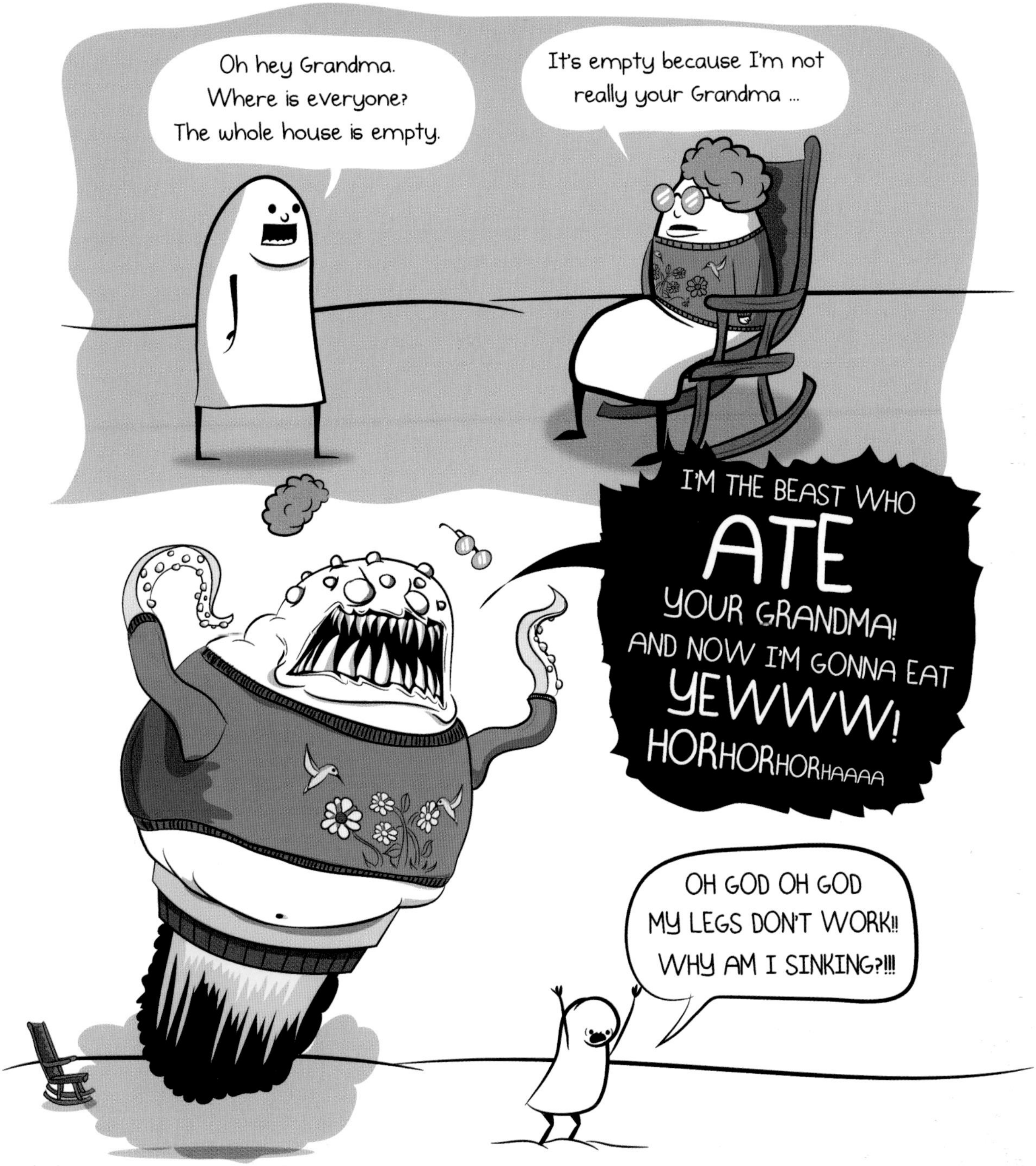
Oh hey Grandma. Where is everyone? The whole house is empty.
It's empty because I'm not really your Grandma ...
I'M THE BEAST WHO ATE YOUR GRANDMA! AND NOW I'M GONNA EAT YEWWW! HORHORHORHAAAA
OH GOD OH GOD MY LEGS DON'T WORK!! WHY AM I SINKING?!!!

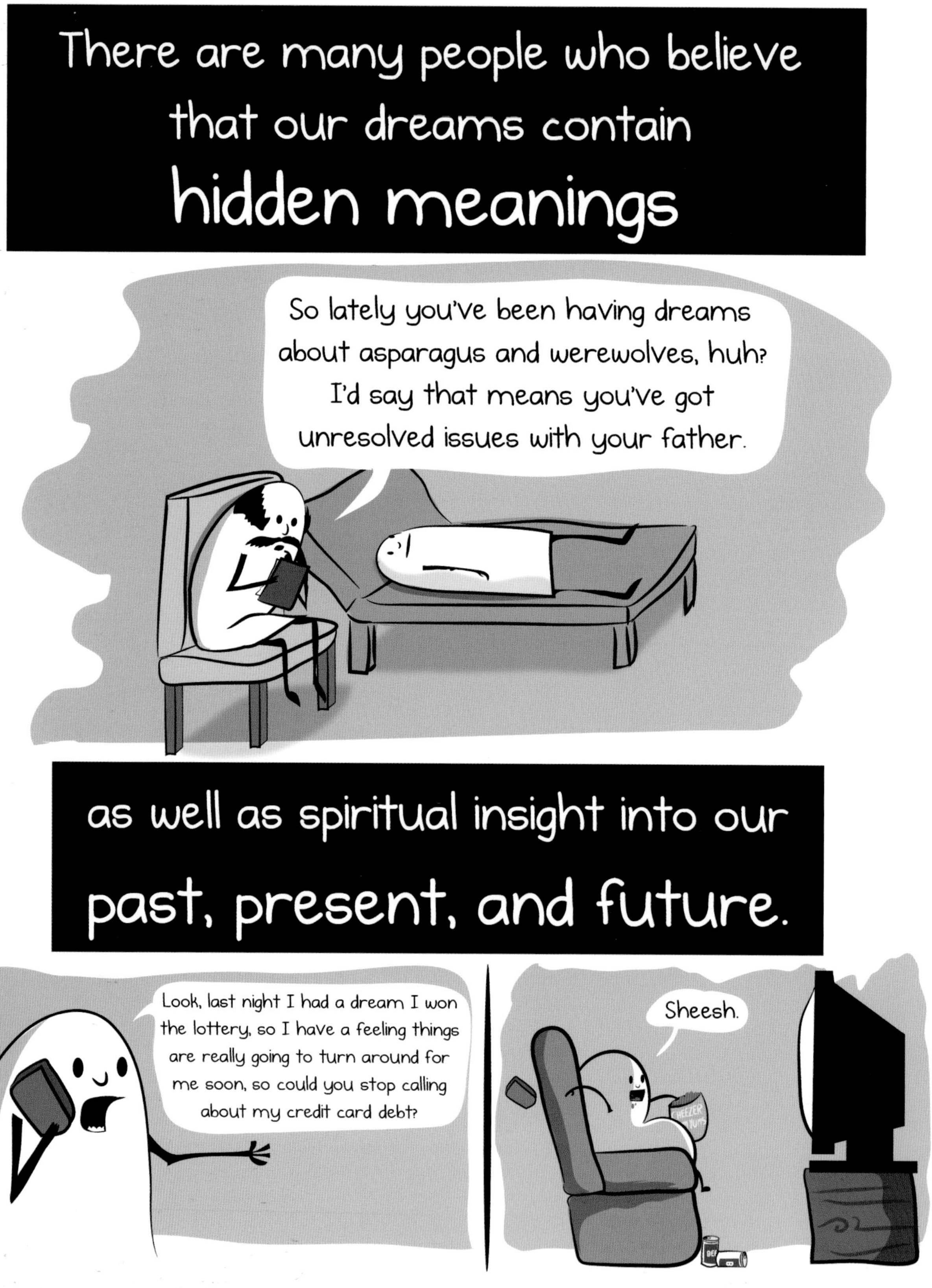
There are many people who believe that our dreams contain hidden meanings
So lately you've been having dreams about asparagus and werewolves, huh? I'd say that means you've got unresolved issues with your father.
as well as spiritual insight into our past, present, and future.
Look, last night I had a dream I won the lottery, so I have a feeling things are really going to turn around for me soon, so could you stop calling about my credit card debt?
Sheesh.

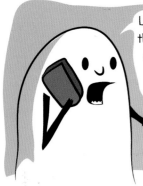

And these people insist on constantly sharing their dreams with others, because to them it was an intensely emotional experience.

But to everyone else ...

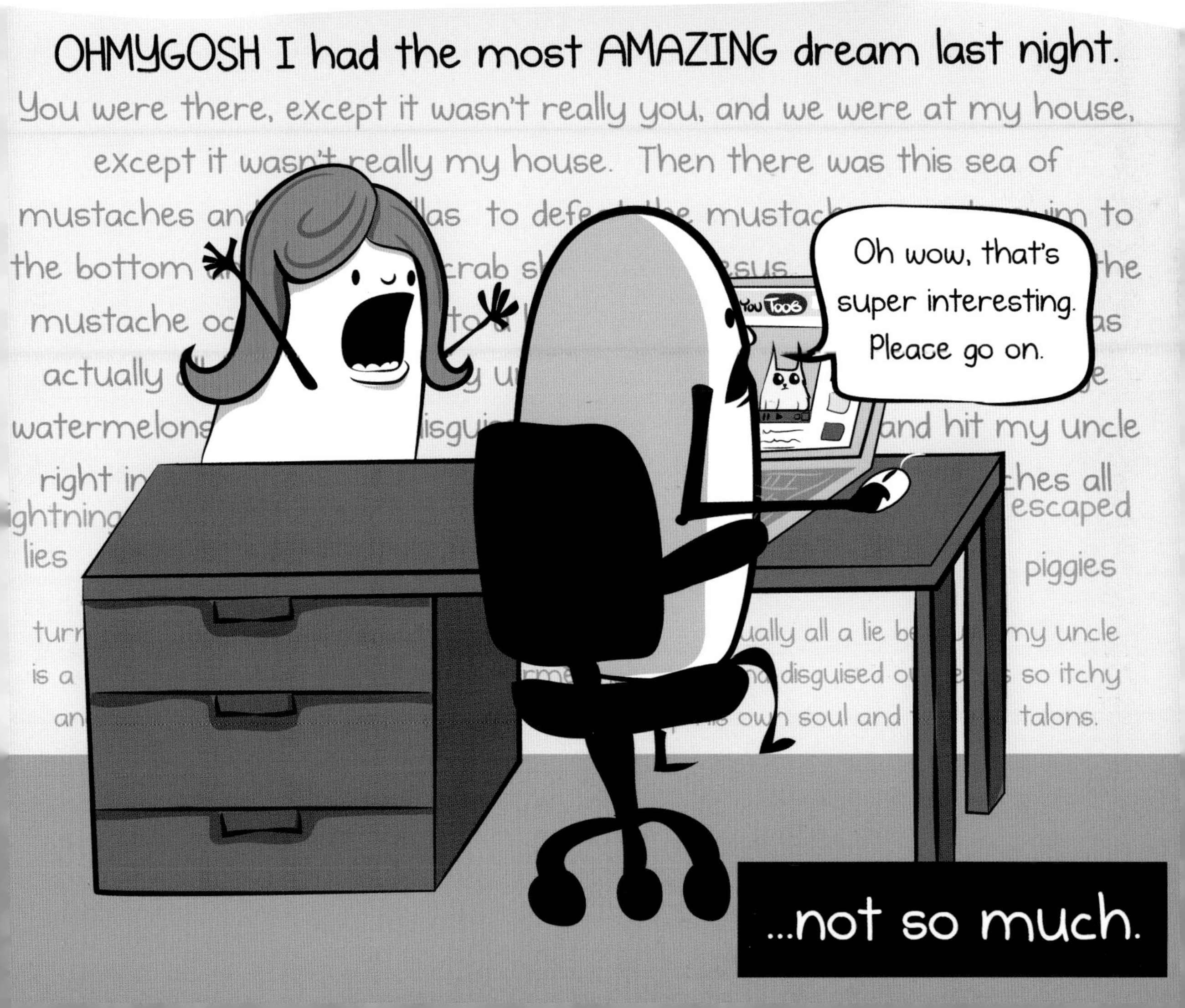
OHMYGOSH I had the most AMAZING dream last night.
You were there, except it wasn't really you, and we were at my house,
except it wasn't really my house. Then there was this sea of
mustaches an
to the bottom
mustache oc
actually
watermelons
and hit my uncle
right in
ches all
escaped
lies
piggies
ually all a lie be
my uncle
is a
disguised o
so itchy
an
own soul and
talons.
Oh wow, that's super interesting. Please go on.
You Toob
...not so much.

In 2005, a study was conducted that measured the effects of CHEESE on dreams.

This study concluded that eating cheese before bedtime produced happier dreams.

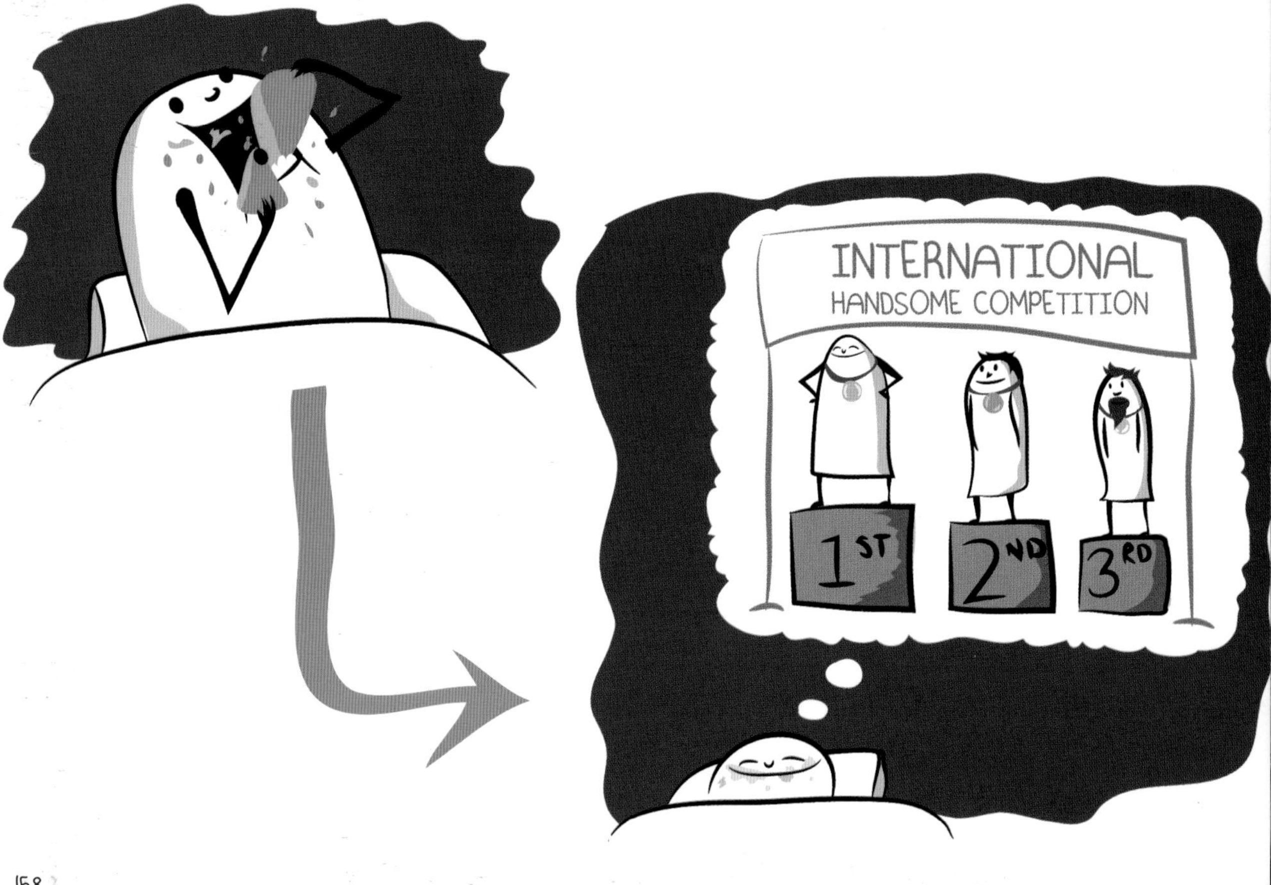
INTERNATIONAL
HANDSOME COMPETITION
1ST
2ND
3RD

And,

I've personally found that if I eat spicy food right before bed, it gives me insane nightmares.

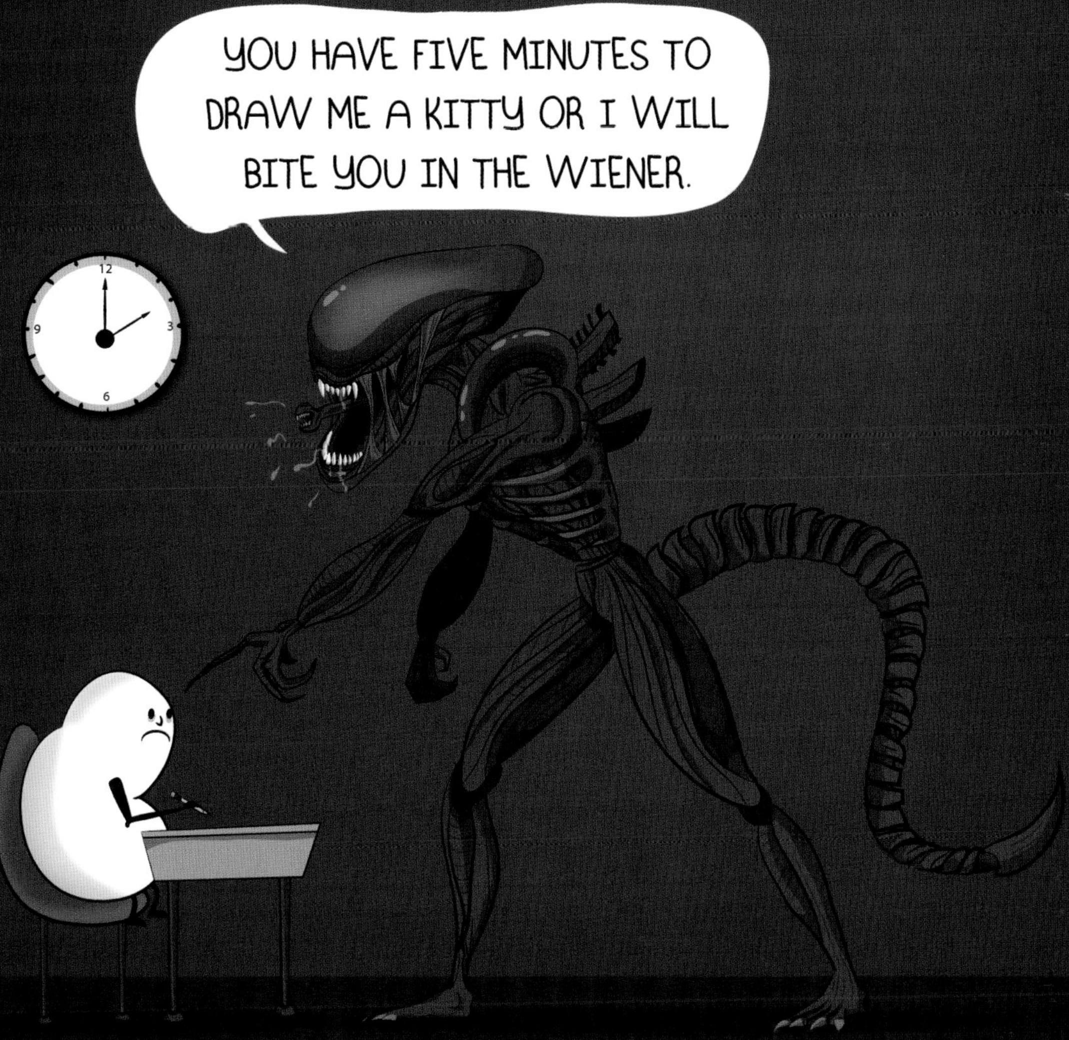
YOU HAVE FIVE MINUTES TO DRAW ME A KITTY OR I WILL BITE YOU IN THE WIENER.
12
9
3
6

Which leads me to the following conclusion:

Dreams are a product of digestion. Poop is also a product of digestion.

THEREFORE,

the insight you can gather by analyzing your dreams

is as profound as the insight you can gather by analyzing your bowel movements.

HOLY SMOKES!
This morning I went #2 and it was shaped like an antelope! What do you think it means?

Well, the antelope could symbolize your feelings of insecurity and regret. Tell me: was it a happy antelope or a sad antelope?

In my supremely unpopular opinion,

dreams are just a grab bag of emotional leftovers from your day, full of thoughts, feelings, fears, and sometimes

cheese.

They're a Rorschach test:

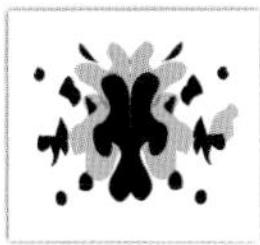

a random inkblot of shapes and colors.

And like a Rorschach test,

the actual pictures you look at are meaningless,

but your **interpretation** of those

pictures can give insight into what you're thinking or feeling.

So I'm not saying dreams are completely useless,

but I am saying that you could get a similar level of understanding of your psyche by watching a steer's butthole and contemplating the shapes that eventually emerged.

Furthermore,
I need to reiterate that my
dog has dreams.

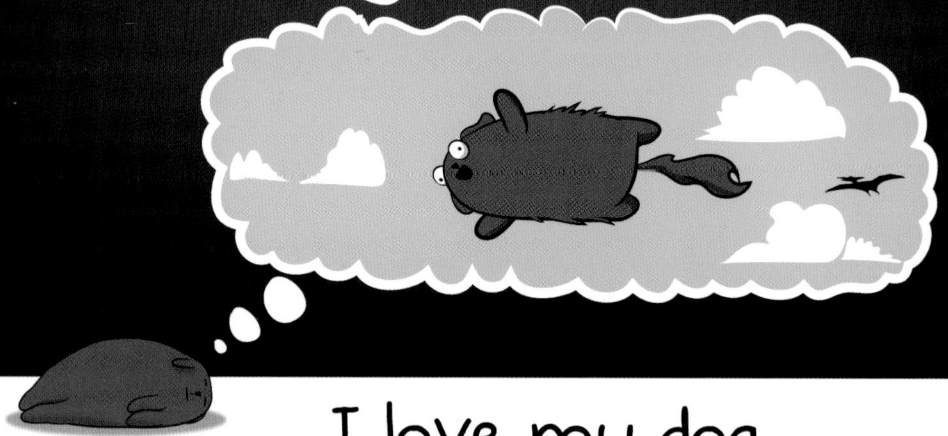

I love my dog,
but he is a simple creature.

His primary concerns in life are eating food and having sex with couch cushions.

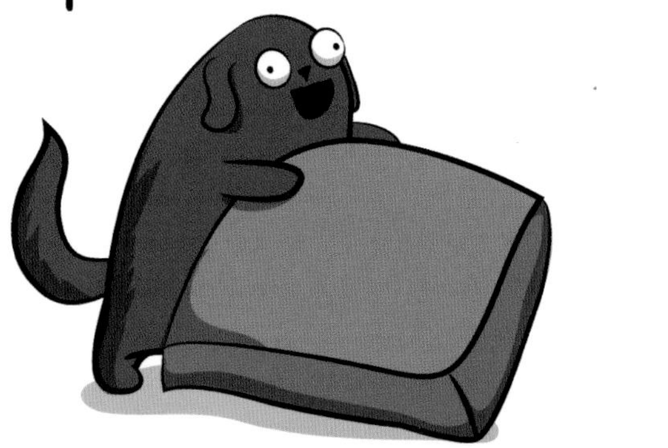

And being a simple creature,
I seriously doubt that while he sleeps he's working through deep psychological issues or channeling messages from the great beyond.

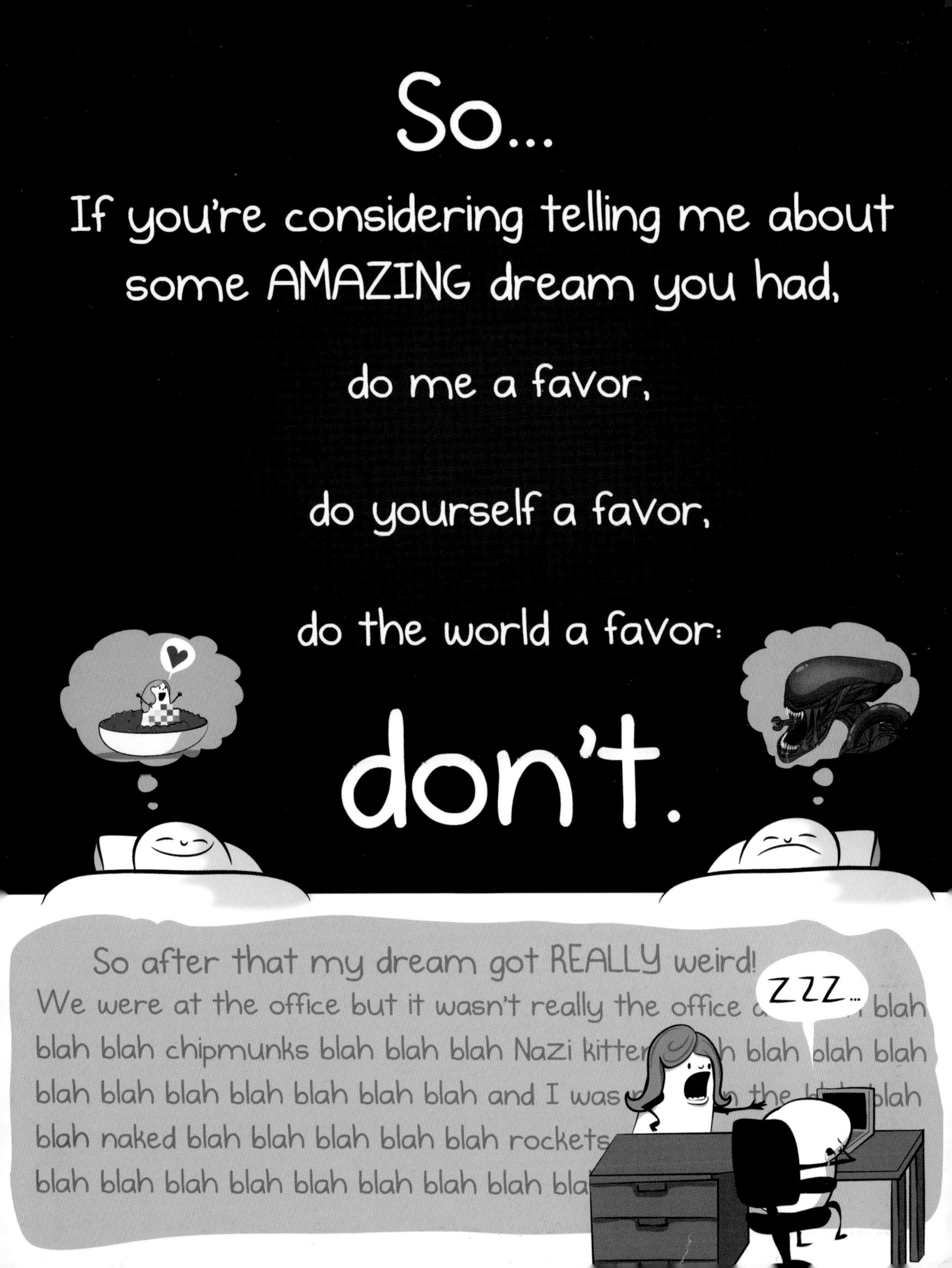
So...
If you're considering telling me about some AMAZING dream you had,
do me a favor,
do yourself a favor,
do the world a favor:
don't.
So after that my dream got REALLY weird!
We were at the office but it wasn't really the office blah
blah blah chipmunks blah blah blah Nazi kitten blah blah blah
blah blah blah blah blah blah blah and I was the blah
blah naked blah blah blah blah blah rockets
blah blah blah blah blah blah blah blah
ZZZ...

The Oatmeal

www.theoatmeal.com

This book was written and drawn by
Matthew Inman.

I AM MOSTLY MADE OUT OF
MEAT

The Oatmeal always wears a party hat, because he's always in the mood to party.

The Oatmeal's real name is Matthew and he lives in Seattle, Washington.

Visit www.theoatmeal.com for more of Matthew's comics, or check out his other books:

↳ 5 *Very Good Reasons to Punch a Dolphin in the Mouth.*

↳ *How to Tell If Your Cat Is Plotting to Kill You*

↳ *My Dog: The Paradox*

P.S.
I want to give a quick thanks to Rebecca Kelley and Jason Arango for suggesting the comic about shrimp being the push-up bras of the sea. Without you two this book would be 100% free of excellent shrimp jokes.